Bayer, 2019

MW00609597

WOMEN, ISLAM, AND ABBASID IDENTITY

WOMEN, ISLAM, AND ABBASID IDENTITY

Nadia Maria El Cheikh

Harvard University Press

CAMBRIDGE, MASSACHUSETTS
LONDON, ENGLAND
2015

Library of Congress Cataloging-in-Publication Data

El-Cheikh, Nadia Maria.
   Women, Islam, and Abbasid identity / Nadia Maria El Cheikh.
      pages cm
   Includes bibliographical references and index.
   ISBN 978-0-674-73636-8 (alk. paper)
   1. Muslim women—History.   2. Islamic Empire—History—
750–1258.   3. Abbasids—History.   I. Title.
   HQ1170.E45 2015
   305.48'697—dc23   2015005995

To Georges, once again
and to Nolan

In memory of my father

Excellent job demonstrating comparative work

Contents

Introduction
· *1* ·

WOMEN, ISLAM, AND ABBASID IDENTITY

Introduction

UPON THE DEATH of the Prophet Muhammad in 11/632, a group of women in South Arabia responded peculiarly: they rejoiced. On learning of the Prophet's death, "they dyed their hands with henna and played the tambourine." These six women were then joined by some twenty-odd other women, the harlots of Hadramaut. These women seem to have been ecstatic at the passing away of the Prophet, hoping that his demise would lead to the obliteration of his recently established order. When the news reached Caliph Abu Bakr, the first successor to the Prophet, he immediately wrote a missive to his commander, stating: "Certain women of the people of Yemen who have desired the death of the Prophet of God . . . have been joined by singing girls of Kindah and prostitutes of Hadramaut, and they have dyed their hands and shown joy and played on the tambourine. . . . When my letter reaches you, go to them with your horses and men, and strike off their hands."[1]

Who were these women, and why were they dismissed as harlots (*baghaya*)? And why such an immediate and brutal punishment? Was Caliph Abu Bakr so fearful of these women's capacity to influence the course of events that he sent a full squadron of warriors to quash their "rebellion"? It is likely that this incident was perceived as challenging belief in the Prophet and as disruptive to the order that Muhammad had introduced; rapid action was hence taken to suppress it. The episode, which is included in *Kitab al-Muhabbar* of Muhammad b. Habib al-Baghdadi (d. 245/859), is especially significant for its singling out of a female group that excluded any male presence from the cohort. One potential implication is that of a strong feminine resistance to the new order that had been established by Muhammad.

Following the death of the Prophet Muhammad, the system of alliances and conversions that had been developed during his last years disintegrated. The refusal of several tribes to recognize the succession of Abu Bakr led to upheavals known as the *ridda* (apostasy) wars. By making a public display of their joy at the death of the founder of Islam, these women in Hadramaut were participating in the *ridda*, celebrating (if prematurely) the resumption of the pre-Islamic order and doing so by reproducing bygone behavior. Their public singing, dancing, and general defiance would be contrasted with the Muslim prescriptions for women, namely, obedience, piety, and domesticity. The anecdote, while it centers on women, provokes commentary on larger issues of essential historical significance to the early Muslims, notably, the ominous possibility of reverting to the pre-Islamic order.

The narrative that the Muslims gradually constructed was that the rise of Islam, that original moment of purity, brought about the elimination of the impurity and corruption of the pre-Islamic "time of ignorance" *(jahiliyya)*. The accepted features of life in *jahiliyya* that we find in the traditional texts were tribal feuds, lawlessness, sexual immorality, lax marital practices, killing by burial of infant girls, the absence of food taboos and rules of purity, and idolatry.[2] Islam was meant to change all of that. The Islamic metanarrative underscored the transformation of the Arabs from the abject, despised people that they had been, governed by passion and violence, into a society of monotheist militants whose defining imperative was to command right and forbid wrong, in obedience to the Qur'anic injunction (3:110): "You were the best community [*umma*] ever brought forth to men, commanding right and forbidding wrong."[3] A text about the early Islamic conquests includes an anecdote in which a Muslim retorts to a Byzantine who had been denigrating the pre-Islamic Arabs: "We were even more unfortunate than what you said. . . . Among us might was for the strong and power to the many and internecine fighting endemic. . . . Blind to the one God, our idols were numerous. . . . During that time it was as though we were 'on the brink of a pit of fire' [Qur'an 3:103], and whoever among us died, died in unbelief and fell into the fire, and whoever among us lived, lived in unbelief as an infidel . . . then God sent among us a messenger."[4] The tone of this narrative reflects gratitude for the Prophet and his installation of a new order; it also includes a retrospective, "enlightened" voice—an insinuation and acknowledgment of one's past wrongs and a new line of reasoning and sense of morality, which would prove to be powerfully persuasive in the early Islamic period.

The confrontation with *jahiliyya* and with *jahiliyya*'s many later incarnations was crucial for the mainstream Islamic cultural construction of itself as a religious and imperial center. The texts' formulation of *jahiliyya* was part of a cultural reorientation that took place over the course of two centuries with the aim of defining ever more sharply what it meant to be an Arab and a Muslim. The accounts that focus on the original community of believers, the *umma*, emphasize the ideological distance between this new community and the pre-Islamic order of *jahiliyya*. *Jahiliyya*, embodied during the lifetime of the Prophet in the behavior of Hind bint 'Utba, wife of his archrival from Quraysh, Abu Sufyan, continued to be an ever-present danger, as witnessed in the actions of the women in Hadramaut, who readily reverted to their pre-Islamic behavior and beliefs as soon as they heard of the Prophet's death. The danger of relapsing into the ways of *jahiliyya* would persist through individuals or groups whose alternative beliefs and behavior would pose a challenge to the integrity and character of the Muslims, both in their formative stages and in the model on which classical Islam would settle—that is, Muslims who professed an established creed and carried out a fixed set of rituals initiated by Muhammad which were distinct from those of the polytheists and the other monotheists.⁵ My study singles out, in addition to the pre-Islamic Arabs of *jahiliyya*, those Muslims who continued to defy restrictions brought about by the new religion—specifically, women's lamenting as part of death rituals; the heretical Qaramita, whose very proximity jeopardized the character of Abbasid Islam; and the Arab Muslims' Byzantine rivals, whose alternative gender relations and sexuality represented a warning of what the future might hold if Muslim society were to relax its controls.

Gender-related and sexual imaginings play an important function in self-construction projects, and this is especially true in Islamic history. Women's proper role and the gender systems in which they operated in temporospatial proximity to *jahiliyya*, Byzantium, or the Qaramita were delineated and reinforced by a variety of texts in order to expose fundamental differences against which the new Islamic center was to be defined. The way the *jahilis*, the Qaramita, and the Byzantines were imagined and interpreted was expressed most vividly in anecdotes that centered on women, sexuality, and gender relations. I take a retrospective look at the temporal alien (the *jahilis*) (Chapter 1); the looming "hybrid," women lamenters (Chapter 2); the heretical stranger within, the Qarmita (Chapter 3); and the geographical outsider, the Byzantines (Chapter 4). The lesson of prescribed female propriety was also to be taught through the sacred stories of the first/seventh-century female exemplars (Chapter 5).

"ISLAM" is a highly complex phenomenon with constantly evolving dimensions. It is difficult to know what Islam was in the decades following its inception, since none of the earliest Islamic texts yet existed. By the time the texts were written down, the normative traditions, as well as the competing parties within Muslim society, were already almost completely formed. This textual tradition informs us that the emerging community of believers, the *umma,* was very early on struggling to define itself as a distinct (singular) community. It was also engaged in debates on questions of leadership. Upon the death of Muhammad, those who thought that he intended his family to succeed him in leading the community looked to 'Ali, Muhammad's cousin and son-in-law, as the obvious successor. The majority of Muslims did not support this family-centered theory, but 'Ali and his descendants continued to play an important role in the Islamic world, and their supporters came to be known as Shi'is. While Shi'ism (and Kharijism, the earliest religious sect in Islam) held strongly defined positions on succession, as Roy Mottahedeh suggests, for most other Muslims "events moved faster than theory, and their theory was to a large extent an explanation of events and a reaction to the more exclusive political theories of the Shi'is."[6] It was only much later on and mostly as a reaction to the development of sectarian movements within the Islamic *umma* that this initially less well-defined theory became the basis of conscious sectarian self-definition, and its upholders came to be called *ahl al-sunna* (Sunnis). The early Muslims, therefore, lived in an intellectually dynamic milieu distinguished by a political diversity extending from those who endorsed the historical caliphate (later designated as Sunnis) to oppositional groups, such as the proto-Shi'a and the Khariji, who strove to establish new politico-religious orders. Lively discourses revolved around issues that were pivotal to the fashioning of the *umma,* most critically the attributes of God, the source and nature of authority, and the definitions of true believers and sinners.[7]

After their success in the *ridda* wars in Arabia, the Muslim armies conquered Syria, Iraq, and Egypt. By 101/720 the Arab empire reached its maximum extent, incorporating North Africa, Spain, Transoxania, and Sind. As early as 41/661, the capital was moved from Medina in the Hijaz to Damascus in Syria by Mu'awiya, who founded the Umayyad dynasty, which ruled until 132/750, the year it was overthrown by the Abbasids. The textual tradition, which derives from materials produced in the Abbasid period, tends to be unsympathetic toward the Umayyads, and particularly their founder, Mu'awiya. Representing them as corrupt and godless, this unsympathetic representation was used to provide a justification for Abbasid rule. The hostility of the Abbasid sources vis-à-vis the Umayyads is an important consideration to bear in mind and is expounded on further in Chapter 1.

The Abbasids established a new capital, Baghdad, in Iraq, in 145/762, and from there they ruled the greater part of the Muslim world for about five centuries. Under the Abbasids, a process of sociocultural symbiosis along with economic integration took place, leading to a new society that was characterized by "the cohesive powers of a common language and currency and a unifying religio-political center."[8] The early third/ninth century saw the flowering of the doctrine of the Mu'tazila, which, while focusing on the question of whether the Qur'an was created or eternal, also represented an effort by several Abbasid caliphs to establish their claims to legal absolutism. It was left to the caliph al-Mutawakkil (r. 232–47/847–661) to reject the rational approach of the Mu'tazila school and support the adoption of the literalist Ash'ari approach. This decisive factor in Islamic history signaled the triumph of Sunni ideology, which was able from then on to direct and construct not only the orthodox canon but also a complete narrative of Islamic history, so that the superiority of the *jama'a* (community) was justified; the *jama'a* became the locus of religious authority. One consequence of the new policy had polemical dimensions, since boundaries were now drawn more rigidly between Muslims and non-Muslims and between Sunnis and Shi'is.[9]

The late third/ninth centuries saw the gradual emergence of a Sunni scholarly elite that secured its religious authority through its command of prophetic traditions defending traditionalist culture against the views of the Mu'tazila rationalists. The fourth/tenth century witnessed the beginning of the disintegration of the Abbasid Empire. Provincial governors became independent, and the caliphal administration in Baghdad fell into the hands of the Shi'i Buyids. The fourth/tenth century has been called the Shi'i century because a considerable number of prominent scholars and literateurs were Shi'i and because several dynasties and rulers were of the Shi'i tendency—namely, the Buyid rulers of Baghdad, the Hamdanid princes of Aleppo, the Fatimid imams in Cairo, the Zaydis in Yemen, and the Qaramita in the rural regions of Syria, Iraq, and eastern Arabia. The most significant ideological challenge to the Abbasid caliphate arose from developments in Shi'ism, and this Shi'i resurgence marked the Sunni metanarrative in a variety of ways.

SCHOLARS DIFFER on how the rise of Islam affected women's status. Judith Tucker has delineated three main interpretations. In the positive view, the previous age, that of *jahiliyya,* comprised a gender system in which women were subject to the arbitrary power of the tribe or their husbands and lacked basic human rights. Islam provided new rights and security for women. Not only were women able to exercise an important level of religious authority in the first/seventh century, most notably through their role in transmitting the words and deeds of the Prophet, but broader improvements in women's status as revealed in the Qur'an outlawed female infanticide and guaranteed women's rights to personal property and to their husbands' economic support. A second, opposed interpretation considers that many of the freedoms and much of the power accorded to women in *jahiliyya* were stifled by the rules and regulations of Islam. In this interpretation, the women of the early Muslim community, such as Muhammad's first wife, Khadija—along with a number of female followers who risked their lives by embracing the new religion—are vital figures precisely because they are not fully Muslim, having lived most of their lives as pre-Islamic *jahili* women. Moreover, both scripture and practice subordinated women to men, granting them lesser rights in divorce and inheritance and as legal witnesses.

A third interpretation offers a more nuanced reading, one that minimizes the Islamic impact on the prevailing gender system. This view emphasizes that much of what came to be called "Islamic" was rooted in pre-Islamic cultural traditions and customs, the novelty of the Islamic gender system residing in the mixing of the tribal peninsular tradition with that of the newly conquered settled states. While these interpretations seem to contradict one another, they all recognize the centrality of gender to an Islamic vision.[10] The historical narrative that has been constructed is that Islam presented a new value system that at once consolidated some pre-Islamic behaviors and modified others.

The Arab Muslim conquests and the organization of the expanding empire produced profound changes in Muslim political, social, and intellectual culture, including major consequences for women and families. The narrative presents a reading to the effect that while the early Muslims had allowed women to participate in public life and had empowered them in their personal lives, the late Umayyad and the Abbasid periods ushered in conditions that debased the position and the conception of women. The new circumstances included the incorporation into the empire of a large non-

Muslim population, the assimilation of Persian customs, and the acquisition of vast wealth and large numbers of slave women, leading to the widespread practice of concubinage. The sources highlight the importance of slavery in shaping the mores of Abbasid society and reshaping the Abbasid family, and scholars have suggested that their presence led to a role reversal affecting the position of free women. This resulted particularly from the overwhelming passion that the slave girls stirred in the hearts of men, as famously expressed by the third/ninth-century humanist al-Jahiz in his *Rislalat al-Qiyan* (Epistle of the singing slave girls). It has consequently been suggested that the concubine became a sort of "antiwife," her presence profoundly affecting the position of the free woman on the actual and affective levels. It is under these ever-evolving conditions that the jurists worked out a legal system to regulate both family and property relations.[11]

An anecdote from the later Abbasid period illustrates the influence of the presence of female slaves, mostly foreign, on the emotional and sexual world of *the Homo islamicus*.[12] *Al-Diyarat*, attributed to Abu al-Faraj al-Isfahani (d. 356/967), tells of a wandering group of Muslim ascetics *(zuhhad)* who came into the vicinity of the town of 'Ammuriyya (Amorium). One of their members saw a Christian slave girl in the market selling bread. She was extremely beautiful, and he immediately fell in love with her. He decided to stay in the town in spite of the pleading of his companions. He spent his days staring at her and ultimately confessed to her his infatuation. The girl reported him to her family and neighbors, who sent a deputation of young men to beat him. They threw rocks at him, causing serious injuries to his head and face; but he was not dissuaded. The girl finally told him that she would marry him if he would convert to Christianity, but he refused the idea, and got a second beating by the neighborhood band. The beating was so severe that the protagonist died.[13]

What does this account tell us about Christians and Muslims, women and men? How can we read this tale and make sense of interactions and fantasies, attractions and desires? This scene takes place in 'Ammuriyya, a Byzantine city that gained its greatest fame in Islamic history when Caliph al-Mu'tasim (r. 218–227/833–842) captured it in 223/838. This conquest was immortalized by the victory ode of the celebrated poet Abu Tammam (d. 231/845 or 232/846), which both reflects and validates Muslim male domination and Byzantine Christian female submission to convey one of the important meanings of this victory. The story related by al-Isfahani tells of the desire of a Muslim man for a Christian female slave from Amorium—a desire so irresistible that the man abandons his fellow Muslim ascetics to fall prey to an uncontrollable attraction. Such was the hold of the Christian maiden, such was the pull of her magnetism, that although he received repeated beatings, he persevered in his longing as if he were in a trance. The Christian woman's appeal imperils the harmony of the Muslim male-centered universe to such an extent that even an ascetic *(zahid)* like our protagonist could not resist the temptation. Women's sexual allure poses a danger in general, and that of a Christian woman in particular, and serves as a warning for Muslim men, cautioning them against the temptation to cross religious boundaries to satisfy their desire. The warning is clear: Christian (slave) women are extremely seductive, and Muslim men would do well to keep away from them, as involvement with them ends in a sure road to perdition.

As with the rogue women who rejoiced at the death of Muhammad, here again women and their perceived roles and character are used as a major organizing principle to articulate cultural differences, draw socioreligious boundaries, and formulate identities. It is with this mode of questioning and analysis that this book is concerned: I investigate the ways in which the discourses on women, gender relations, and sexuality and those on identi-ties intersect and are informed and constructed by each other in the Abbasid texts. Historians have examined other periods and geographical entities in this way, but the early Islamic period down into the Abbasid period has predominantly been left untouched. Postcolonial historians have, for instance, analyzed the sexualization of cultural difference and the ways in which the gender constructs of the dominant imperial culture were used to explain the "uncivilized" nature of the colonized. Studies on nationalism have similarly stressed the uses of the categories women, gender, and sexuality in national self-definitions.[14] Such analyses have demonstrated that depictions of women, gender relations, and sexuality are at the heart of the cultural construction of identity and collectivity. Historians of early Islam have yet to adopt a similar approach in scrutinizing Islamic texts. I hope to drive the field in a new direction, bringing in a methodology and an awareness to bear upon the early traditional Islamic texts.

Recent developments of scholarship on early Islam have shifted the focus away from notable female figures, giving way to new analytical methods that explore different historical categories. An assessment of the field, published in 2010, listed, among others, publications pertaining to social rank, personal status, veiling and seclusion, women's visibility in public spaces, women's role in dynastic policies, female slaves and concubines, women's ownership of property, women's piety, and attainment of religious knowledge.[15] One important development has occurred in sexuality studies. The pioneering monograph of Salah al-Din al-Munajjid on the sexual life of the Arabs, published in 1958, represented a first attempt to give a comprehensive account of sexual desires and practices in Arab society from pre-Islamic times to the end of the Abbasid period. Important works that relate to the early Islamic period have since been published; they range from studies on birth control to Islamic attitudes toward homosexuality and concubinage.[16] The most important contributions to the history of women, gender, and sexuality in Arab Muslim societies, however, have been produced by historians of the Ottoman Empire and the modern Middle East who created theoretical breakthroughs and rereadings for their respective periods and geographies, thanks in large part to the richness of the archives. An edited volume published in 2008, for instance, explores different genealogies of sexuality in order to determine the boundaries of Islamic discourses on male and female sexuality and desires, while one of the historians at the forefront of theorizing gender has reread the history of Iranian modernity through the lens of gender and sexuality.[17] This scholarship has generated models of analysis that can inspire new approaches to rereading the early texts. However, the fundamental historical differentiation between these diverse eras, compounded by the variant nature of the sources—notably the absence of archival material for the early period—precludes direct methodological and even conceptual borrowings.

Manuela Marin confirms that for the earlier period, the lack of archival evidence drives scholars to produce historical analyses based on literary works, chronicles, biographical dictionaries, and juridical writings.[18] Since access to the medieval Islamic past is dependent upon its texts, and history is conditioned by them, it is necessary to shift attention from the narrative and the descriptive toward an analytical approach that studies the texts while considering the ideologies behind them, the possible patron supporting their execution, the potential audience to whom they are addressed, their relationship to other sources, and inquiries into their genre.[19] It is imperative not to read literary texts as if they were windows to the past, but rather to realize that they require a methodological "turn" to the textual mechanisms of ideology construction and representation. This is precisely what I seek to achieve, by adapting and employing methodologies that distinguish institutional, cultural, and discursive mechanisms of inclusion and exclusion, using techniques to interpret from silence and to write "a history in confrontation with the extant sources rather than in conformity with them."[20] I explore the ways in which identities were negotiated in the Abbasid textual production by analyzing how women were produced discursively as a means to embody communal and sectarian identities through the affirmation of difference. The goal is to tease out the role of women, but also of sexuality and gender relations, in order to reveal the degree to which mainstream Islamic representations of other groups served to define Islam itself.

I begin Chapter 1 by exploring the accounts of Hind bint 'Utba, mother of the Umayyad caliph Mu'awiya b. Abi Sufyan, within two different temporal axes: Hind as a construction of *jahiliyya,* and Hind's function in anti- and pro-Umayyad rhetoric. *Jahiliyya* constitutes one of the central axes around which Muslim self-definitions are posited. Hind's excessive behavior, as it was portrayed in the Abbasid texts, constitutes a prototype of *jahiliyya* behavior. It is an intentional construction, and tracing it allows us to begin to understand the elaboration of the *jahiliyya* concept. But while Hind symbolizes *jahiliyya,* she also has a function in anti-Umayyad rhetoric. Hind was central in the campaign to vilify her son Mu'awiya, founder of the Umayyad dynasty. I posit that the image of Hind is a construct of Muslim ideologues interested in defining, by opposition, the ideal Muslim ways of behavior as well as furthering Abbasid legitimacy in opposition to the Umayyad dynasty.

Chapter 2 focuses on women's role in death rituals. Rituals are always crucial in demarcating boundaries between communities and religious identities, and so it is hardly a surprise that early Muslims strove to create new, uniquely Islamic practices for death rituals. Often these changes were evidenced in the very different comportment expected of Muslim women at funerals. The "Islamization" of death rituals implied the stifling of emotional outburst, specifically of wailing, *niyaha.* However, many women resisted total assimilation, indicating the survival of *jahili* mourning behavior, in the guise of women's wails of lamentation; this inability to conform to the new standard meant an incomplete transition from one cultural norm to another.

The disruptive presence of the "alien" arises not only in the ways people imagined groups of people temporally and geographically distant from them, but also as they viewed groups close to home. Chapter 3 analyzes the mainstream textual output on the Qaramita, a Shi'i sect that emerged in the third/ninth century. The Qaramita were viewed as heretical extremists and were accused of preaching and practicing communism of goods and women. Such representations of heretics are a rhetorical construction and reveal how these (re)imagined dissenters were perceived, described, and categorized in order to define sociopolitical borders and secure in-group identities. The Qaramita dwelled within the geographic confines of early Muslim society but outside its ideological framework, its models of comportment, and its institutional cadres. Such ideological conflict between a majority and its minorities sparks perhaps the greatest fear in transitional societies that are in the process of consolidation. Whenever the majority feels threatened by the existence of minorities, it tends to demonize them, depict them as "monstrous," and use them as a catalyst to identify and characterize its construction of itself as justifiably contra and superior to the minorities.[21]

Chapter 4 examines geographical outsiders—specifically, the Byzantines. Here again the Arabic Islamic representations of Byzantine women and men and gender relations served as a polemical focus for the belittlement of Byzantine culture, one salient theme of which is Byzantine women's threatening sexuality. Gendered and sexualized representations of Byzantium fulfilled a particular function in the process of Islam's self-definition, as the vision presents an ominous picture of what Muslim women would become if they were to exceed the bounds set for them by their normative Islamic culture. Rejecting the moral and ethical systems of the Byzantines as debased and indulgent, the Abbasid texts reinforced adherence to what was believed to be a superior moral system.

The final chapter, Chapter 5, focuses on the wives and female companions of the Prophet, projected as exemplary Muslim women, and their textual uses in the process of defining the new Muslim identity. The Arab monotheists who had coalesced around Muhammad became the Muslim *umma* through the articulation of a distinct narrative of its own past, placing themselves within the history of late antiquity and elaborating on their own specific character. Muslims were trying to define what it was to be a true Muslim and to identify and safeguard the bounds of comportment that defined the Muslim *umma*.[22] The formulation of a distinctive identity required an array of opposites, centering as much on what it meant to be *jahili*, Byzantine, or Qarmati as it did on what it was to be a "Sunni" Muslim. It was the search for validation that made the construction of these categories necessary and provided an affirmation of the new identity brought forth by the establishment and consolidation of Islam within the new *umma*.

THE HISTORICAL FRAMEWORK of this study stretches from the first/ seventh century to the fifth/eleventh century. I have consulted a wide array of Arabic Islamic sources, both religious and secular prose texts, to discern how Muslim society marked its internal and external boundaries through the categories of gender and sexuality. Texts of a highly literary, rhetorical, and ideological nature participated in the construction of this gendered realm, shaping the modalities of social reality and accommodating the writers and readers, the performers and audiences, to assume multiple and ever-shifting subject positions within the world that they themselves constituted and inhabited.

The "generation of 800," that is, the narrators, authors, and compilers of the Abbasid period, were those who fashioned the texts that we still consult. While not all conform to the Abbasid agenda, each has been shaped

ℵ in response to it.[23] The Abbasid period is the classical tradition's defining moment, since it produced a vast body of literature and also left a mark on the Arabic canon by preserving and codifying the texts of previous eras. The literary production of Baghdad aspired to give coherence to the entire inhabited world; at stake was the weaving of new links that looked to the past to give sense and legitimacy to a transformed present.[24] The overarching structure of many historical chronicles seems to have been dictated by a master narrative whose purpose was to confirm Muslims as the only followers of the true faith and to explain how Islam had attained its superior position over the course of the third/ninth and fourth/tenth centuries.[25] These texts were of a hybrid lineage, part *jahiliyya*-style Bedouin war narrative, part pious tale in the late antique tradition. It was, according to Thomas Sizgorich, "the union of these two traditions of remembrance . . . that created a specifically Muslim mode of recalling the past."[26]

The most enduring of the early Islamic historiographical filters was the one imposed following the return of the caliphate to Baghdad in 279/892 (consequent to an interlude in Samarra'). The late third/ninth and early fourth/tenth centuries witnessed a profound reorganization of the past and of historical knowledge, leading to the crafting of a then widely accepted and agreed-upon version of the early Islamic past.[27] Thus the major challenge in examining Islam's formative period, from the rise of Islam until the fall of the Umayyad dynasty, is that the available evidence dates from the late second/eighth century at the earliest and is constituted of Abbasid narratives which were used to depict new conflicts as old ones. Dialogue in the Abbasid historical texts responded to episodes in ancient legend as well as to events that occurred in the second/eighth and third/ninth centuries. Thus, answers about one historical phase are reached through studying another, and the historian's task becomes that of discovering similarities among the accounts and investigating their various ramifications through new correlations.[28] It is critical to emphasize that the present endeavor does not strive to confirm or refute a core of data about early Islamic history, but rather to study the ways in which this Arabic Islamic corpus came to define communal boundaries through its use of the discourse on women and sexuality. I have investigated this complex process by inquiring how such gender-charged representations exclude, silence, or exaggerate other groups.

The standard sources for historical study were authored by male elite members of the bureaucratic government and the religious establishment. Bearing in mind that it is the literate in society who form the metanarrative and imagine the "true Islamic" identity and the *umma* in textual form,[29] these prescriptive accounts describe the normative gender system that existed in the minds of the educated urban male elite. However, "reading women in male-authored texts" requires special attention to the "problematic of referentiality." In other words, the intention of the male elite who wrote about women was not to refer to women (qua women) but rather to write to and about men and to depict relationships to traditions of male textual activity and male social and political privilege. Analyzing these writings about women becomes, thus, methodologically complex, since definitions of "woman" reflect back and redefine the definitions of "men."[30]

During the period of the consolidation and expansion of the Islamic state, Muslims clung to memories of the Prophet and the first Muslim community of Medina. A multitude of anecdotes and historical reports about the life of Muhammad and his companions were recalled by word of mouth, giving rise to conflicting and at times fanciful accounts. In their wish to apply Qur'anic vision to all segments of their lives, it became imperative for the believers to know what the practice of the early Muslims had really been like. The Prophet's example was to be a major source of guidance and, amid the conflicting accounts, religious scholars in the second/eighth and third/ninth centuries collected reports about the Prophet and wrote them down, subjecting the information to a rigorous test of authenticity. These reports were compiled in hadith collections that provided a record of the Prophet's utterances and actions and came to serve, along with the Qur'an, as a basis for decisions about law and ritual. The *Al-Jami'al-sahih* of Muhammad al-Bukhari (d. 256/870) and the *Sahih* of Muslim al-Naysaburi (d. 261/874) brought together everything that was recognized as genuine in the Sunni orthodox circles of the third/ninth century. Hadith institutionalized Muhammad's exemplary behavior for the benefit of all Muslims, and they asserted their authority as a repository of early religious and historical experiences.[31] Early Muslim women have a notable presence in these collections, both as protagonists and as transmitters.

Oral reports that had no bearing on legal matters fell into a different category, that of *akhbar* (accounts). *Al-Sira al-nabawiyya,* a biography of the Prophet composed by Muhammad b. Ishaq, which survived in the edition made by 'Abd al-Malik b. Hisham (d. 213/828), relied on *akhbar* in its effort to present the Prophet's life, his pacts, his victories, and his contacts with his female relatives and other female members of the first community. Scholars such as Ibn Sa'd (d. 230/845) also relied on such accounts to collect information for a biographical dictionary on the Prophet and his companions. Ibn Sa'd's *Tabaqat,* the earliest extant biographical dictionary, devotes a volume to women, divided into the women of Quraysh who converted; women of other tribes who immigrated to Mecca; the women who took the oath of allegiance to the Prophet; and the Medinese women who became

Muslim. The hadith material, the *Sira* of the Prophet, and the *Tabaqat* literature are vital to the discussion of *jahiliyya,* Hind bint 'Utba (Chapter 1), the subject of women's lamentation (Chapter 2), and female exemplars (Chapter 5).

Other scholars used *akhbar* to compile histories. Historical chronicles and narratives are central in the Abbasid textual production of the third/ninth and fourth/tenth centuries. The preeminent example of the annalistic historiographical tradition was achieved in the work of Abu Ja'far b. Jarir al-Tabari (d. 310/923) in his *Tarikh al-rusul wa al-muluk.* Al-Tabari's *Tarikh,* a monumental corpus that begins with the creation and ends with the year 302/915, is fundamental for studying any aspect of early Islamic history, as he delves into the history of ancient nations, pre-Islamic Arabia, a biography of Muhammad, the conquests, and the history of the Muslims down to his own time. It offers a presentation of Muslims' identities and roles in the third/ninth and fourth/tenth centuries. Other late third/ninth and fourth/tenth-century compilers similarly influenced the material by selecting and arranging preexisting *akhbar*—breaking them up, rephrasing, supplementing, and composing new ones.[32]

In Chapter 3, on the Qaramita, I examine religious polemical texts in the genre of *al-milal wa al-nihal* (the religions and the sects), which constitute the "heresiographical" literature; they are fundamental, as they enumerate the religious doctrines and the groups or schools which profess them.[33] Heresiological treatises were designed to provide information about the constituents of correct belief partially by attacking what was held to be incorrect. One notable work is *Al-Farq bayn al-firaq* by 'Abd al-Qahir al-Baghdadi (d. 429/1037), a learned heresiographer much given to antagonistic stereotyping of his adversaries. Another prominent author in connection with the Qaramita is 'Abd al-Jabbar al-Hamadhani (d. 415/1024), whose *Tathbit dala'il al-nubuwwa* served to prove that Muhammad was a prophet, a task that led him to invalidate competing systems of thought. In addition to including strong criticisms of the Qaramita, he developed an Islamic narrative of Christian history, values, and morality.[34] As such, his writings remain directly significant for their comments on Byzantine women and Byzantine sexual morality (Chapter 4).

Material on Byzantium is also present in a variety of works of *adab,* traditionally defined to include the best of what had been said in the form of verse, prose, aphorisms, and anecdotes on every conceivable subject an educated man, an *adib,* is supposed to know. *Adab* also purports to address a wide range of problems of language, literature, and ethical and practical behavior.[35] One of the most famous authors of works of *adab* and politico-religious polemics was 'Amr b. Bahr al-Jahiz (d. 255/868–869). His *Risala fi al-radd 'ala al-nasara* includes important material on Christian/Byzantine women, especially relevant to the present study (Chapter 4). Some larger *adab* works, such as the anthology of Ibn 'Abd Rabbih, *Al-'Iqd al-farid,* includes significant sections on women, notably their role in mourning and lamenting (Chapter 2). The anthologies of al-Muhassin b.'Ali al-Tanukhi (d. 384/994), which contain material for the social history of the third/ninth and fourth/tenth centuries—namely, *Nishwar al-muhadara wa akhbar al-mudhakara* and *Al-Faraj ba'da al-shidda*—include anecdotes on women's lives in Abbasid Baghdad, vividly illustrating many practices and attitudes (Chapter 4). While anecdotes in *adab* texts do not usually convey a sense of real time and place, individual persons, or concrete events, these fictions of gender nevertheless participated in confirming and replicating the existing order of women's role(s) and gender relations.

The texts I have examined represent a broad spectrum of genres and styles developed over a long period of time. While this investigation yields relatively little empirical knowledge, it seeks, through its examination of well-known sources, to suggest that for these authors, the ideological backdrop behind these varied discussions aimed to give legitimacy to their own history, culture, and society and to reinforce identification with the *umma*.

WOMEN, sexuality, and gender relations are strongly affected by their presence in such narrative texts, which serve to determine moral and social boundaries and evolving roles and identities. Probing intention, context, and readings that attend to gaps and absences is essential for a critical reading of the Abbasid texts if one hopes to introduce a new understanding of these narratives. The Abbasids were struggling with the complexities of self-definition across their own internal linguistic, sociocultural, and religious models of identity. The sexualization of cultural difference and the ways in which the gender constructs of the dominant imperial culture were used to explain the "uncivilized" nature of other groups are the central threads that run through this book.

Women, gender relations, and sexuality are at the heart of the cultural construction of identity, as they are discursively used to fix moral boundaries and consolidate particularities and differences. In her monograph on medieval French epic, Jacqueline de Weever shows that the portraits of the Saracen princesses were meant to mirror "the binary oppositions of the culture of the time, the foundations of which are the oppositions of Latin Christian/oriental pagan, white/black, orthodoxy/heterodoxy, truth/error."[36] Louise Mirrer also emphasizes that depictions of women in medieval Castilian literature were bound up in issues of political and military power, religious difference, and language.[37] In a similar fashion, Abbasid textual projections of women, gender relations, and sexual conduct achieved the broader purpose of defining identities and delineating the character of the *umma*. The discourse used gendered metaphors and sexual differentiation as a means to embody communal and sectarian identities through the affirmation of difference; in so doing, it created its own temporal, internal, and geographical "subalterns." The mechanics by which these categories and Muslim identity were simultaneously constructed is the larger context for this book.

I

Hind bint 'Utba

Prototype of the *Jahiliyya* and Umayyad Woman

IN EARLY Muslim historiography, accounts of the past were always tied to the present, as if the past was invoked only to be useful to the present.[1] The historical narratives, all recorded during the early Abbasid period, were not, according to Tayeb El-Hibri, intended "to tell facts but rather to provide commentary" on political, sociocultural, and religious/moral causes deriving from controversial historical episodes. The history of the Rashidun caliphs was, for instance, represented according to political, legal, and rhetorical/artistic concerns that were prevalent in the early Abbasid period. Stories about the choice of Abu Bakr as first caliph, therefore, were more akin to polemical pieces than actual history, reflecting third/ninth-century debates on whether non-Arab converts had the right to partake in ruling the Islamic state or "whether the merits of Quraysh established its continuous political primacy."[2]

The prehistory of Islam, in particular, in addition to being a conceptual notion for Abbasid historians seeking to understand the emergence of Islam, remains so for contemporary Muslims as a way to understand their relationship to their religion and their cultural heritage. The ruptures that are ascribed to the rise of Islam are represented in Islamic historiography as having been fundamental with respect to religion, comportment, and mentalities. The migration *(hijra)* of the Prophet Muhammad from Mecca to Medina in AD 622 was a major turning point signifying the end of the pre-Islamic era, commonly called *al-jahiliyya*. This momentous journey was a defining moment for the traditional periodization of Islamic history, constituting the starting point of the Muslim calendar. *Jahiliyya* indicated the negative image of a society seen as the opposite pole to Islam. It was portrayed as a state of corruption and immorality from which God delivered the Arabs by sending them the Prophet Muhammad.[3] By describing rupture rather than transformation, the notion of *jahiliyya* represented a state of being and a belief, rather than history—"a belief in the uniqueness of a particular moment, when the laws of history . . . are suspended . . . a belief that Islam . . . and Islamic history are exceptional."[4]

Jahiliyya thus served as a historical, ideological, and ethical counterpoint to the Islamic ethos. In this representation, the pre-Islamic period is equated with ignorance and savagery. The sharp distinction between the pre-Islamic and Islamic periods meant that the people of *jahiliyya* lingered in the imperial Muslim imagination. They functioned as a signifier of a new Muslim identity emanating from the heritage of *jahiliyya,* a Muslim identity that could not exist without the constant remembering and retelling of the story of *jahiliyya.* As such, *jahiliyya* could not be totally eradicated because it continued (and continues) to be the mark of conversion itself. The alterity of *jahiliyya* was, thus, integrated into the victorious Muslim present.

Thus, knowledge of pre-Islamic history was filtered through "the theologically inspired picture of the past provided by the later Muslim sources."[5] Abbasid rhetoric relied on the concept of *jahiliyya,* which supplied it with the image of a common past as well as an ulterior mode of existence against which the Abbasids could define themselves. Similar to the European Middle Ages, which are not merely a period in history, but rather "a vastness of time ripe for colonial exploitation,"[6] *jahiliyya,* likewise, can only exist through typologies that define it as void of a positive meaning of its own. *Jahiliyya* took on meaning only in the context of another term, "Islam." This juxtaposition explains the continued role of *jahiliyya* in the historicizing projects of the Abbasids. *Jahiliyya* was essentialized and reduced to a set of morally negative core features. To cultural critics, this historicizing is a familiar process whereby one social group tries to "intensify its own sense of itself by dramatizing the distance and difference between what is closer to it and what is far away."[7]

The representation of Hind bint 'Utba in the early Islamic texts provides a case study that needs to be reexamined within the context of *jahiliyya.* Hind bint 'Utba is the *jahiliyya* woman par excellence. Her actions, as portrayed in the Abbasid texts, seem to constitute a prototype of *jahiliyya* behavior. The material on Hind provides an example of contrasts that contributes to the wider depictions of difference between Islamic values and those of the cultural system that existed before. The accounts pertaining to Hind express two levels of discourse, the pagan and the Islamic. It is an intentional construction, and tracing it allows us to begin to understand the elaboration of the *jahiliyya* concept and its significance as the antithesis to Islam.

Not only did Hind symbolize *jahiliyya,* but she also had a function in anti-Umayyad rhetoric. Hind, who was the mother of the first Umayyad caliph, Mu'awiya b. Abi Sufyan, was central in the campaign to vilify the founder of the Umayyad dynasty. Henri Lammens suggests that Hind's depiction is probably an Abbasid invention;[8] William Muir thinks that the opposition of Hind and Abu Sufyan was not held against them until later, when "civil strife burst forth."[9] The analysis of the material posits the image of Hind as a construct of Muslim ideologues interested in defining, by opposition, the ideal Muslim ways of behavior as well as furthering Abbasid legitimacy in opposition to the Umayyad dynasty. I explore the accounts pertaining to Hind within these two different temporal axes: Hind as an embodiment of *jahiliyya* and Hind the Umayyad.

ONE OF THE EARLY REFERENCES in al-Tabari's *Tarikh* puts Hind in contact with Zaynab, the Prophet's daughter, who was planning to join her father in Medina. Knowing of her intentions, Hind offered her support: "Cousin, do not deny it. If you need anything which will make your journey more comfortable or any money to help you reach your father, I have whatever you need, so do not be ashamed to ask; for men's quarrels have nothing to do with the women."[10] In spite of her family's involvement in the conflict against the Prophet, solidarity with a relative took precedence and explains Hind's offer of support. This brief anecdote demonstrates her strength and solidarity with others of her sex but also evokes a high degree of self-confidence.

Hind's family opposed the Prophet Muhammad, who was forced, along with his supporters, to leave Mecca for the safety of the oasis of Yathrib/ Medina in 1/622. Hind's rage against the Muslims increased following the battle of Badr in 2/624. There she lost her father, 'Utba b. Rabi'a, her uncle Shayba b. Rabi'a, her brother al-Walid b. 'Utba, and her son Hanzala b. Abi Sufyan. Al-Waqidi relates that Abu Sufyan, upon his return to Mecca, instructed the Quraysh neither to cry over their killed relatives, nor to use a *na'iha* (professional mourner) to lament over them, nor for a poet to eulogize them lest their anger vanish and they fall prey to the derision of Muhammad and his companions. Hind reiterates these concerns, stating that she will not cry until she takes revenge: "If I knew that my sadness would leave my heart, I would cry; but nothing would take it away except seeing my revenge with my own eyes."[11] Not all proved so strong, and Hind

herself fell short of her words. The first/seventh-century Kufan poet Ayman b.
Huraym recalls scenes of lamentation spurred by these heavy losses:

> The calamity that befell the Banu Harb left their women dazed.
> Had you seen Hind and Ramla, crying and beating their cheeks,
> You would have cried like a mother whose only son was carried off by fate.[12]

Indeed, Hind challenged the claim of the grieving female poet al-Khansa'
as being the most bereaved of all the Arabs, and declared that she, of all
Arabs, had suffered the greatest of catastrophes. Dwelling on her grief, Hind
set out for the fair of 'Ukaz, sought out al-Khansa', and challenged her
claim, whereupon both women composed elegies on their dead. Hind said:

> What an eye which saw a death like the death of my men!
> How many a man and woman tomorrow
> Will join with the keening women;
> . . . I was afraid of what I saw
> And today I am beside myself.
> How many a woman will say tomorrow
> Alas Umm Mu'awiyya![13]

The above-cited verses call us to emphasize Hind's role as a learned poet
in the genre of *Marathi* (elegies), which was, in pre-Islamic Arabia, reserved
for warriors killed in battle.[14] Often composed by women, such elegies immortalized the fallen hero, calling for vengeance as an act of purification
to cleanse the tribe of disgrace and revitalize its kin by shedding enemy
blood. According to Suzanne Stetkevych, women of the warrior class were
allowed or even required to have a public voice on restricted occasions,
namely, *niyaha*, lamenting for their adult menfolk, and *tahrid*, inciting their
menfolk to battle.[15] Hind was thus performing a quintessential role as a
free woman in the pre-Islamic context.

In retaliation against their defeat at Badr, the Quraysh set out for the next
battle of Uhud, taking their womenfolk with them, hoping that the women
would spur them in battle and shame them from running away.[16] The
women, led by Hind, encouraged the men, singing, dancing, and beating
their tambourines. Hind chanted:

> If you advance we will embrace you and spread cushions
> If you turn your backs we will leave you and show you no tender love.[17]

Hind seems to have been especially keen on avenging her father, 'Utba, killed
by the Prophet's uncle, Hamza. The *Sira* mentions that whenever Hind
passed the Abyssinian slave Wahshi, she would say, "Satisfy your vengeance

and ours." Wahshi had been asked by his master, Jubayr, to kill Hamza in return for his freedom.[18]

On the battlefield, Hind incited the warriors into battle with such aggressiveness, belligerence, and fearlessness that she barely escaped death. Abu Dujana recounts how he took the sword of the Prophet and headed toward the battlefield. At some point he was seen with his sword hovering over the head of Hind. Then he turned away from her. Abu Dujana explains his action in the following way: "I saw a person inciting the enemy violently, and I made for him, and when I lifted my sword against him, he shrieked and I realized it was a woman. I so honor the sword of the Prophet so as not to hit with it a woman."[19] Hind's close encounter with death was not enough to calm her, and when Wahshi hurled his javelin, killing Hamza, she seized the opportunity for retaliation. In a transport of vengeance, Hind and the women with her mutilated the corpses of the fallen Muslims. They strung their cut-off ears and noses into anklets and necklaces. Hind finally ripped out Hamza's liver, biting on it. She was, however, unable to swallow his liver, and spat it out.[20]

In the next scene, Hind is seen standing on a high rock screaming verses at the top of her voice. The Prophet's companion, 'Umar b. al-Khattab, recalled this moment to the poet Hassan b. Thabit: "You should have heard what Hind was saying and seen her insolence as she stood on a rock reciting *rajaz* poetry against us and recounting how she had treated Hamza."[21] Hind's feat of voicing her deed in language completed the act. Not only did she verbally acknowledge her crime; she had the audacity to proclaim it. Hind recited verses in which she expressed the deep sorrow she had been feeling as well as describing the act of revenge that appeased her anger:

> We have paid you back for Badr
> And a war that follows a war is always violent
> I could not bear the loss of 'Utba
> nor my brother and his uncle and my first-born.
> I have slaked my vengeance and fulfilled my vow
> And you, Oh Wahshi, have assuaged the burning in my breast[22]
> . . . I slaked my vengeance on Hamza at Uhud
> I split his belly to get his liver
> This took from me what I had felt
> Of burning sorrow and exceeding pain.[23]

Answering both her verses and her posture, the poet Hassan b. Thabit satirized her:

> The vile woman was insolent and she was habitually base
> May God curse Hind, distinguished among the Hinds with the large clitoris

And may He curse her husband with her
... And did you forget a foul deed which you committed?
Hind, woe to you, the shame of her age [*subbat al-dahr.*][24]

A few years later, at the conquest of Mecca by the Prophet Muhammad,
Hind appears to have opposed her husband Abu Sufyan's policy of appease-
ment and surrender. She took him by his beard and cried out, "Kill this old
fool for he has changed his religion!" Once she realized that the day was
lost, she vented her wrath this time toward the powerless idols, smashing
them and lamenting the fact that she had put her trust in them.[25] According
to the traditions, when the Prophet entered Mecca, he gave security to everyone except five men and four women. Hind was among those few.[26] The
impudence she revealed in defying and defeating her enemies, allowing herself to tumble into violence and unbridled emotion, typify her in Islamic
memory as an archetypal *jahiliyya* or fallen heroine. Hind escaped the sen-
tence by becoming Muslim and taking the oath of allegiance to the Prophet.

Hind and the Construction of *Jahiliyya*

Jahiliyya constitutes one of the axes around which Muslim self-definitions
are posited. The *Encyclopaedia of Islam* defines it as "a term used, in almost all its occurrences, as the opposite of the word *Islam,* and which refers to the state of affairs in Arabia before the mission of the Prophet, to
paganism, . . . the pre-Islamic period and the men of that time."[27] The concept of *jahiliyya* is slippery. Is it a state of being, or does it refer to a precise
period of time? Is *jahiliyya* the antithesis of knowledge (*'ilm*)? Is it the antithesis of gentleness *(hilm)*?[28] The attestations of *jahil* and of *jahiliyya* in
the Qur'an scarcely allow a precise determination of their meaning; however, most commentators on the Qur'an feel that *jahil* opposes *'alim,* "one
who knows God." *Jahiliyya* is thus applicable to the period during which
the Arabs did not yet know Islam and the divine law, as well as to the beliefs current at that time. S. Pines posits that *jahiliyya* and its derivatives as
they occur in the Qur'an imply an antithesis between those who participate in the kind of knowledge *('ilm)* that the Prophet had received from
God and the ignorant who reject this knowledge, and that this seems to be
an essential part of the self-definition of the *umma* (the community of believers) envisaged in the Qur'an.[29]

The early dictionaries stress the opposition of *jahl* to *'ilm,* and they also
suggest that *jahiliyya* was a period lacking knowledge or religious guidance.
Dictionaries of the sixth/twelfth century add new layers of meaning, de-

fining it in reference to the rancor or zealotry of *jahiliyya (hamiyyat al-jahiliyya)*, thus evoking passion and antagonism to Islam.[30] This definition was expanded in the medieval dictionary of Ibn Manzur (d. 711/1312), *Lisan al-'arab:* "In the tradition that states: you are a person who has *jahiliyya* within him, the explanation is that this was the way *(hal)* of the Arabs prior to Islam, as they were ignorant *(jahl)* of God, his Prophet, and the religious laws, upholding instead pride in ancestry, haughtiness and tyrannical behavior *(tajabbur)*."[31] This idea led Ignaz Goldziher to explain the word *jahiliyya* as a "time of barbarism," suggesting that the primary meaning of the root *j-h-l* is not ignorance but barbarism, especially the tendency to go to extremes in behavior. The *jahil* is the antithesis of *halim*, the latter being someone who is firm and strong; has moral integrity; and is unemotional, calm, and mild in behavior, deliberation, and manner.[32] The *hilm* of the famous al-Ahnaf (d. 67/686–687) included self-control, indulgence toward adversaries, seriousness, and discretion. Echoing these beliefs, the third/ninth-century humanist al-Jahiz wrote that a *halim* must "have control over himself, make reason curb passions, master anger, repress bursting satisfaction, overcome lusts, refrain from giving expression to malicious joy, impudent happiness, misplaced affliction and undue anxiety; from praising or reproaching without enough reflection . . . from passing too fast from anger to contentment or from contentment to anger."[33] The *jahil*, by contrast, is wild, violent, impetuous, indulges in unrestrained passion, and is cruel because he follows his animal instincts.

Consequently, the term *jahl* came to convey a number of meanings, including pride, baseness, obscenity, indecency, stupidity, filth, abusiveness, impudence, shamelessness, and profligacy.[34] When Muslims say that Islam ended the customs and habits of *jahiliyya*, they are thinking of "the arrogance of *jahiliyya*, the tribal pride and eternal feuds, the cult of revenger, rejection of forgiveness."[35] In this conception, *jahiliyya* was not a period of time, now past, but rather a dynamic force or state of mind, latently existing in the minds and memories of believers, ever ready to surface, and serving as a threat to the new religion.[36]

Texts support the belief of feeling "saved" by the birth of Islam and demonstrate the expansiveness of the ideological shift and difference in attitude toward faith and against a barbaric past. The early Muslim construction of *jahiliyya* finds expression in a statement by the cousin of the Prophet, Ja'far b. Abi Talib, to the Christian negus of Abyssinia: "Oh King . . . we were a people of *jahiliyya*, worshipping idols, eating corpses, committing abominations, breaking natural ties, treating guests badly[,] and our strong devoured the weak. Thus we were until God sent us an apostle."[37] Ja'far then contrasts the *jahili* way of life to the new order brought about by Muhammad and Islam: "He [Muhammad] summoned us to acknowledge God's unity and to worship him and to renounce the stones and images that we and our fathers had worshipped. He commanded us to speak the truth, be faithful to our engagements, mindful of the ties of kinship and kindly hospitality[,] and to refrain from crimes and bloodshed. . . . He forbade us to commit abominations and to speak lies, to devour the property of orphans, to vilify chaste women. He commanded us to worship God alone."[38] The moral and faithful transformation, as well as the praise for and obedience to the Prophet for elevating society from moral baseness, is evident in these passages.

As Geraldine Heng remarks, events occur in historical time but become historical phenomena only "by being placed in a signifying process determining their intelligibility."[39] The vastness of *jahiliyya* had to be described and claimed. *Jahiliyya* was, to a large extent, invented and given a particular historical agency; its meaning was derived from the Abbasid gaze. In the second/eighth century, discovering and processing images of the pre-Islamic era became a major endeavor. Not only was a body of *jahili* prose and poetry recovered, but with it the *jahili* ethos and history were also resurrected. One of the key controversies in the early Abbasid period between the so-called ancients *(qudama')* and moderns *(muhdathun)* was associated with the rediscovery of *jahiliyya*. The view of the ancients was that *jahili* Arabic was purer and that the Bedouins were the last surviving speakers of Arabic in its pristine form. The implication of this position was that life was also purer and that manners, morals, and knowledge were superior to what followed later.[40] The recollection of this Bedouin past developed into an all-encompassing antiquarian industry, as the collection, study, and canonization of Arab antiquities became the foundation for collective and imperial self-definitions.[41]

The cultural capital represented by the ability to recite poetry indicates, in the words of Rina Drory, "the special status accorded to the pre-Islamic past in the Abbasid cultural repertoire of self-images."[42] In early Islamic literature, nomadic Arabs are often represented as uncouth, given to hypocrisy and covert sensuality, and addicted to pagan practices. This was to change, and they would become characterized as the origins of the Arabs and a validation for Islam. The rehabilitation of the Arabs occurred once scholars came to regard them as a crucial source for the Islamic sciences.[43] From its condemnation as "an age of wrong belief, dominated by conflicting tribal interests and rivalries," the pre-Islamic era gradually came to be seen as "a unified Arab past, in which the true values of Arab ethnic identity were manifested."[44] The past was embraced as an elemental, remembered part of the present.

Hind's behavior was constructed in a way that would reflect the proto-type of *jahiliyya,* the age of barbarism characterized by wild acts as yet untamed by the revelation of Islam. Her excessive arrogance and tribal pride, her inability or unwillingness to curb her passions and master her anger, her expression of malicious joy, and especially her thirst for revenge epitomized the "chaos of pre-Islamic times."[45] Although in one version Hind restrained herself, refusing to mourn those killed at Badr lest her yearning for revenge be quenched, in most versions Hind's mourning is represented as excessive—crying and beating her cheeks and calling for revenge. This attitude is to be contrasted with the proper attitude toward death that Islam came to emphasize. Strong emotional reaction to death was condemned, since it implied a skeptical attitude toward the divine promise of eternal life and a preference for earthly values. Instead, a Muslim's reaction to death should reflect steadfastness, *sabr,* and contentment with the divine judg-ment. Reassurance for the fate of the eulogized and acceptance of God's decree was to replace pre-Islamic emotion, anguish *(jaza'),* and wails *(walwala).*[46]

Even before the battle, as the Quraysh were heading toward Uhud, they arrived at al-Abwa', and Hind told Abu Sufyan, "Try to search for the grave of Amina, the mother of Muhammad, which is here in al-Abwa' so that if one of you were to be captured, you could ransom him with one of her limbs." Her request to search and unearth the grave of the Prophet's mo-ther was deemed extreme by the rest of the Quraysh, who asked Abu Su-fyan not to cross such a threshold lest their enemies search for the graves of their own dead.[47] Hind's entreaty to exhume the cadaver of the Proph-et's mother represented, once again, a particularly intense level of fierce-ness, since all the leaders of the Quraysh recoiled from it. But it was Hind's excesses in the battle of Uhud that exposed her entrenched *jahili* ways. Her excessive behavior manifests itself in her acts of brutality and vindictive-ness, verging on cannibalism. While mutilation of enemy corpses does not seem to have been uncommon, what was uncommon was her extreme intemperance, the overload of her behavior, her chewing of Hamza's liver. Stetkevych states that Hind's persona reflects a mélange of human and animal traits, because it is vultures and hyenas that defile and devour fallen warriors: "The sacrificial dialectic of animal sacrifice versus blood vengeance . . . is thrown into confusion, producing the abomination of cannibalism."[48] This comparison is mirrored in another parallel, namely, in the verse, cited above, by Hassan b. Thabit which refers to Hind bint 'Utba as Hind "with the large clitoris." This parallel foregrounds sexual organs, as hyenas are notorious for their large clitorises. Other references to Hind's sexuality occur during the battle of Badr when she, along with other women from Quraysh, encouraged the warriors of Quraysh by promising sexual intercourse for the courageous: "If you advance we will embrace you and spread cushions." Hind's words, which expose and offer up her sexuality and that of the other women, are further proof of the temporal view of Hind as crass and animalistic, characteristic of *jahiliyya*'s quintessence.

The Prophet's kinswoman Hind bint Athatha described Hind's actions in terms of whoredom, sexual exposure, and disgrace, implying that although Hind bint ʿUtba may have been dishonored by the death of her kinsmen at Badr, the way in which she avenged their deaths at Uhud tainted her still more. Hind bint Athatha launched a bitter attack on the shameful way in which Hind bint ʿUtba wrought vengeance, entrusting it as she did to a hired slave, thereby violating the conditions of honorable vengeance. Hind had stepped beyond the traditional female role of inciting the menfolk to battle *(tahrid)*. Her revenge left her more polluted than ever. She ends her poem by asking, "What have the harlots to boast after [Hind]?"[49]

Hind's actions at Uhud, with her desecration of the corpses, followed by her bursting into triumphant poetry brimming with malicious joy, all express the depravity of *jahiliyya*, the *jahl* of *jahiliyya. Jahl* can be so strong, especially as a reaction to other acts of *jahl,* that the Prophet himself was tempted by it, vowing, on seeing Hamza's corpse, to mutilate thirty of his opponents. The sight was horrible: Hamza's belly was ripped up, his liver was missing, and his nose and ears were cut off. The Prophet is said to have uttered at once: "Were it not that Safiyya [Hamza's sister] would be miserable and it might become the custom after me, I would leave him as he is, so that his body might find its way into the bellies of the beasts and the crops of birds. If God gives me victory over [the] Quraysh in the future I will mutilate thirty of their men."[50] Seeing the Prophet's grief and rage, the Muslims vowed, on their next victory, to injure their enemy in a way that none of the Arabs had ever seen.[51] Verses, however, descended proscribing excessive vengeance and advocating patience (Qur'an 16:127): "And if you chastise, chastise even as you have been chastised; and yet assuredly, if you are patient, better it is for those patient." And so the Prophet forgave, was patient, and forbade mutilation.[52] The *Sira* mentions, further, that "the Prophet never stopped in a place and left it without ordering us to give alms and to forbid us from committing mutilation." Only Islam, in specific Qur'anic verses and particular utterances of the Prophet, could abrogate the stronghold of *jahl*.

It is commonplace to find cultural enemies depicted as cannibals, especially in narratives of territorial invasion and conquest. In demonizing *ja-*

hiliyya, its people were given barbarous qualities, notably cannibalism. Ruth Morse suggests that, in historical writing, the ultimate mark of savagery is cannibalism, "a mark of the wickedness of those who perpetrate such deeds."[53] The accusations of near-cannibalism were part of a project to render Hind, and by extension such behavior, utterly outside the bounds of culture and civilization. The accounts cautiously point out that Hind was unable to swallow Hamza's liver and that that resulted from a divine intervention, as reported by the Prophet himself. Ibn Saʿd relates that Hind chewed on a piece of Hamza's liver in order to swallow it, but she could not, and so she spat it out. This account reached the Prophet, who said, "God has forbidden for the fires to ever taste of Hamza's flesh." Another rendering has the Prophet ask: "Did she eat anything of it? They said, no. He said: God would not have allowed that anything of Hamza enter the fires."[54]

Hind, the violent and near-cannibalistic *jahili* woman, becomes a prototype of anachronistic humans: irrational, regressive, existing in a permanently anterior time within the "modernity" that Islam came to represent. The description of Hind's savagery is rife with moral, aesthetic, and political connotations. Hind's act of near-cannibalism functions as a temporal marker, and thus her savagery expresses temporal distancing: "it is a marker of the past, their time, not ours."[55] *Jahiliyya* becomes, then, a historical period defined exclusively by its relation to the observer. The remote, the savage, belong not to extreme geographical locations, as is the case in medieval European literature and *mappae mundi,* but rather to an entirely different temporal zone, that of pre-Islam. Muslims situated the monstrous, a category that was "central to a discourse about the limits of humanity," in a different time zone.[56] "Monstrous" figures are found patrolling key sites of demarcation as they embody the oppositions between which they erect a boundary. Abiding on the edges of the familiar, they serve as a warning of what is at stake regarding the observance of boundaries.[57] Hind's act was monstrous, and with it the whole of *jahiliyya* was defined as a "temporal monstrosity." The conflation of the female and the monstrous needs to be emphasized: it is a female who became, ultimately, the principal locus for the cultural monstrosity that defined *jahiliyya.*

The manipulation of the motif of cannibalism played an important role in the Muslim construction of the category *jahiliyya,* defining the cultural distance between the Muslims who would never engage in cannibalistic practices and the *jahilis* who did. Hind's cannibalism functioned as an efficient marker in the discourse between civilization and barbarism and also as a marker of cultural distance between the people who told the stories and those about whom they were told. The key categories were now Muslim, representing the cultural norms of humanity, and *jahili*, representing deviations from those norms.[58]

Hind, the Umayyad

While Hind symbolized *jahiliyya,* she was also assigned a significant function in anti-Umayyad rhetoric. Scholars who associated with the circles hostile to the Umayyad dynasty, predominantly in Iraq, took a leading role in the collecting, arranging, and editing of the material. Adding to this the fact that the centuries-old material was produced in the Abbasid period, it is not difficult to understand its hostility toward the Umayyads in what the tradition reports and the way in which it reports it.[59] Indeed, what we know about the Umayyads is a tributary of what men in the Abbasid period wished to know and to pass on, bearing in mind how crucial the control of the caliphal past remained for the early Abbasids. Profound reinterpretation and rewriting took place during the third/ninth–fourth/tenth centuries that aimed to establish an official past in the service of the Abbasid dynasty. It was necessary to provide a justification for the toppling of the Umayyads by the Abbasids; the Umayyads were hence branded as a symbol of the corrupt and godless alternative to Abbasid rule. More fundamentally, it was essential to determine the circumstances that led to the betrayal of the pact of the Prophet, notably in the civil wars that destabilized the *umma* in the first/seventh century. Culprits were needed, and the Umayyads fit the profile; the official interpretation produced by the Abbasid court was to lay the responsibility on the corrupt Umayyads, and especially on Mu'awiya (r. 41–61/660–680).[60] This tradition recounts that the Umayyad family was prominent in the opposition to Muhammad and that most of the family members accepted Islam at the last hour, when it was obvious that the Prophet was going to be victorious. Once they accepted Islam, the Umayyads managed to acquire power by skillful political manipulation, and once in power "they pursued policies which at best paid no regard to the requirements of Islam and at worst were positively anti-Islamic."[61]

Anti-Umayyad voices in the Abbasid sources took a variety of forms. The representation of Hind is one of these forms, which, like the multitude of anecdotes that populate the Abbasid texts about the vanity and decadence of some Umayyad caliphs, go a long way toward discrediting the whole dynasty. Hind was, after all, the mother of Mu'awiya, founder of the Umayyad dynasty and its most famous caliph. He continues to be a controversial figure, as Muslims have been ambivalent about his character and role. On the one hand, he remained a symbol of the conflicts and anxieties that afflicted the community of believers; on the other hand, he did not fit into the moral categories that later Muslims devised to evaluate a person's religious standing.[62]

Mu'awiya's clan bitterly opposed Muhammad, and Mu'awiya's father, Abu Sufyan (who was also Hind's husband), led the wars to oust Muhammad and his followers from Medina. Al-Tabari even includes a report in which Abu Sufyan himself is spotted mistreating the corpse of Hamza. He was reprimanded by a follower: "Banu Kinana, can this be the leader of the Quraysh acting as you see with the corpse of his cousin!" Abu Sufyan answered, "Keep it quiet, it was a slip."[63] It was a reflection of his prestigious standing, however, that upon entering Mecca, the Prophet, expressing his conciliatory policy, stated that whoever enters the home of Abu Sufyan is secure.[64]

The official interpretation that developed in the second/eighth and third/ninth centuries, and was circulated by the Abbasid court, laid the blame for the community's disasters on the corrupt Umayyad clan, especially on the usurper Mu'awiya. Systematic public campaigns to vilify Mu'awiya and the entire Umayyad clan were, for instance, planned by the Abbasid caliphs al-Ma'mun and al-Mu'tadid.[65] For the Kharijites and the Shi'i, Mu'awiya was someone who knowingly and cynically worked to destroy the new covenant established by the Prophet and to return the *umma* to the ignorant brutishness of the *jahiliyya*.[66]

Hind was central to the campaign vilifying Mu'awiya, who was tainted by his mother's action and was textually connected to her in her capacity as *akilat al-akbad,* eater of (human) livers. During the struggle between the fourth caliph, 'Ali b. Abi Talib, and the then governor of Damascus, Mu'awiya, and as the rumors of the latter's death were spreading in Kufa, 'Ali is said to have uttered the following prediction: "You have exaggerated in reporting Mu'awiya's death. By God, he did not and will not die until he rules the land where I stand. The only wish of the son of the liver-eater is to hear me predict this."[67] In one anecdote Mughira b. Nawfal is said to have proposed to marry Umama, the granddaughter of the Prophet. Hearing that she had also been approached by Mu'awiya, Mughira exclaimed, "Would you marry the son of the liver eater!" Consequently, Umama chose him over Mu'awiya.[68] This derogatory epithet for Mu'awiya followed him even in the references to the Sufyanid legend, which mushroomed in the early Abbasid age. One prophecy stated, "And when this happens watch for the son of the Liver-eating Woman *(ibn akilat al-akbad)* in the Wadi al-Yabis."[69]

In one anecdote we find the Prophet's companion Ibn al-Zubayr comparing himself to Mu'awiya in the following way: "Do you know that my father was a follower of the Prophet, blessings of Allah be upon him, while his father is Abu Sufyan, who fought against the Prophet; my mother is Asma', daughter of [the first caliph] Abu Bakr al-Siddiq, while his mother is Hind, *akilat al-akbad.*" Mu'awiya's answer in self-defense was that "Abu Sufyan was of great importance in *jahiliyya,* and his position was well preserved in Islam. On the day of the conquest [of Mecca] he was given what no one else was given: the caller of the Prophet said: whoever enters the mosque is secure, and whoever enters the house of Abu Sufyan is safe; it was his house that became a sanctuary, not the house of your father; as for Hind, she was a woman from Quraysh; in *jahiliyya,* she was of great portentousness while in Islam she was of honorable reputation."[70] It is important to point out in connection with this comparison between Asma' bint Abu Bakr and Hind bint 'Utba that while Hind became more laudable after conversion, Asma' was a steady paragon of faith, known as "she of the two girdles" because she tore her garment in two to assist the Prophet when he fled Mecca. She became Muslim early on and was so loyal to the new cause that she refused to receive her nonbelieving mother, Qutayla, Abu Bakr having divorced her in *jahiliyya,* or to accept her gifts until she inquired the Prophet's opinion on the matter.[71] Thus, while Asma' was an exemplar for the early Muslim believing women, Hind's actions, in *jahiliyya,* stained Mu'awiya's memory.

The recollection of Hind's immoderate pride lingered so that the half brother of Caliph 'Uthman, al-Walid b. 'Uqba, urged Mu'awiya to take quick revenge on Caliph 'Uthman's blood, reciting:

> By God, Hind will not be your mother if the day passes
> without the avenger taking revenge for 'Uthman
> Can the slave of the people kill the lord of his household
> And you [pl.] do not kill him? Would your mother were barren![72]

Her excessive pride toward Mu'awiya's career is highlighted in the texts. When Mu'awiya was still a youth, a man looked at him and said, "I think that this man will rule over his people." Hind heard him and said, "May I lose him if he were to rule only over his people."[73] In another instance she tells him, "A free woman has rarely brought forth to the world someone like you."[74] Were such statements a reiteration of Hind's excessive arrogance, or did they constitute a later acknowledgment of the prominent role that Mu'awiya played in the first century of Islam? In any event, her pride and defiance, epitomizing her quintessential *jahili* identity, continue to be underscored. Ibn Sa'd includes the following dialogue between Hind and the Prophet: "Women came to the Prophet to give him allegiance, and among them was Hind bint 'Utba b. Rabi'a, the mother of Mu'awiya. When the Prophet said: You should not commit adultery, Hind answered: Can a free woman commit adultery? He said: And they should not kill their children; she said: But did you leave us any sons that you did not kill at the battle of Badr?"[75]

The Umayyads, who came to serve as precedents in the art of ruling as well as an affirmation of political continuity, gradually progressed from an adversarial position to one of alterity. By the third/ninth century, the Abbasids finally adopted what was to become Sunni "orthodoxy," and the crystallization of this religious orientation saw the emergence in the historiography of this period of a friendlier image of the Umayyads.[76] Mu'awiya, anathematized by the Shi'is, was defended by the followers of Ahmad b. Hanbal, who had prohibited the cursing of Mu'awiya because it went against the prophetic hadith upholding the righteousness of all the Prophet's companions; the Prophet had trusted Mu'awiya enough to make him a secretary transcribing his revelation and was thus guaranteed by the Prophet to enter paradise. This favorable representation of the Umayyads is linked to the late third/ninth-century Sunni resurgence which tried to reshape much of the history of previous scholars and eminent political figures to fit these new politico-religious considerations. A subsidiary zealous strand fostered panegyrics and hagiography for Mu'awiya and his family. This was in large part an expression of protest against the Shi'i currents.[77]

The rehabilitation starts with Abu Sufyan's ambivalence about the mutilations perpetrated at Uhud. While he was the leader at the fateful battle of Uhud, he sought to distance himself from the acts of his wife, Hind, stating: "A day for the day of Badr, war has its ups and downs. You will find that some of your dead have been mutilated. I neither commanded it, nor does it displease me."[78] Al-Waqidi's report clarifies the fluctuating position of Abu Sufyan, not utterly *jahili* but not quite Muslim yet: "Abu Sufyan said, raising his voice: Indeed you will find corruption and mutilation with your dead that is not the result of an opinion from our elders. The zeal of *al-jahiliyya* overtook him, however, and he added, when it happened we did not detest it."[79] These pronouncements reveal not only a temporal confliction about, but also a tolerance or acknowledgment of, *jahiliyya,* reflecting a cultural pride and a forbearance of such behavior.

In a positive strand, Abu Sufyan attains a notable place in Islamic tradition for his role in informing the Byzantine emperor Heraclius of the emerging Prophet and his community of followers. This report, found in al-Bukhari's collection of traditions, the *Sahih,* has Abu Sufyan enumerating to Heraclius the qualities of the new Prophet, presenting the portrait of a perfect man.[80] Abu Sufyan is also praised by way of Hind. When he asked to marry her, she described him as a man of noble lineage and intelligent opinion, a man of great pride who defends his home well. Hind chooses him as a man who "befits to be the husband of a free noble woman."[81] The daughter of Abu Sufyan, Ramla, is another medium for the rehabilitation of Abu Sufyan's family. Better known as Umm Habiba, she accepted Islam in defiance of her father, migrated to Abyssinia with her husband, and later married Muhammad. She stood firmly by him against the interests of her father at a critical time when Abu Sufyan was losing ground as the leader of the Meccan opposition.[82] The Prophet's marriage to Umm Habiba, the daughter of one of his staunchest opponents, is the occasion for the Qur'anic verse (60:7): "It may be God will yet establish between you and those of them with whom you are at enmity love. God is All powerful; God is All-forgiving, All-compassionate."

The pro-Ummayad strand also includes a report of Mu'awiya's early conversion. In the biographical dictionary of the Damascene Ibn 'Asakir (d. 571/1176), Mu'awiya states that Hind cautions him against defying his father or else Mu'awiya may be cut off from support; and so Mu'awiya accepted Islam, and in doing so "purified" himself.[83] This version wishes to confirm the voluntary conversion of Mu'awiya but also that he enjoyed a certain priority *(sabiqa)* in the adoption of Islam.

In addition, the pro-Umayyad current necessitated a rehabilitation of Hind herself. On her first encounter with the Prophet Muhammad, when she went to meet him with a group of women to offer him their allegiance, Hind, in Ibn Sa'd's *Tabaqat*, spoke to him in words that reflected the Muslim woman she had now become: "Messenger of God, praise to Allah who gave victory to the religion of his choice so that I may benefit from your mercy. O Muhammad, I am a woman who believes in God and his messenger." Lifting her veil *(niqab)*, she presented herself: "I am Hind bint 'Utba, and the messenger of God answered: welcome to you." Upon becoming Muslim, she struck an idol in her house with an axe until she broke it into pieces while repeating, "We were deluded about you."[84] Ibn 'Asakir, moreover, relates that Hind told her son Mu'awiya that she dreamed on three successive nights that she was in utter darkness, then she would see a spot of light, and it was the Prophet calling her to Islam. She consequently destroyed the idol in her house, went to the Prophet, proclaimed herself Muslim, and gave him allegiance.[85] Prophetic tradition includes one hadith via 'A'isha, the wife of the Prophet, stating that Hind bint 'Utba came to the Prophet and told him, "There were no people that I wished to be humiliated more than the people of your tent; and now I do not wish for a people to have more glory as much as your people."[86] Positive reports also emphasize Hind's aggressive role in the defense of the new cause. Once her son became governor of Syria, she took part in the battle of Yarmuk (13/636) against the Byzantines with undiminished ardor, exhorting the Muslims to "circumcise their uncircumcised" adversaries with their swords.[87]

Hind is also rehabilitated by way of her son Mu'awiya: Hind, the most excessive of the *jahilis*, is counterbalanced by the most *halim* of the Muslims. *Lisan al-'arab* states that *hilm* is "patience and reason," while *Taj al-'arus* defines *hilm* as "the act of reining one's soul and holding back one's nature from the violent emotion of anger." *Hilm* in Islamic ethics not only extols self-control and forgiveness but also, in the words of Charles Pellat, exhorts "an assemblage of features denoting moral pre-eminence as against the state of barbarity presented by *jahl*." It thus extends from justice and moderation to forbearance and leniency, including self-control and dignified behavior.[88] The pro-Umayyad thread portrays Mu'awiya as one of the most humane of Muslim rulers. He was not an austere, self-disciplined moralist, and he had no special profile in Muslim piety but represented the human bridge between the *jahili* virtues *(muruwwa)* and tribal solidarity *('asabiyya)* on the one hand and the new order of Islam on the other. Mu'awiya's *hilm* became proverbial.[89]

Hind's rehabilitation is also visible in *adab* texts. Here the stories are different. One such story takes place in the early period of her life, when she was accused by her first husband of adultery. He had returned home early to find a stranger leaving his house. Hind swore to her father "in the ways they used to swear in *jahiliyya*"—that her husband was a liar.[90] Like 'A'isha when she was accused of adultery, Hind was unable to convince her family or her husband of her innocence. Despite her protestations, her (own) words alone could not exonerate her. It was a pre-Islamic priest in Yemen who proclaimed her innocence: "Stand up, you are not ugly and you are not an adulterer and you will bring to the world a king who will be called Mu'awiya."[91] Thus the saving of Hind's honor was accomplished in a supernatural way, as was that of 'A'isha's reputation with the descent of the Qur'anic verses 24:11–20.[92] These anecdotes at last sketch Hind as a righteous figure but also reveal the significance and trust in reverence and prophecy, casting the ideal female as virtuous and pious.

Renate Jacobi points out the tendency in *adab* texts to upgrade Hind morally. Here Hind's image casts her as a heroine of 'Udhri love and links her to the poet Musafir, who, like other 'Udhri poets, falls in love and perseveres in the face of hopelessness and despair. Most of the 'Udhri stories follow a common pattern: the poet and his beloved fall in love and seek marriage, but the promise is broken as the woman is married to a richer man. The lover remains faithful and eventually dies of sorrow.[93] *Kitab al-aghani* relates how Musafir fell in love with Hind and wished to marry her after her separation from her first husband, Fakiha. Not being wealthy enough, Musafir traveled to the court of al-Nu'man b. al-Mundhir in Hira and, while there, met the rich merchant Abu Sufyan, who was on a business trip and who informed him that he had married Hind. Musafir fell sick and died; *Al-aghani* states, "He is one of those who were killed by *'ishq.*"[94] It is significant that 'Udhri lovers are chaste, since a physical union would destroy the idealism of true love. *Adab* foregrounds Hind's chaste nature and invalidates the accusation of adultery brought against her by her former husband.

Hind, the highly disquieting female, is thus feminized by becoming a woman who fits the dominant conceptualization of the normative feminine and the new patriarchal economy. Consequently, Hind is shown as having converted to Islam and to proper femininity. The battle was finally over. In time, Hind manages to slowly slide from *jahiliyya* to Islam. Her *jahili* attributes, her ferocity and brutality, are gradually tempered through a moral rehabilitation that only the civilizing force of Islam was/is capable of achieving.

Marking *Jahiliyya,* Rehabilitating the Umayyads

In the Abbasid texts *jahiliyya* came to be recalled as a temporal era that ended with the triumph of Islam, whose benefits could only be truly appreciated if measured against the darkness of the time of ignorance. *Jahiliyya* became a "resource for communal and imperial self-fashioning."[95] A central hermeneutical problem for the history of *jahiliyya* and that of Umayyad memory is that they have been transmitted through texts from the post-Umayyad age. The shaping of both historical periods, but especially that of the Umayyads, went through several stages, influenced by the evolving discourses of religious authority, dynastic legitimacy, and regional politics, so that while it was necessary for the purposes of Abbasid legitimacy to remember the Umayyads as impious and tyrannical sinners, attempts were also made at rehabilitating the memory of the Umayyads.[96]

The anecdotes and the context in which they appear provide an important playing field for commentary on pre-Islamic history and the Umayyad past. The Abbasid polemic which opposed *jahiliyya* to Islam in terms of depraved/righteous suggests that Hind bint 'Utba is more than a minor figure at the edge of this unfolding drama, as she resonates with wider circles of meaning in the historical discourse. There was something "too much" about the *jahili* Hind, and the texts needed, at some point, on some level, to reduce this "too-muchness" to manageable proportions.[97] Hind's behavior in *jahiliyya* signifies an immoral, inferior culture, and she is highlighted as one whose expression must be dissociated from Islamic behavior. This backwardness represents Islam's common, rejected past and thus unifies the discursive Muslim community in the construction and definition of a new order. The transformation of the Arabs of *jahiliyya* from a barbarous, idolatrous, desperate, and abject people into the morally, ethically, and politically formidable people that they had become was a measure of the superiority of the Prophet Muhammad and his revelation. A Muslim author writing in the third/ninth century described the transformation of *jahiliyya* Arabs to respectful Muslims in the following terms: "They were the greatest of communities with regard to unbelief . . . they worshipped idols and poured out blood . . . killing their own children. . . . They were conquered by their own pleasures and their own desires. But [Muhammad] moved them away from the worship of idols and to the worship of the one God. . . . And he made them judicious and wise, whereas before there had been ignorance. . . . He tamed their hearts . . . and he ennobled their characters, those who before had been wicked."[98]

Islam had redeemed the Arabs from the/their *jahiliyya,* and while Muslim chroniclers present Islam as a decisive break in world history, supplanting what had previously existed, the Muslims of the time of Muhammad and the Muslims of all times constantly confront the temptation to slacken and turn away from the rigors of obedience to God. One hadith by the Prophet predicted the failure of the civilizing mission of Islam when he announced that the Muslim community would not abandon four *jahiliyya* practices: "Glorying in the deeds of one's own ancestors, calumniating the pride of another's genealogical descent, seeking rain by the configuration of the stars, and wailing."[99]

Jahiliyya is not a closed-off, inert space but was rather contiguous with Islam, and hence the threat of a cultural backsliding from Islam to *jahiliyya* is ever-present. The history of Islamic origins is filled with such moments: when the Prophet's companion Khalid b. al-Walid beheaded Islam's enemies after having promised them safety, the Prophet sent out his son-in-law 'Ali, ordering him to examine the affair thoroughly "and trample down the custom of *jahiliyya.*"[100] The caliphate of 'Uthman provides a similar example. When sedition against the third Rashidun caliph, 'Uthman (r. 23/644–35/656), started in Kufa, his staunchest opponents were described as *ahl al-ayyam,* as still accustomed to the pre-Islamic lifestyle of raids, tribal negotiations, and rejection of singular leadership—in other words, men who were still operating within the framework of *jahiliyya.* In the narrative,

Muʿawiya is made to issue a warning about the dangers the *umma* would incur if Caliph ʿUthman were killed. Here there are none of the pragmatic and opportunistic characteristics that one usually finds in portrayals of Muʿawiya. Instead, he gives fair warning about "the kinds of *jahili* politics that might once again come to prevail if the fabric of the *jamaʿa* is torn."[101] Hind is not simply overcome by the display of Muslim power following the conquest of Mecca. She is altered and absorbed into Muslim subjectivity, thus signaling the interpenetrability of the religious categories that seem so overdetermined in narratives of the Islamic triumph over *jahiliyya*. Hind represents the *jahili* past that has been mastered as well as the *jahili* past that has ceded place and been absorbed into the Muslim present. The traces of *jahiliyya*, nevertheless, necessitated constant reconquest and appropriation, thus continuously reminding the Muslims of the threat that *jahiliyya* will always present.[102]

The Umayyad Hind is more complex. The successive rewritings (of history) correspond to new meanings that were given to the past in order to make it serve the needs of a present constantly transformed. The changing political circumstances could not be satisfied with one monochord discourse for the entire period. The redemption of the memory of the Umayyads should be seen in this light, becoming not only possible, but necessary, in the second part of the third/ninth century.[103] In his third/ninth-century *adab* work, Ahmad b. Abi Tahir Tayfur includes an anecdote in which Caliph ʿUmar b. al-Khattab prohibited Abu Sufyan from sprinkling the entrance to his house with water lest the pilgrims slip on it; when Abu Sufyan did not obey and ʿUmar himself slipped in front of it, he lashed him and then said: "Praise to God who showed me Abu Sufyan in the plain of Mecca; I hit him and he does not defend himself and I order him and he obeys. Hind heard him and she said: Praise Him O ʿUmar for if you praise Him you will be bestowed greatly."[104] Positive and negative traditions resulted in a more nuanced projection of the Umayyad Hind. Here the motive is clear. She is the mother of the first Umayyad caliph, and her upgrading results from reaction to the pro/anti-Umayyad propaganda. El-Hibri has expressed surprise that pro-Umayyad historical voices could have originated amid Abbasid hostility, leading one to speculate on the role the Abbasids played in nurturing this image and, specifically, how they stood to benefit from it. El-Hibri suggests that a moralizing current underlies the representation of the Umayyads, notably the portrayal of Muʿawiya. The contradictory messages, about Hind in this case, "can [even] constitute a cohesive message on their own regarding human behavior and its variability in response to changing conditions."[105]

But whether *jahili*, Umayyad or in fact Abbasid, since ultimately Hind's representation is an Abbasid production, there is no doubt that, of all its meanings, the pre-Islamic past was especially significant as a locus for the moral warning, the consolation, and "amazement at the world's mutability which contemplation of that poignant past evoked."[106] The vastness of pre-Islam had to be described, demarcated, and claimed. It is the peculiar emptiness of *jahiliyya*, emptied of historical agency, that creates its meaning; its very being can only derive from the Abbasid gaze that is fixed on it. As medievalists have shown, the colonization of the past is an indispensable companion of empire, as it constitutes the invention of a past complementary to their own.[107]

A powerful conjunction of the *jahili* and the feminine was brought forth in the actions that Hind perpetrated. But the fact that Hind became a *sahabiyya* (a female companion of the Prophet) created a problem with the narrative. As a result, Hind, like all *jahilis*, is absorbed into the civilization of the conquerors. Indeed, Islam considers itself to be the most authentic representative of a universal, supranational religion. This is clearly manifested in the traditions about *fitra,* the natural inborn religion which stands for the inherent religious status of a child before any religious education turns the child into a conscious member of a distinctive religious congregation. Muslim scholars believe that this *fitra* is synonymous with Islam.[108] Hind thus represents an ideal of the "natural" Arab with all the goodness and all the wickedness we (each) possess; she is also the exemplar who was transformed by Islam, becoming a new person, bypassing the hatred and the pain inherent in *jahiliyya*. Her story constitutes one of the ways in which the Abbasid discourse brought order to the chaos of the "primitive" and ever-threatening landscape of *jahiliyya*.

Women's Lamentation and
Death Rituals in Early Islam

THE MUSLIMS were building a new world, fashioning a mode of living and a communal discipline that distinguished them from their pagan (and Jewish) neighbors. Muhammad's mission was to usher in a radical departure from the religious and social mores of pre-Islamic Arabia. A sweeping transformation of society was required. The opposition between righteous Islamic conduct and unrighteous *jahiliyya* conduct is clearly stated in the following verse, which addresses the wives of the Prophet and teaches them the new exemplary comportment, as contrasted with *jahili* practices:

> Wives of the Prophet, you are not as other women. . . .
> Remain in your houses; and display not
> your finery, as did the pagans of old.
> And perform the prayer, and pay the alms,
> and obey God and His Messenger.
> People of the House, God only desires
> to put away from you abomination
> and to cleanse you. (Qur'an 33.33)

The identity of the *umma* (Islamic community) was to be defined partly by its adherence to specific social and ritual practices so as to affirm its distinctiveness from pagans and from the other monotheist confessions. In accentuating the discontinuity between *jahiliyya* society and the *umma*, gender roles were especially potent for conveying meaning. Women protagonists in the Islamic religious texts consequently have to be read within this context of social realignment that characterized the transformation from pre-Islamic *jahiliyya* to the Islamic *umma*.[1]

Islam, being orthopraxic, carefully delineated correct practice understood to be emblematic of belief. Muslims therefore erected boundaries between the acceptable and the reprehensible and between an old and a new order, mobilizing, as seen in Chapter 1, the concept of *jahiliyya* to create distance from certain types of non-Islamic practices and behavior, notably death rituals.[2] Death practices came to constitute a barometer of faith and piety—death being the one moment common to all, arguably "the ultimate expression of society's beliefs, and also the ultimate opportunity for shaping and controlling a society's behavior."[3] Death creates an occasion for self-fashioning, and death rituals become charged social and cultural spaces in which issues of identity are negotiated with precision.[4]

With the rise of the new Islamic order, ritual mourning, notably the act of lamenting, entered into crisis. The Muslims rejected ritual mourning because it was grounded in an ideology of death incompatible with the new faith's emphasis on salvation in the afterlife. Moreover, establishing a new social order brought with it deliberate restrictions that fostered the interests of the emerging state and public unity over those of family and tribe. This entailed the reshaping of women's roles in death rites. The two concerns that weighed on the minds of traditionalists and jurisprudents, who valued social order and social uniformity, were the ideal ritual order and the role of women in society. The wailing of women was offensive because it represented an act of complaint against God's judgment and of rebellion against his decree and wisdom. According to Leor Halevi, the "struggle over wailing" was a conflict between two distinct modes of religiosity: the *jahili* mode, characterized by "spontaneous, emotional and violent rituals," and the Islamic mode, defined by "conformity to dogmatic beliefs and by emphasis on routinization."[5]

Ritual lamenting had similarly met with little accommodation from the Christian church, which upheld that the separation of the living and the dead is temporary and that believers will be reunited in heaven, and so a true Christian's grief should be measured and moderate.[6] The Catholic Church would persist in associating lamentation with non-Christian behavior. The converted Jews in Guadalupe, for instance, were identified in the AD 1485 persecution as heretics on the basis of customs inherited from their Judaic past, including mourning rituals, with one trial specifying that women sang mourning chants for the deceased. In the early 1520s, Isabel Garcia from Hita was accused of having gone with other women "to the home of a certain deceased person, [where they] climbed on top of the bed of the said deceased and sang and cried and wailed." Thus, keening lingered as a sign of both paganism and Judaism, and according to a Sevillian humanist, "loud funeral processions were abolished by the Inquisition for smacking of pagans and Jews and as a matter that little benefited the soul."[7] As religious beliefs developed, moral and ethical codes were tightened and rendered more modest to reflect the new creeds. Such propriety and humility were reflective of the theological and philosophical evolutions taking place across religions. Collectively, women's roles were the reflections of these shifts, but were also individually the catalysts for acceptance or resistance to such societal transformations.

Women were of course the main culprits in these Inquisition trials because women are central to the process of making sense of death and responding to it. It has been argued that the gendered division of labor extends into the sphere of emotions, with the result that true femininity requires intuitive sensitivity and emotional expressiveness, in contrast with true masculinity, which is predicated on rationality and emotional control.[8] Death is associated with emotionality, and it is women who express bereavement through crying and self-mutilation. Several theories have been advanced to explain the factors that underlie the sex difference in emotional expression—specifically, that crying may represent a female form of aggression; that women, through their roles as nurturing, sympathetic mothers and wives, develop stronger attachments to the deceased; or that women may simply be used as the persons who symbolize publicly the loss that all have experienced.[9]

It is thus understandable why the campaign to reform mourning practices in the new Islamic order would have a gender dimension. The leading and almost exclusive role women played in keening made mourning an explicitly female ceremony. In hadith literature, specifically in *Kutub al-jana'iz* (Books on funerary practice), this behavior was exemplified as one of the hallmarks of idolatrous behavior associated with the *jahiliyya*. Women's roles in death rituals were critical in providing new normative guidelines, which were to be contrasted with *jahili* practices; their personality and participation in death rituals during this pivotal era served as markers for religious and ideological shifts constitutive of the period. But another dimension is also added—namely, the tenacity of women's behavior, which would result in the survival of *jahili* mourning behavior, particularly in the guise of female lamentation.

Islam and Lamenting the Dead

Al-'Iqd al-farid, the *adab* compilation of Ibn 'Abd Rabbih (d. 328/940), incorporates a long section entitled "Kitab al-durra fi al-nawadib wa al-ta'azi wa al-marathi (The Book of Lamentations, Condolences, and Elegies)." The subsection entitled "Crying for the Dead" includes three traditions relating to the Prophet Muhammad. In the first tradition, he is seen crying over his dead son Ibrahim and is asked about his crying. The Prophet answered, "The eyes become tearful and the heart is saddened but we say only what is agreeable to God." The next tradition has the Prophet's companion 'Umar b. al-Khattab rebuking women for crying over a dead man. The Prophet told him, "Leave them, O 'Umar, the soul is stricken and the eye is tearful, and the fulfillment of the promise is close at hand." The last tradition in this series takes place following the battle of Uhud, when the Prophet heard the sound of weeping and wailing over the dead. The Prophet said, "But there are no women weeping for Hamza!" *(lakin Hamza la bakiyata lahu)*. "The people of Medina heard that and from then on, no funeral ceremony took place which did not begin with the women weeping for Hamza."[10]

The inherent tension between the need to mourn and lament the dead and the proper Islamic attitude toward death is reflected in these traditions. Indeed, Islam changed the notion of death. The Qur'an portrays close relationships among the concepts of death, life, and God, who does not just create humans and bring about their death, but rather is the source of life renewal: "It is He who gave you life, then He shall make you dead, then, He shall give you life" (Qur'an 22:66). Consequently, a basic premise of Qur'anic teaching concerning death becomes evident: in his omnipotence God determines the span of human life; he creates man and also causes him to die.[11] Death, like all else in the created order, belongs to the will of God and cannot occur without his leave. In Ira Lapidus's words, "Death is the ultimate test of a Muslim's capacity to accept God's decree with fortitude and trust."[12] Death in the Qur'an and Islamic theology was no longer annihilation and nonexistence; death is not an end but a step in a larger scheme and a necessary passage into the afterlife; it is merely the end of the appointed period *(ajal)* in which humans are tested in the world. Human existence, which in Islamic belief has been extended to eternity, renders death a merely transitional phase. Since death is not the end, it can be accepted with solemnity and calm, for it is the transition to a new phase of existence, to a truer life. Thus, the pious Muslim has nothing to fear from death. Without wishing for it, it is his or her duty to accept death with serenity as a prelude to a new life and to carry hope for those who have died. It was only natural, in line with these new religious conceptions, for Islam to modify certain funerary practices, in particular, sacrifices and lamentations.[13]

In the new order, traditional acts of mourning such as crying out loudly, throwing dust on one's hand, and the tearing of one's hair were abhorred, as the pietists stated that "the plaintive groan and the snort came from the devil."[14] Strong emotional reaction to death was condemned by religious pronouncement because it implied a skeptical attitude toward the divine promise of eternal life and a preference for earthly values. If the former flamboyant expression of excessive grief was no longer considered appropriate, then a new psychology, that of *sabr* (steadfastness) and contentment with the divine decree, was offered in its place. One hadith narrates the actions of Abu Talha's wife to exemplify the virtue of *sabr*: When her child died, she did not inform her husband until she conceived the following night. The hadith has the Prophet endorsing her behavior post facto. Later consolation treatises, designed to comfort parents, included this tradition as typifying the exemplary behavior of the Prophet's companions.[15]

Lamenting, *niyaha,* was condemned by the Islamic tradition. The root *nwh* does not occur in the Qur'an, nor does any term associated with the practice, such as *ranna* (to wail), *'awwala* (to bewail), *khamasha* (to scratch the face with the nails), *shaqqa jayban* (to tear the front of a garment), *nashara sha'ran* (to let the hair down), *latama* (to strike the cheek), or *nadaba* (to bewail).[16] These omissions exemplify the rejection of the instinctive, uncivil practices of *jahiliyya*. Whereas the Qur'an is silent about this practice, Muslim exegesis puts forward one verse in which a prohibition of *niyaha* is, according to commentators, implied in *Surat al-Mumtahana:*

> O Prophet, when believing women come to thee,
> Swearing fealty to thee upon the terms that
> they will not associate with God anything,
> and will not steal, neither commit adultery,
> nor slay their children, nor bring a calumny
> they forge between their hands and their feet,
> nor disobey thee in aught honorable,
> ask forgiveness for them; God is all forgiving, All-compassionate.
>   (Qur'an 60:12)

The generally accepted explanation in the exegetical tradition for "nor disobey thee in aught honorable" is that this refers to *niyaha,* the tearing of clothes, the cutting of the hair, and the scratching of faces.[17] This explanation is also found in Ibn Sa'd's *Tabaqat*. In his chapter on the allegiance given by women to the Prophet Muhammad, Ibn Sa'd relates that Isma'il b. 'Abd al-Rahman b. 'Atiyya stated that he asked his grandmother Umm 'Atiyya about the meaning of the portion of the Qur'anic verse "nor disobey thee in aught honorable," and she answered, "He forbade us to lament." Abu Bakr b. 'Abadallah similarly states that the Prophet received allegiance from women "on the condition that they do not tear their clothes, nor wail, nor scratch their faces." A third story refers to a woman who came to give allegiance to the Prophet, who recited to her the aforementioned verse; and "once he [the Prophet] reached the part 'nor disobey thee in aught honorable,' he said: do not lament."[18]

Condemnation of *niyaha* is explicit in the compilations of hadiths, which include traditions admonishing crying over the dead and extravagant shows of grief. *Niyaha,* as an established institution of *jahiliyya,* was considered to be a legacy of paganism. As such, it was condemned by the Prophet, who said, as recorded in Muslim al-Naysaburi's *Sahih:* "Four pre-Islamic *(jahili)* customs will be retained by my community. They are: boasting of the family's achievement *(ahsab),* attacking genealogies, invoking the planets in order to receive rain, and lamenting the dead *(al-niyaha).*"[19] The Prophet is said, however, to have made a distinction between lamenting and weeping, *niyaha* and *buka'.* Grief and sorrow for the loss of a relative can be expressed, as the Prophet himself did when his only son died: "At the death of his son Ibrahim, the Prophet wept *(baka).* Someone said to him: O Messenger of God, did you not forbid weeping? He said: I forbade *nawah,* the raising of one's voice, in two instances: A voice raised in a state of happiness . . . and a voice in times of misfortune which shows itself in mutilating one's face, tearing of clothes and a diabolical mourning cry. My personal tears express my compassion *(rahma).*"[20] Thus, while lamenting (as wailing) was forbidden, weeping was permitted if discreetly done.

Another tradition in Muslim's *Sahih* mentions that one of the Prophet's daughters sent him a message that her son was on his deathbed. The Prophet ordered her to be patient, but she sent after him asking for his presence. He went and, upon lifting the child in his arms, his eyes became tearful. He explained his reaction by saying, "This is a compassion that God brings into the hearts of mankind."[21] The *Musnad* of Abu Dawud includes the following tradition, which similarly distinguishes between *niyaha* and *buka':* "He [the Prophet] permitted singing during weddings and also weeping *(buka')* over the dead without lamenting *(niyaha).*"[22] While consolation was a very desirable *sunna* (prophetic custom) which must be given to all, lamenting the dead was forbidden. The most important collections of prophetic traditions—namely, those of al-Bukhari, Muslim, Abu Dawud, and al-Nasa'i—have transmitted that the Prophet instructed Muslims "not to bewail over a dead person."[23] Some traditions prohibit striking the head with the hands and the tearing of clothes when a calamity occurs. One tradition specifically states that the one who strikes the face, tears the clothes, and summons the cause of *jahiliyya* does not belong to Muslims.[24] What the prophetic tradition condemned was the gesturing and public histrionic manifestations of grief, a theatricality verging on a lack of sincerity. Moreover, the tradition was meant, perhaps, to discourage actions of lamenting that would increase rather than obliterate the grief of the bereaved person. But most of all, wailing and manifestations of abandonment to grief were deemed to be incompatible with resignation to God's will and submission to his decisions.

Women and *Jahili* Lament

If death ritual and response to fatality were dramatic acts, it was of course women who were the main actresses in the performance. According to al-Mubarrad, in *jahiliyya,* if women wished to exaggerate their sadness, they would shave their heads and strike their faces with their sandals.[25] The woman who lost her husband would shave her hair, scratch her face, and redden a piece of cotton with her own blood and place it on her head.[26] One of the most famous pre-Islamic scenes of lamentations provides glimpses into some of the practices that women followed in lamenting their dead:

> Whoever is happy with the killing of Malik,
> let them come to our women early in the day
> He will find the women uncovered lamenting him,
> hitting their faces . . .
> Scratching their faces over a young man
> of good predisposition and reputation.[27]

Pre-Islamic poetry functioned as a form of public register serving both as a method of communication and as the storehouse for collective memory, with poets representing their respective tribal interest. Within this system, women were entrusted with lamenting the dead as well as inciting men to war and to blood vengeance. The lament, which had ritualistic dimensions, was performed at grave sites, tribal gatherings, and festivals.[28] The poet Hassan b. Thabit describes the ways in which keening women expressed their mourning:

> O Mayya, arise and weep sadly at dawn as the keening women do;
> As those who carry heavy burdens cannot move for their weight
> Who cry aloud scratching the faces of free women.
> . . . They let their hair loose and their locks appear . . .
> They weep sadly like mourners whom fate has wounded,
> Their heart scarred by painful wounds.[29]

The *Sira* reports that when the Prophet's grandfather 'Abd al-Muttalib knew that his death was at hand, he summoned his six daughters and asked them to cry over him so that he might hear what they would be saying upon his death. His daughter Safiyya recited verses beginning with "I could not sleep for the voices of the keening women." His other daughters started their verses with something like "Be generous O eyes, with your pearly tears,"[30] reflecting *jahiliyya* poetry recited on the occasion of death.

Women's role in lamentation during *jahiliyya* is epitomized in the person of al-Khansa', the most famous of all the lamenting poets and the best-known female poet in the classical Arabic poetic tradition. Upon the death in battle of her two brothers, her poetic potentialities burst forth in a never-ending strain of lament. Her hero and her obsession was her brother Sakhr.[31] While al-Khansa' lived most of her life in pre-Islamic times, post-conversion stories reflect the embarrassment al-Khansa's newly converted kinsmen experienced at her continued mourning, both in the guise of elegies and in her wearing of the pre-Islamic mourning garb. Anecdotes relate that al-Khansa' revealed the reason of her deep grief to 'A'isha, wife of the Prophet, when she asked her about the coarse camel hair shirt she was wearing: "What is this Khansa'? The Prophet, may God's mercy be upon him, died and I did not wear it for him!" Al-Khansa' answered by relating the unfailing support that Sakhr had given her in all moments of distress in her life. Three times she approached him in dire need, and he gave her half of his wealth. When she came a fourth time, his wife tried to persuade Sakhr not to give her anything, but he rejected this counsel, reciting, "Were death to destroy me, I am sure she would tear off her head-gear and put on a camel-hair bodice."[32] 'A'isha and Caliph 'Umar b. al-Khattab, on separate occasions, told al-Khansa' that the brothers she was mourning and for whom she was composing elegies were in hell, since they died before the appearance of Islam. Her answer both times was that this was all the more reason for her distress.[33]

These stories substantiate the disapproval in which pre-Islamic mourning institutions were held after the rise of Islam but at the same time emphasize the strength of will of women like al-Khansa' in maintaining their mourning and expressions of grief, even in the face of societal censure.[34] James Bellamy states that it is hard to believe that al-Khansa's grief for her brothers was so intense that it could only be purged by a hundred poems.[35] But was al-Khansa's grief a solitary instance, or was it a reflection of the uncontrollable passion that grief could unleash, of the primitive irrational taking hold?

The *jahili* lament can be paralleled with anthropological representations that globally framed lament as primitive to civilized societies. Spaniards, who described the funeral customs of non-European peoples, talked about the calm way in which Mexican Indians died and were buried, in contrast to the people of Guinea, who were wild and uncivil, displaying their grief by howling and crying. Such remarks suggest that mourning customs helped Europeans distinguish between primitivism and savagery.[36] Similarly, the new Islamic order found violent displays of grief offensive in that they allowed nature to completely overwhelm culture. The poet Labid, for instance, warned his two daughters not to act, upon his death, in the manner of the people of *jahiliyya*:

> Behave and declare what you have been taught
> do not scratch your faces or shave your heads.[37]

The fashioning of a new society that would deal with the drama of an individual's death in an Islamic way meant that in contrast to pre-Islamic reactions, forbearance was, from now on, the correct Islamic response. In the context of the conquest of Khaybar, the *Sira* relates the reaction of one woman who upon seeing her slain fellow (Jewish) tribesmen, "shrieked and slapped her face and poured dust on her head. When the Apostle saw her he said: 'take this she-devil from me.'"[38] It is, moreover, perhaps revealing that one of the few women commanded by the Prophet to be killed was Sara, a singer and mourner *(nawwaha)* from Mecca who had gone to Medina asking for the Prophet's help, stating, "I have abandoned lamenting and singing." The Prophet ordered that she be given food. However, when she returned to Mecca, she resumed her old religion, and started chanting insulting poetry about the Messenger of God. On the day of the conquest of Mecca, she was killed.[39]

The purpose of Islam's injunction against excessive lamentation was to contain mourning. There were thus religious prescriptions prohibiting lamenting and traditions that explicitly condemned the work of the *na'iha* (professional mourner). The Prophet is reported to have said that the deceased would be punished if a professional mourner was hired to keen by the grave. Another tradition has it that this punishment is reserved only for those who during their lives gave explicit instructions for professional mourners to attend their funerals. The opinion of the Prophet on professional female mourners is further expressed in the following utterance: "The professional mourner, if she feels no remorse before her own death, will arise on the Day of Judgment, but be held fast in skirts of tar and underskirts of sulfur."[40] One hadith states that the Prophet disapproved of the *saliqa*, the one who raises her voice in lamentation; the *haliqa*, the one who shaves her hair in lamentation; and the *al-shaqqa*, the one who tears her clothes in lamentation. Abu Dawud also includes in his collection a tradition that states that God's curse is on the *na'iha* and the listener, *al-mustami'a* (in the feminine form).[41] The hired female mourner is, moreover, criticized by Caliph 'Umar b. al-Khattab. She is someone who deserves no deference, as she hurts the dead in their tombs and prevents patience, whereas God has ordered it. She is cursed and promised punishment unless she repents before she dies.[42] Nevertheless, as mentioned above, the Prophet himself required that the women of Medina lament Hamza's passing. The seeming contradiction between the Prophet's personal demand to lament Hamza and his general injunctions against lamentation produced the following hadith: "Every *na'iha* is in hell except for the *na'iha* of Hamza."[43]

Female Lamentation and the Construction of a New Order

Grief organically arouses passion, as observed in Hind bint 'Utba's behavior after the battle of Badr, when her lamentation and call for vengeance prolonged and exacerbated tensions. Such behavior threatened to let the temporary chaos of death and mourning spill over into society at large and threaten its stability. Hind used lamentation to keep alive her family's cause and to stir up the desire for revenge. Mourning women were indeed considered dangerous, especially since the themes developed by women who lament were at odds with the rhetoric of the public ideology of the emerging *umma*. The *jahili* women's behavior symbolized the forces of kin, nature, and emotion, while the Islamic discourse and rituals surrounding death suppressed personal feeling. Women's lamentations were thus deemed to be a reflection of the impulsive, emotional human reaction to death, which momentarily rules over self-control and piety.[44] Passionate lamenting was dangerous, all the more since it was inseparable from its status as a principally women's genre, and women are represented as emotional and irrational, always requiring male control.[45]

Anthropologists have pointed to lament's potential as an effective channel for venting dissatisfaction or protest. Indeed, linking lament too closely with emotion might obscure its character as an often politically charged act. Laments were performances not only of grief but also of grievance, moving some to violent revenge on behalf of the bereaved. In the ancient city of Athens, Solon blamed the emotional excesses of women's laments for causing barbaric blood feuds. The excessive mourning of Electra, Antigone, and Medea obscured their judgment and threw them into the realm of madness and death. In a similar fashion, perhaps, Hind mingled grief with rage and hatred to such an extent that it could be quenched only by an act of irrational violence. And like Shakespeare's Queen Margaret, who demanded recognition of the priority of her suffering, saying, "If ancient sorrow be most reverend, / Give mine the benefit of seniory,"[46] Hind challenged the claim of the lamenter without peer, the grieving poet al-Khansa', of being the most bereaved of all the Arabs, declaring herself to be the greatest of the Arabs in terms of catastrophes suffered. This was not simply a listing of catastrophes but rather a deliberate inflammation of hatred. Queen Margaret said, "Bear with me. I am hungry for revenge. . . . Cancel his bond of life, dear God, I pray, / That I may live to say, The dog is dead,"[47] in much the same way that Hind cursed and raged, giving vocal expression to her pain. She waits until the next battle to avenge father, son, and uncle. The passion of her grief is such that it potentially threatens the new order. Hind's excessive call for revenge and her outrageous irrational acts stand, in the texts, in direct opposition to the accepting and quietist attitude with which Muslim women were supposed to react to the death of their male relatives.[48]

Lamentation has, historically, allowed women to articulate their sorrow, to incite rage, to reveal their vulnerability when faced with a loved one's death, and to remember and connect with the deceased.[49] Ritual lamentation provided al-Khansa' and Hind with a public platform from which they could speak and express their pain and need for revenge. The work of grief and the articulation of a grievance go together, as grief and grievance are linked in a linguistic sense as well as "within the psychic economy of loss."[50] The women who grieve at the same time that they protest and contest articulate their rage in uncompromising tones, making reconciliation impossible.

The narrative of Hind following the battle of Badr and at the battle of Uhud brings together violence, the female voice, and female lament, aligning each of these expressions with the irrational, the precultural, revealing the vacillation between the wild and the civilized, nature and culture. It is also a scene or freeze-frame, a marker of time between the pre-Islamic and Islamic eras and the opposition to assimilation to the new—or any sense of—order. The verses recited by Hind incorporated passion and discontent with aversion and fantasy, thus developing a feminine mode of expression that challenged the new order. The Islamic answer to Hind's excessive lamentations after the battle of Badr is reflected in Safiyya's response to the mutilation of her brother Hamza at the battle of Uhud. The new Islamic ethos that Safiyya now represented called for a modification of behavior, a display of restraint and forbearance. When Safiyya came to see the corpse of her brother, the Prophet told her son al-Zubayr to take her back "so that she does not see what has happened to her brother." Safiyya refused, saying: "Why? I have heard that my brother has been mutilated for God's sake . . . I will be calm and patient if it is God's will."[51] Safiyya eulogized her brother

Hamza in verses that confirm the profound belief of a Muslim woman and her acceptance of God's divine decree:

> Are you my sisters asking in dread
> The men of Uhud, the slow of speech and the eloquent?
> The latter said Hamza is dead,
> the best helper of the apostle of God.
> God the true, the Lord of the Throne, called him
> To live in paradise in joy. That is what we hoped and longed for.
> Hamza on the day of gathering will enjoy the best reward.
> By God I'll never forget thee as long as the east wind blows,
> In sorrow and weeping, whether at home or in travel
> . . . I said when my family raised their lamentation,
> God reward him, fine brother and helper as he was![52]

Safiyya was mirroring the new paradigm of how the women of the emerging *umma* were to confront mortality. Safiyya's patient reaction and words at the sight of the corpse of Hamza reflect a withdrawal from the female world of lament, shifting emotions away from the morbid relish of female grief, giving instead the death of the fallen martyrs its full meaning. In this case, it is a woman, a Muslim woman, who translates the new mood, the new *Sabr* ideology, which prohibits lamentation over the dead and promotes an ethic of patience when confronting the tests of time and the decrees of God. Even the reactions to the Prophet's own death were to follow Islamic prescriptions. When Umm Ayman, the Prophet's nurse *(hadina)*, cried upon hearing of the Prophet's death, she is said to have defended herself by saying, "By God, I do not cry over him knowing that he has departed to what is better for him than this world; I cry for the termination of revelation."[53] This was again emphasized by Muhammad's companion Asma' bint 'Umays, who, upon hearing of the Prophet's death, shrieked. Someone called out: "Are you crying over the Messenger of God? Are you shrieking over the Messenger of God? Asma' answered: We are neither crying over the Messenger of God nor are we shrieking over him but for the termination of revelation *(inqita'al-wahi 'anna)*."[54]

The audible female voice in ritual lamentation induced anxiety, since it gave vent to the uncontrollable and irrational, that is, essentially feminine, emotions. The devaluation of feminine utterance is the consequence of anchoring the female voice in the female body, which confers upon it the conventional associations of femininity with emotion and irrationality.[55] Women's lamentation came to constitute an offense against the new Muslim community. While the death of members in the *jahili* context may bring disorder, for the Muslims, death of individual members does not threaten the sacred communal ties of the *umma,* since the loss involves not only the blood relatives of the fallen but also the entire community.[56] Muslim women were to become the medium through which "correct" grief and emotion would erase the offense of their *jahili* past.

In the *Sira* of Ibn Hisham, the death of the Prophet is grieved only by the official male poet Hassan b. Thabit (d. 40/659 or 54/673), whose long poem forms the closure to this lengthy biography. There, no women are found lamenting. In the Muslim *umma,* women's lament, the female voice at once stigmatized, ideologically "marked" and construed as a problem, is now superseded by the culturally sanctioned male voice of Hassan b. Thabit. And, indeed, while Ibn Sa'd's *Tabaqat* includes a large number of elegies recited on the occasion of the Prophet's death, by, among others, the companion Abu Bakr, the poet Ka'b b. Malik, and the daughters of 'Abd al-Muttalib, the majority of verses are by the official poet, Hassan b. Thabit.[57] The verses reflect a change from the pre-Islamic style, genre, and method of composition, away from the ideals of pagan tribalism and toward the new Islamic ideal defended by an emerging political and religious community. Unlike the pre-Islamic poet who defended his tribe against rival tribes, the new polarity, depicted in Hassan's poetry, was one between the faithful and their adversaries.[58]

Islam was not alone in eliminating the role of women in mourning rituals. In ancient Greece, the outlawing of public female mourning by Solon in the sixth century BC had given way in Athens to two new discursive modes of mourning, namely, the tragedy and the official state funeral oration. A predominantly female oral tradition was rewritten as a set of performance conventions that excluded female performers and female members of the audience. Mourning was reappropriated in a process that negated the female. It is as if the attempt to impinge on women's ritual authority through suppressing their lamentations was a move to silence them. Regulating mourning equaled regulating women, so strongly does the reciprocal relation between women and mourning assert itself in the ancient Greek texts.[59] Similarly, in the emerging Muslim *umma,* there was a binary and gendered opposition between the official (male-performed and male-attended) and the unofficial (female lamentation) modes of mourning. Death was to leave the private, personal domain of the female and enter into the public and political world of the male. Lamenting women who symbolized disorder and *jahili* ways were to be replaced by institutionalized poets such as Hassan b. Thabit, who were henceforward allotted the task of expressing the new Muslim community's reaction to a given loss.

But such reformed discipline in ritual lament was not easy to follow, since it is through the acts of tending the dead that women carry out the soul's serious work necessary upon loss of a loved one.[60] Denying the veracity of certain beliefs, practices, and rituals was not enough to eradicate them. A gap would persist between official theology and popular practice. The new models of behavior would not easily displace the ancient mourning customs. For instance, Nu'm, wife of Shammas b. 'Uthman, a Muslim woman whose husband was martyred at Uhud, elegized him in verses that did not conform to the attitude of forbearance expected from a Muslim woman. Her elegy followed the manner of pre-Islamic elegies:

> O eye be generous, let thy tears flow spontaneously
> For the noble and victorious warrior
> . . . I said in anguish when news of his death came,
> The generous man who fed and clothed
> others has perished.[61]

A similar reaction was observed upon the death of Hanzala, one of the companions of the Prophet. His wife lamented him, and neighbors reprimanded her, warning her that such an attitude would thwart her.[62] The reaction of Hamna bint Jahsh, another of Muhammad's companions, reflected the dangers of women's emotionality, although she tried to abide by the new Islamic injunctions of controlled mourning. Having been told of the death of her brother 'Abdallah, she responded, "We belong to God and to God we return." Then she was told of the death of her maternal uncle Hamza, and she uttered the same words for him. But when told of the death of her husband, Mus'ab b. 'Umayr, she shrieked and wailed.[63] While the temporal culture urged conformity to the new order of Islamic propriety, women ignored the social expectation to self-suppress their emotions when enduring grief, and hence continued at least part of the death practices left over from *jahiliyya*.

During his lifetime, the Prophet had to constantly teach the proper attitude toward death that was compatible with the new belief and, thus, to draw the line between the old and new order. For instance, when Ja'far b. Abi Talib was killed at the battle of Mu'ta, someone informed the Prophet that the womenfolk of Ja'far were crying. The Prophet twice ordered them to refrain from such behavior, and twice they desisted. 'A'isha claims that the Prophet said, "Go and fill their mouths with sand."[64] In one version, Ja'far's wife, Asma' bint 'Umays, relates that upon learning that Ja'far was killed: "I stood up and screamed, and the women came to me. The Prophet began to say: O Asma', do not speak obscene words or beat your chest!" Another version, which projects a more appropriate response on the part of Asma', has the Prophet asking her, "O Asma', will you not rejoice?" She replied,

"But of course for you are dear to me." He said, "Indeed, God most high has made two wings for Ja'far that he may fly with them to paradise!" She replied, "By my father and my mother, O messenger of God, inform the people of that."[65] Hadith compilations have included, moreover, specific directives as to the mourning restrictions that Asma' was to follow: "Asma' bint 'Umays said that when Ja'far was killed, the Prophet came to see us and he said: stand up, wear the clothes of mourning *(al-hidad)* for three days, and then do what you please."[66]

The nuance involved between crying and lamenting, but more specifically the potential for excessive behavior around death, is yet again connected to the death of the Prophet's uncle, Hamza. When the Prophet returned from Uhud, women came to cry for Hamza by the Prophet's home upon the latter's request: "The Prophet slept and later woke up and they were still crying so he said: woe unto them! They are still here! Let them go back and never cry again over a dead person."[67] The Prophet had expected controlled and restricted weeping over Hamza and thus reprimanded the women when he saw that they were extending their emotional outburst beyond the newly instituted norms.

Women's continued connection to lamenting is evoked by Umm 'Atiyya, who states: "The Prophet ordered us when we came to give him allegiance not to lament. Not a woman among us kept her promise except for five women."[68] Even on his deathbed, as his daughter Fatima started to cry, he told her, "Do not cry, child, and say when I die: we belong to God and to Him we return."[69] The tension persisted, nevertheless, between what the official religion allowed and what would actually be done: the grandson of the Prophet, Husayn, instructed his sister Zaynab before his death, "O sister find solace in God's consolation . . . I beseech you not to rend your garment on my behalf, not to scratch your face or break out in wailing."[70] Such texts imply that women instinctively resisted the newly prescribed suppression of their lament, echoing the primal, human urge to physically express their grief in public or private, and demonstrating a lack of concern for their audience and for their new faith.

Ignaz Goldziher collected information about the persistence of lamentation practices, including the following episodes: the wife of al-Hasan erected a tent over his grave and maintained it for a year; the women of the Mughira clan placed their hair on the grave of the Muslim hero Khalid b. al-Walid; a poet saw girls beating their faces by the grave of an Abbasid prince in Samarra'; Ibn al-Athir al-Jazari, a court secretary under Saladin, quoted a decree containing instructions which he wrote on the nomination of a *muhtasib* (market inspector): "To matters often practiced contrary to the religious *sunna* belong the holding of assemblies of condolence, the wearing of black or blue mourning clothes, and imitation of the *jahiliyya* with wailing, excessive weeping and heart-rending grief bordering on deliberate provocation of God's anger." Goldziher provided these examples as proof that several features of *jahiliyya* practice endured in Islamic culture despite the opposition of the pious Muslims.[71]

This female contestation of the many prophetic injunctions to follow restraint and accept God's decree seems to have continued all the way down to the Mamluk period. Usama b. Munqidh, the prince of the Syrian locality of Shayzar, described a mother whose son had been killed by the Franks as an elderly woman, who would perform dirges for the deceased and lament for her son.[72] Upon the death of the Ayyubid sultan al-Malik al-'Adil in 615/1218, his son, al-Mu'azzam 'Isa, ripped his clothes and struck his head and face; when al-Mu'azzam himself died, women who never left their homes stood with their children in the streets and marketplaces, ripping their clothes and disheveling their hair, lamenting him for a full month.[73] We also read that when the Mamluk sultan al-Ashraf died in 693/1294, his *jawari* (slave girls) went out uncovered, slapping their faces in lamentation. His children and his *ghulman* (slave youths) stepped out as well, splitting their clothes and clamoring. His young slaves and the wives of the officers who were attached to his service put on the vestments of mourning and deambulated in the streets in the company of professional mourners who celebrated his funerary oration.[74]

In the eighth/fourteenth century, the jurist Ibn al-Hajj (d. 737/1336–1337) denounced the numerous "innovations" and un-Islamic manners that he observed in the female customs associated with death rituals, stating that "women expose their faces and spread their hair, they blacken both face and body, and lament and wail in loud, shrieking voices."[75] Ibn al-Hajj expounds how a *na'iha* was hired to intensify the atmosphere of mourning, leading female relatives and friends to the beats of the tambourine, the wailer orchestrating a powerful scene of lamentation. Women indulged in these scenes, in defiance of the sharia (religious law), for several days and nights after the death.[76] Social and religious inhibitions were little regarded, and the women gave vent to their sorrow and their pain in a most vehement manner. A woman coming to present her condolences would enter while shouting her distress, striking and scratching her face, and "the *nawa'ih* (professional mourners) [would] receive her in their usual reprehensible ways."[77] The continuance of women lamenters and professional mourners revealed their hesitancy to integrate into their new religious selves and kept them at the border between pagan and Muslim, wild and subdued.

The use of professional mourners thus continued in spite of clear condemnation, and Islam came to understand wailing as a common, intractable pagan rite that survived despite religious efforts to abolish it.[78]

While the evidence so far provided comes from mainstream Sunni sources reflecting behavior within the Sunni community, the Shiʻi carried lamentation to a far higher level after the martyrdom at Karbala' of the Prophet's grandson al-Husayn in 61/680, an event that caused Shiʻism to be described as a religion of lament. Lamenting the family of the Prophet carried with it an elite connotation, certainly of prestige. Although the Shiʻi legal books record opposition to violent lament, the tone of some traditions is ambivalent, since wailing for the imams was deemed appropriate.[79] Weeping was to be a reminder of the sufferings of al-Husayn, whose death serves as a basis for identity and cohesion in the Shiʻi community. It is significant that here again lamenting for al-Husayn was initiated by a woman, his sister Zaynab, who is said to have instituted the *majlis*, the mourning assemblies held to commemorate the tragedy of Karbala', as a fundamental ritual. Al-Tabari says that as the women passed al-Husayn and his family, they shrieked and tore at their faces. Passing by al-Husayn's body, Zaynab cries out: "O Muhammad! . . . Here is al-Husayn in the open, covered with his blood; his limbs torn off."[80] In a further statement that cannot but evoke the martyrdom of the Prophet's uncle Hamza at Uhud, she exclaims: "Do you know what liver of the Prophet you have split? What blood of him you have shed?"[81] Women's lament here reflects a righteous voice and a mature transition from unruly, sacrilegious wailing to reverent lament; it is evidence of the evolution of the emotional presentation, yet at the same time proof that the act of lamenting itself, by virtue of its own primal power, could not be eradicated.

While in the first/seventh and second/eighth centuries Shiʻi lamentation sessions *(majalis al-niyaha)* were held in private or around the shrines of the imams, the third/ninth century witnessed the appearance of professional mourners, both men and women, who used lamentation elegies that they composed to commemorate al-Husayn and his family. By the fourth/tenth century, Shiʻi men and women were parading in the streets of Baghdad in processions, mourning al-Husayn. Al-Tanukhi talks about Khilb, a *na'iha* in Baghdad, who lamented al-Husayn and the family of the Prophet in private houses, because at the time people were unable to lament publicly for fear of the intransigent Hanabila. Khilb's work posed a threat to her own life, for the head of the Hanabila said, "I have heard that a *na'iha* known as Khilb is lamenting; get her and kill her."[82] The attack on lamenting and its professional practitioner, the *na'iha,* thus sometimes resulted from such intersectarian tensions. The death of al-Husayn would continue to serve as a fundamental basis for identity and cohesion in the Shi'i community, especially so in the continuity of sorrow which is most powerfully presented in the mother of the martyred imam, Fatima, who remains the mistress of the House of Sorrows, both in this world and in the world to come.[83]

Shi'i lamenting and weeping, which, as noted, were performed by both women and men, appear in the mainstream texts as excessive; by extension it is the entire community that appears as dangerously extreme. Given that this grief- and grievance-triggered response is of a reflexive nature, we may understand the fact that it was forbidden but still practiced as evidence of the innate difficulty that human nature has in complying with the repression of an intrinsic impulse—it is as if lament is unleashed all the more because it is felt and seen as unacceptable, thereby rendering its release all the more urgent. In so doing, women's resistance demonstrated not only the immediacy of their emotion but also the weakness of their faith. Moreover, since mourning and lamenting are primarily female occupations, is a community whose redemptive suffering enjoins and provokes weeping hence feminized? But in either case, whether Sunni or Shi'i, it is women who are the main offenders, blurring the boundaries between the old and new orders through their excessive lamenting and emotional indulgence, and in some ways prolonging a more complete evolution from pagan behavior to Islamic comportment, hence jeopardizing the order required by the new regime. Emotion, especially when it is passionate, is seen as subversive, destructive, and dangerous.

The Persistence of Female Lamentation and the Enactment of Islamic Identity

The stubborn adherence to lamentation, despite the Islamic injunctions, buttressed and reconstructed ideologies of the illogicality of a woman's nature and her essential lack of authority and control.[84] Such manifestations, whether in any way real or merely textual representations, reflected and consolidated the new gender constructions, which regarded such behavior not only as unmasculine but also as un-Islamic, having been undertaken by those who were the opposite of both constructs—in other words, women and *jahilis* (or sectarians). These displays reinforced the belief that if left uncontrolled, women would revert to a wild and untamed condition, to the era of *jahiliyya*.

The theologian Ibn Taymiyya, in the eighth/fourteenth century, criticized the tenacity of pre-Islamic customs among Muslims of his time, which, to his mind, constituted a *jahiliyya* in a restricted sense. He explained that the term *jahiliyya* is applied to a certain state *(hal)* or to the carrier of that state *(dhu al-hal)*. *Jahiliyya,* Ibn Taymiyya confirms, exists in Muslim lands and among many Muslims, just as the Prophet had stated: "Four characteristics dating from *jahiliyya* persist among my people."[85] Women were clearly responsible for carrying on at least one of these, namely, lamenting the dead.

The *jahili* rituals that survived, notably female lamentation, were the source and the field of a struggle for power between the religious creativity of the masses and the establishment's need for control.[86] The rationale for prohibiting excessive grieving practices was based on the conviction that the show of great sadness on the deaths of friends and relatives implies a denial of the promise of being brought back to life on the Last Day. It was necessary to convince believers that death is the beginning of eternal life instead of something mournful. But the rejection of ritual mourning went beyond such associations to involve proper comportment, especially the avoidance of *jahili* excesses, epitomized by Hind as well as by the extreme emotionality of women lamenters.

The emerging Islamic community, in this period of great historical transition, strove to establish a new order that sought to replace kinship and the power of blood relations with the emergent ethical order based on the principles of the new *umma*. The intense acts of lamentation of Hind and other *jahili* women stood in contrast to the controlled, quietist attitude the women of the new Muslim order were expected to follow in reaction to the death of their loved ones, thus highlighting a binary construction of an ideal type of Muslim womanhood against an equally constructed *jahili* womanhood.[87] The "Islamization" of death rituals implied, first and foremost, the stifling of emotional outbursts, most specifically of lamenting *(niyaha)*, that pietists associated with *jahili* practices. However close to actual pre-Islamic practice, *niyaha* became the construct of ideologues striving to define by opposition the ideal Islamic ritual.[88]

Ritual lament was perhaps the foremost medium in which women expressed themselves and their concerns publicly and could therefore exert some influence on their community's affairs, posing a subtle challenge to the dominant ideology of the early Muslim *umma*. The rites of mourning are a society's means of performing and containing grief. The political is not only tightly related to, but perhaps even arises out of, the rites and rituals of mourning, since "there is no politics without an organization of the time and space of mourning, without a topolitology of the sepulcher."[89] Seeing the danger and political potential of extreme grief, the emerging *umma* tried to bring funerary behavior under state control, and thus establish masculine (that is, rational) control over death rituals. Male pietists feared that wild, wailing women would counteract the good intentions of the reserved Muslim men who obeyed God's will and wished to establish the new order's death rites.[90] But all of this was an ideal scheme frustrated by the reality of wailing women, whose spontaneous poetry and unpredictable behavior epitomized the chaos of pre-Islamic times and who gave in to their instinctive urges. Death rituals, especially lamentation, became one of the *lieux de mémoire,* an institutionalized realm where true memory is stored, taking refuge "in gestures and habits, in skills passed down by unspoken traditions, in the body's inherent self-knowledge, in unstudied reflexes and ingrained memories," in the words of Pierre Nora.[91]

Our texts saw women's lament as an inferior model of comportment: pagan, feminine, and emotional. Grief was to be regulated and governed, and clear rules were formulated for its performance. *Jahiliyya* as a point of origin became the domain that needs to be controlled, a historical moment that is to be put decisively behind. The self-mastery of the early Muslims operated in ways to help them distinguish themselves from the unruliness ascribed to both the period of *jahiliyya* and women's behavior. The new order sought to bring women's laments and public displays of grief under control and to adapt them for its purposes. The early Muslims recognized the threat of leaving this daring resource in the control of women, whose ritual behavior had its roots in *jahiliyya* custom.

The canon of Islamic funerary practices set forth in *fiqh* (jurisprudence) literature provides a structure of order and meaning for the bereaved. But to understand Islamic beliefs and practices relating to death, we must stress that Muslim bereavement practices took shape between what is prescribed and what is performed, as death produces reactions that challenge, condone, or bargain with religious prescriptions, which consist of formalized rules and gain power by being embedded in divine will and prophetic example. The performed dimension of religion, however, is suppler and gives people the freedom to appropriate, contest, adapt, and change religious and cultural norms.[92] Elisheva Baumgarten has reflected on the "religiousness" of certain practices and on how medieval women rendered some daily actions as "religious proclamations."[93] In this particular case women's continued involvement in lamentation suggests, even if obliquely, the weakness of their faith. The anthropologist Lila Abu Lughod has concluded that the "traditionally gendered rituals where women lament the people they have lost and men instead invoke God will become an important means by which women publicly enact their own moral and ultimately social inferiority."[94]

The cultural authority of the women lamenters was overtaken by the civilizing power of the transformation. However, women (some of them, at least), as the protectors of cultural identity, withstood assimilation and maintained the rituals related to death. The women who continued to lament the dead were, in a sense, societal in-betweens and spiritual go-betweens, entering as they did the "in-between" spaces that initiate new representations of identity and pioneer points of cooperation and contro-versy.[95] Thus, while their resistance reflected at the surface a certain pas-sivity, it was latently a boundary-maintaining mechanism against the new male-dominated order.

The new instructions regarding behavior about death created a temporal boundary between the time of *jahiliyya* and the time of Islam. The construc-tion of "Islamness" required the invention of Islam as a religion, as an or-ganized body of belief and ritual severed from earlier cultural practices, no-tably those that surround death. Women's lamentation will continue to represent, in the age of rapid religious change, a retarding effect of attitudes and rituals from the pre-Islamic past which remain operative in the Islamic present. Their repetition, which is the very nature of rituals, represents, ac-cording to Clifford Geertz, "an enactment, a materialization, a realization of the worldview encapsulated in myth and symbol,"[96] implying continuity with the past. The textual examples give a pivotal role to the figure of the lamenting woman, underscoring the degree to which women participated in the shaping—through acceptance or opposition—of changing religious practice. Whether they were performing *jahiliyya* or articulating their re-formed Islamic selves, through lamenting or abstaining from lament, women were inherent markers of identity and belonging.

3

The Heretical Within

The Qaramita and the Intimate Realm

IN HIS ANALYSIS of the rise of persecution in medieval Europe, R. I. Moore suggests that "the very process of identifying and rebutting heresy [gives] it greater coherence," transforming disparate and inarticulate heresies into an image of a threatening monster. Heresy, when acknowledged and attacked, gains greater visibility and prominence, but its exposition is not necessarily representative of the actual peril it poses to an established regime or orthodoxy. The heresiological literature misrepresented the heretics, exaggerating their number, their indulgent behavior, their convictions, and their sphere of influence.[1] Europe developed a tradition of persecution of outsider groups, including heretics, defined according to well-established stereotypes that placed women and sexuality at center stage.[2] Indeed, charges of sexual deviance have been generally attached to heretical movements. In twelfth-century Europe, the Waldensians were described as unrestrained hedonists, forsaking the spiritual for sensual experience. The Cathars were also accused of teaching free sex, and the Council of Rheims in AD 1157 condemned sex orgies as a part of their heretical behavior. A century earlier in the Byzantine Empire, the theme of sexual transgression was similarly deployed in the polemic against the Paulicians who were accused of partaking in orgiastic and incestuous behavior.[3]

All these attitudes render the study of women and sexuality in premodern heretical movements problematic. The heresiological sources were written from the point of view of self-identified orthodoxy; moreover, they were authored by men who used the heretical woman as a vehicle to assert their own orthodox male selfhood.[4] Such narratives reveal, consequently, little about the women in the groups in question and a lot about how male writers used stories of women to drive and challenge conceptions of gender relations and sexuality, and, more broadly, determine how women functioned as tropes in this discourse.[5] I analyze the way antiheretical polemic was used in mainstream Sunni sources regarding one Islamic heretical group, the Qaramita; more specifically, I examine how women and sexuality were used as ploys for boundary definition and differentiation. Sunni texts imply that the Qaramita promoted a sexual ethic that radically differed from the "correct" Muslim one. Their purported sexual licentiousness was used as a polemical tool to exclude them from the body politic.

Heresy in Islam

There is no specific Islamic term for heresy. In a sense there is no heresy in Islam, if one is to follow the Christian definition, as in the Abbasid era there was no dominant religious voice with the moral or coercive authority to impose its views to the exclusion of all others. There could, therefore, be no orthodoxy but rather a variety of opposing parties competing for the right to define doctrine.[6] In theory, every Muslim was free to propagate his or her own vision of Islam while condemning other visions as "corruptions." This meant that every theological school of thought upheld its own version of orthodoxy while accusing other groups of delusion and heresy. As orthodoxy had been contested in this fashion, it seemed rather fluid. But, nevertheless, *ijma'*, the unanimous opinion of qualified jurists belonging to the classical Sunni schools of law, had the ultimate claim to define Islamic orthodoxy. All other opinions came to be considered heterodox.[7]

The authority of consensus became an established principle in Sunni jurisprudence by the fourth/tenth century, with the consequence that violating it risked accusations of heresy. Orthodoxy is a process, and its history is one of how claims to truth come to be enshrined in social practices such as rituals and in institutions such as the "community of scholars," the *'ulama*.[8] As Hamid Dabashi points out, "orthodox" and "heterodox" are polemical rather than hermeneutic terms, and it was the political success of a particular interpretative reading that rendered a religious position "orthodox."[9] The Sunni Muslims represented early Islam as a single, uniform community with a firm canon and foundation from which sects developed and strayed from the whole. Theologians who were determining the content of the *sunna* had to indicate who would belong and who would remain outside it. They identified when an individual's error or a deed beyond the scope of the *sunna* was considered unbelief.[10] However, even within the Sunni branch of Islam, the complexity of doctrinal developments prevented a single idea of "orthodoxy."

The Arabic term that comes close to defining heresy is *zandaqa,* which originally connoted believers in dualist doctrines who nominally professed Islam, but which was later generalized to include holders of unorthodox, unpopular, and otherwise suspect beliefs.[11] The term *zandaqa* came to be used for all kinds of heretical deviation until eventually it designated more than simple error—namely, unbelief. Another term connoting heresy, *ghuluww,* is related to exaggeration or excess in one's religious belief, such as the denial of prophecy and Islamic law or the preaching of antinomianism. The term *ilhad* came into use in the early Abbasid age to signify not so much adherence to false religious doctrine as rejection of religion as such—materialist skepticism and atheism. With the consolidation of Sunni orthodoxy in the fourth/tenth century, heresiography came to employ set designations for those considered opponents of Sunnism: Batiniyya (those groups rejecting the literal wording of the sacred text and stressing instead *batin,* the inward meaning, most especially the Isma'ilis), Qadariyya (theologians embracing the principle of free will), and Ibahiyya (antinomian groups). However, consistency in these definitions was never achieved.[12]

Marina Rustow suggests that to challenge the power the Qaraites wielded in the Jewish community, the fifth/eleventh-century Rabbanites of the Fatimid Empire accused them of heresy. Rustow underlines that beliefs in Islam and Judaism became heretical when religious majority authorities applied the use of force.[13] Similarly, according to Sherman Jackson, in the absence of a formal ecclesiastical hierarchy, all that is needed to establish and sustain any orthodoxy is authority, which may be formal or informal. Orthodox creed, elusive as it was, could be established only through state support.[14] The question of which movement constituted a sect and which set of beliefs constituted heresy was not decided by dogma but by the views of the majority or by a minority's lack of success. Persecution was founded in the temporal mind-set and on chance rather than on dogma and law;[15] and thus, in some sense, orthodoxy came to mean the acceptance of the existing order, whereas heresy represented its criticism or rejection.

According to Daniel Boyarin, the invention of heresy is essential to the creation of the discursive category of orthodoxy; hence the two notions "come into the world of discourse together," always to be defined in each other's context, "borders within" being constructed so as to eradicate semantic and social fuzziness and produce fully separate entities.[16] This is how many religions and regimes have originated—by standing in opposition to the beliefs or mores of a predecessor or neighbor who in some way is seen as a threat. As long as orthodoxy and heresy are codependent, the antagonism they share for each other, the innate sense of conflict, will live and breathe—constantly grating against each other and redefining their own and each other's boundaries. In his account of the transition from paganism to Christianity in late antiquity, Peter Brown has described such a tactic as conductive to peaceful coexistence: "Clear cut enemies and firm codes of avoidance, based on a sharp sense of pollution, can have the effect of protecting religious groups from each other. It gives them room to back off."[17]

Most heterodox information has not been preserved and is available only through the mediation of the heresiographers, whose texts are late, schematic, and frequently hostile to the doctrines and groups they describe. The opacity of the sources, given what we know about heretical groups and what the mainstream Sunni historians and traditionalists wanted to preserve, reflects the biases of the emergent Sunni orthodoxy. Historical developments have, therefore, been hidden behind a polemical image and a negative paradigm.[18]

The Sunni literature, in particular, sought to define the doctrinal basis for a Sunni orthodoxy by applying a sectarian label to all those who did not fit the mold. This became the basis for exposing their infamies, leading to either a legally derived charge of heresy or outright demonization. The genre of *firaq* (heresiography) included discussions of comparative religion, sectarian beliefs, and religious polemic, the authorial aims focusing on "the encyclopedic and taxonomic desiderata of the heresiographical genre, such as the delineation and establishment of communal boundaries."[19] The *firaq* literature has been described as an effort to form a conception of an orthodox center in Islam and to reveal the presence of the heterodox bodies as distinct from the center.[20]

The interest in describing sects partly owes its impetus to its usefulness in defining Sunni doctrine by contrasting it with heretical views. Debates about "heresy" brought basic beliefs into focus as notions of orthodoxy and heresy led to more coherent religious communities and, in turn, reinforced group identities. And indeed, the formulation of Sunni doctrine evolved from counteracting or renouncing the heresies.[21] The Shafi'i Ash'ari theologian 'Abd al-Qahir al-Baghdadi (d. 429/1037) aimed in his *Al-Farq bayn al-firaq,* a classic in the heresiographical tradition, to construct an apologetical treatise in order to advocate the Sunni doctrine and to denounce the heresies that were threatening it. His aim was not to write a history of the sects but to elaborate a normative classification of the sects in terms of their relative distance from the Sunnis, the only repositories of the whole truth. Since he considered these sects to be guilty of apostasy, he thereby provided legitimacy to all the repressive measures that the state undertook in the past and that it would undertake in the future against the extremist and redoubtable sects that survived, namely, those of the Batiniyya. Under the appellation Batiniyya, *Al-Farq* includes the Qaramita of Iraq, Syria, and Bahrain as well as the Fatimids of Egypt. In his treatise, al-Baghdadi demonstrates that the credo of the Batiniyya is incompatible with the Muslim religion. The thesis of the *Al-Farq*, which is repeated by the heresiographers and other sources, is that Batiniyya, Qaramita, Isma'iliyya, and 'Ubaydiyya designate, under different names, the diverse manifestations of one movement whose main aim is to demolish the religious and political edifice of Islam.[22] These terms, it should be emphasized, were often used interchangeably in the sources, as will become obvious in the following discussion.

Historical Background of the Qaramita

The history of early Isma'ilism, extending from the mid-second/eighth century to the establishment of the Fatimid caliphate in the early third/ninth century, is obscure, and until recently the Isma'ilis, like all movements of contestation which are described mostly through their opponents' opinions, were judged primarily on the basis of evidence provided by their adversaries. The anti-Isma'ili version of the Sunni polemists has been traced to a work written by Abu 'Abdallah Muhammad b. 'Ali b. Rizam in the early fourth/tenth century. While Ibn Rizam's polemical treatise has been lost, excerpts of it have been preserved and were used in another anti-Isma'ili work written about 370/980 by Akhu Muhsin (d. ca. 375/985–986). Most of Akhu Muhsin's work has also been lost, but important portions of it have been preserved by three Egyptian historians. It is this account by Ibn Rizam-Akhu Muhsin aimed at discrediting the whole Isma'ili movement that constituted the basis for most subsequent Sunni writings on the subject.[23] Indeed, it became one of the main sources from which heresiographers and polemicists drew their knowledge about the secret doctrines of the Batinis. According to Wilfred Madelung, they discovered in the account enough atheism, libertinism, and blasphemy to justify the disrepute in which the heretics were held.[24]

After its underground beginnings, the Isma'ili movement erupted on the historical stage around the mid-third/ninth century as a dynamic revolutionary organization conducting intensive missionary activity. Its adherents began to attract the attention of the Abbasid authorities and the public at large under the name al-Qaramita. Initially used for the followers of Hamdan Qarmat, an Isma'ili leader in the environs of al-Kufa in the third/ninth century, the term "Qaramita" came to be generally used for those Isma'ili groups who refused to recognize the claims of the Fatimid caliphs to the imamate. This split took place in 286/899. In addition to the peasantry of southern Iraq, the Qaramita gradually attracted Bedouins in northeast Arabia and the Syrian desert, especially after opportunities to serve in the military, obtain government subsidies, and have any control over trade decreased.[25] The Qaramita succeeded in founding a powerful state in Bahrain under the leadership of Abu Sa'id al-Jannabi starting in 273/866, and they soon disposed of one of the most effective fighting forces in the Islamic world.

The early fourth/tenth century witnessed a great burst of activity. Abu Tahir al-Jannabi, Abu Sa'id's son, began a series of devastating campaigns into Iraq. The Qaramita repeatedly and seriously threatened the caliphate of Baghdad, plundering, assassinating, sacking Kufa and Basra, and attacking the pilgrim caravans. Some Qaramita believed that the Mahdi, the prophesied savior, would come in the year 300/912, end the era of Islam, and initiate the seventh and final religious era. The Qaramita intensified their attacks on their opponents as the anticipated date approached. It was in preparation for this event that, in Iraq, they pooled their property and moved to an abode of emigration *(dar al-hijra)* where they exchanged their life as villagers for one as soldiers on the Mahdi's behalf.[26] The sources relate that the Qaramita peasants of Kufa were ordered to give up increasingly large proportions of their wealth to their religious leaders on the grounds that doing so would ensure true harmony *(ulfa)* and that one-fifth of their booty should be given to God. The Egyptian encyclopedist and historian Shihab al-Din al-Nuwayri (d.733/1333), relying on Ibn Rizam, stated the following: "They assessed their net worth, whether cloth, or other things, and they paid him the one-fifth with such rigor that a woman paid one-fifth of what she wove and men one-fifth of the product of their work. Once this was established, he imposed on them the duty of *ulfa,* which meant that they should gather all their possessions in one place to benefit from them in common."[27]

An alternative date to the advent of the Mahdi, following the conjunction of Jupiter and Saturn, was in the year 316/928, when the Qaramita of Bahrain and Iraq made what they expected to be their final attack on Iraq and even threatened Baghdad itself. Abu Tahir's activity reached its climax when he conquered Mecca during the pilgrimage season in 317/930. The Qaramita of Bahrain committed a terrible slaughter of the pilgrims and inhabitants, carrying off the sacred Black Stone of the Ka'ba to their capital at Hajar. It was not until twenty-two years later that the stone was returned after payment of a high ransom. The sources stress that their extreme military actions were accompanied by radical religious alterations, a frank admission that for the Qaramita of Bahrain the external rites of Islam had come to an end.

According to Hugh Kennedy, the Qaramita attacked certain areas of Iraq because they wished to have access to Basra and other Gulf ports. They also wanted to secure the right to protect the pilgrimage caravan, the *hajj*, in return for payments and military salaries from the Abbasid government. Thus, it is not that the Qaramita disapproved of the *hajj* on religious grounds but rather that for them the *hajj* was the best economic opportunity in Arabia.[28] The Qaramita justified their actions by proclaiming the sovereignty of the Mahdi, the rightly guided imam from the house of the Prophet who would establish justice and order.[29]

And, indeed, in Ramadan 319/931, Abu Tahir handed the rule over to a young Persian captive from Isfahan, recognizing him as the expected Mahdi. The young Persian took a series of actions that ended up demoralizing the movement: he ordered the cursing of the prophets and the worship of fire; he initiated the abolition of the external *(zahiri)* law by issuing strange and, by normal Muslim standards, repulsive rules, with much recourse to Zoroastrian ideas; and he had some prominent Qarmati leaders put to death. After some eighty days, and after having turned against the pillars of the community, Abu Tahir had him killed and confessed that he had been duped by an impostor. The episode severely hurt the reputation of the movement, especially with the accompanying manifestations of libertinism and the ritual violation of the law in shocking and outrageous manners.[30]

While the attempt to abolish the Islamic sharia by the Persian captive in Bahrain failed, a second, later attempt was more successful, for we read in the text of the Isma'ili traveler Nasir-i Khusraw that Bahrain had acquired a new political organization and abolished ritual worship around the mid-fifth/eleventh century: Muslim ritual and dietary law had vanished, the locals did not pray, and social relations were egalitarian. Politically, he described it as a sort of oligarchic republic governed by a council of six who ruled with equity and justice.[31] Nasir-i Khusraw is one of the rare sympathetic sources; most of our information, as already mentioned, comes from sources that viewed the Qaramita as heretical extremists and relate sensational accounts composed of a strange mixture of truth and fiction. One anti-Qaramita voice, for instance, was Abu Bakr al-Nabulsi, chief jurist in Damascus, who said, "Holy war *(jihad)* against those [al-Qaramita] has priority over holy war against the Byzantines," arguing that the Qaramita were polytheists and hostile to the prophets, though they falsely claimed to be Shi'a, while the Byzantines really were People of the Book. Moreover, "the Byzantines do not conceal their religion, but on the contrary, they proclaim it; while those atheists *(kuffar)* and polytheists *(mushrikun)* harbor polytheism *(shirk)* and deceive people by claiming to be Shi'a."[32]

This constituted a major problem. While orthodoxy is represented as the negation of heresy, heresiological discourse frames the association of heresy and orthodoxy as one of emulation.[33] Heretics who skillfully mimic orthodoxy represent a deeper threat, as the heretic runs the risk of being indistinguishable from the true orthodox. The Qaramita, as Muslims, although of an ultra-Shi'i doctrine, could play the game without really accepting its rules, and as a result be able to bludgeon Islam with its own weapons.[34] The danger they represented was consequently extremely acute, as stated by al-Baghdadi: "Beware that the harm inflicted by the Batiniyya on the different Islamic groups *(firaq)* is greater than the harm inflicted by the Jews, Christians and Zoroastrians . . . even greater than the harm to be inflicted by the Dajjal [the anti-Christ]."[35] In his chapter entitled "Those Who Pretend to Be Muslim While They Are Not," Fakhr al-Din al-Razi (d. 606/1209) also cautions that the harm inflicted by the Qaramita on the true religion is greater than the harm that befalls it from all types of unbelievers, since their ultimate goal is nothing less than to completely obliterate the canonical law.[36] Much later on, the Hanbalite scholar Ibn Taymiyya (d. 728/1328) issued a religious decree stating that the Nusayriyya and other Qaramita are more harmful to Muhammad's *umma* than the Turks and the Crusaders.[37] This censure summarizes the authoritative Sunni perception of a damning linkage. The Qaramita, as Muslims themselves, were more of a threat to the regime, as they could potentially twist their knowledge of the faith and Islamic rituals to their will and acquire followers who would bring down the state.

The actions of the Qaramita—notably the killing of thousands of innocent pilgrims, the burning of Qur'ans, and the defiling of the Ka'ba—revealed the true face of their heresy in all its manifestations: externally they feign the Shi'i faith, internally they hide pure unbelief. The secrecy in which the Batinis enveloped part of their doctrine, as well as their early history, furthered this direction in the hostile sources. They were considered to be the worst heretics and were regarded with suspicion and prejudice for a host of reasons, notably for their doctrine of the "inner meaning" *(batin)* and the specter of license *(ibaha)*.[38] The charge of allowing the forbidden *(ibahat al-maharim)*, with its intended libertinism, served to categorize certain groups on the fringe of the Shi'a, namely, the Ghulat (those who practice *ghuluww)*, as a class apart, especially since for them knowledge of the imam was the most essential religious obligation, and consequently reduced all other obligations to insignificance.

By the fourth/tenth century, with the rise of the Isma'ili Fatimids in Egypt, the Abbasid caliphs and the Sunni religious scholars *('ulama)* launched a widespread anti-Isma'ili propaganda campaign with the aim of discrediting the Isma'ili movement so that the Isma'ilis could be condemned as heretics. Polemicists concocted accounts of the sinister teachings and practices of the Isma'ilis, attributing to them a variety of shocking beliefs and practices.[39] The entire Isma'ili enterprise represented a complete contrast with which compromise was not possible. Their violent tactics and their alternative social lifestyle posed a threat to the integrity of the Muslim community and were regarded as un-Islamic. The Isma'ilis, and in particular their extremist offshoot, the Qaramita, were emblematic opponents against whom the vocal majority defined itself and its beliefs.

Deviance can either challenge or reinforce rules or law and either encourage social change or uphold social hegemony. In this case, sexuality was the main vehicle for the expression of deviance from mainstream cultural norms. The violent campaign against the Qaramita (and the Batiniyya in general) was unscrupulous, and defamation and calumny strengthened these prejudices. The diffusion of malicious accounts of the Qaramita's teaching and of slanderous stories about alleged excesses practiced by members of the sect proved especially harmful to them.[40] Unlike the *jahilis*, who were ignorant of the new Muslim norms, the Qaramita were the perpetrators of deliberate transgressions upon Muslim society, all the more dangerous because they were secretly located in the heart of the norm. In this intolerable situation, concern for sexual conduct was textually deployed in an attempt to keep the groups apart.

The Qaramita Women and Sexual Conduct

When discussing the Late Antique landscape, historians point out that accusations of heresy were often accompanied by charges of immoral behavior, a well-known rhetorical technique. The pagans are said to have leveled three charges at the early Christians as a ground for persecution: atheism, Thyestean banquets, and Oedipal unions. Sexual promiscuity was widely alleged, and it was reported that they had sexual intercourse with all women (sisters and mothers) and children, regardless of their age.[41] One Roman consul accused the Christians of immorality under the guise of religion, stating that they come together for a feast with their children, sisters, and mothers, and after much feasting, the light is put out, and "in the shameless darkness, they embrace one another with unspeakable lust, as chance brings them together."[42] Similarly, a pagan description of a communion service of a Gnostic Christian sect, the Phibionites, states: "First they have their women in common . . . the man . . . says to his own wife stand up and make love with the brother."[43] Some Christians accused Gnostics of extreme sexual license, while Roman pagans accused the Christians of incest, misinterpreting the Christian custom of calling those unrelated to them "brother," "sister," "father," and "mother."[44] Later on, in medieval Europe, the heretical sects preparing for the return of Christ dreamed of abolishing sexuality. In that spirit, the men attempted to live with the women in purity as brothers and sisters, a shocking proposition that struck at the fundamental armature of society. The detractors of these sects believed that they were lying and that in reality, at night, they practiced communal sexuality. Paul of Chartres wrote what was whispered, namely, that at the end of their reunions, each one got hold of the woman next to him, be it his mother or his sister.[45] What we can gather from these comparisons is the similarities in the accusations and attacks of the reigning majority against the deviant minority, the "ethical" against the "primitive," the modest against the indecent. This is also the case with the Qaramita.

One of the main charges brought against the Qaramita by their Sunni opponents was that they preached and practiced communal sexuality. Judge 'Abd al-Jabbar states in *Tathbit dala'il al-nubuwwa* that the Qarmati man who has achieved the seventh degree of initiation is to share his wife with others who have achieved similar degrees of initiation, since "sharing wives is like sharing food and the generous man is he whose wife has sexual intercourse with another man in his presence, the way food is eaten in his presence."[46] The fourth/tenth-century *Tarikh akhbar al-Qaramita* by Thabit b. Sinan al-Sabi' includes the following anecdote, which relates a specific encounter and names the protagonists involved: Ibrahim al-Sa'igh reports that he was at one time with Abu Sa'id al-Jannabi when Yahya b. al-Mahdi visited the latter. They ate, and once they finished, Abu Sa'id left the room after ordering his wife to sit with Yahya and not to stop him if he wished to have sexual relations with her.[47] The judge 'Abd al-Jabbar includes the same anecdote, adding that Abu Sa'id told his wife, "If this holy man *(wali)* wants you, don't prevent him from yourself, he is more deserving of you than me."[48]

A Sunni jurist from the fifth/eleventh century from Yaman talks about the "ghastly scene" *(al-mashhad al-a'zam)* in which these heretics, after drinking, would gather their womenfolk, blow out the candles, and grab hold of whoever fell into their hands.[49] Abu Hamid al-Ghazali (d. 505/1111), affirming these suspicions, stated that what is known about the Batiniyya in general is that they allow complete licentiousness, including the lifting of the veil, the permission of forbidden sexual acts, and the disavowal of canonical laws.[50]

The best-known such account is related by Ibn Rizam and transmitted by al-Nuwayri in his *Nihayat al-arab fi funun al-adab:* "He ordered his representatives (the *da'is*) to collect all the women one night so that they might mix indiscriminately with all the men and he told them that this was the perfect and last degree of friendship and brotherhood."[51] Muhammad b. al-Hasan al-Daylami, whose work dates from the early eighth/fourteenth century, reiterates more fully the accumulated accusations concerning the behavior of the Qaramita: "They abandoned praying and the call to prayer, Islamic canonical laws and belief, they made light of the Prophet and of the Ka'ba, they killed the pilgrims, destroyed the mosques and made everything forbidden by religion permissible . . . [allowing] sexual intercourse with daughters and sisters and the marriage of two males. . . . It is the sect of comfort, licentiousness, the devil and the passions. . . . It releases them from the restrictions of the law . . . and permits them what is forbidden from God's sacrosanct laws *(maharim)*."[52]

Al-Daylami lists fifteen different names for al-Batiniyya, including al-Qaramita, al-Isma'iliyya, al-Ibahiyya, al-Malahida, and al-Zanadiqa. He explains that they are referred to by the name Ibahiyya because "they are people of licentiousness who do not follow the laws . . . and they allow what God has forbidden in terms of money, people and women."[53] Having written about their affiliation with Babik al-Khurrami, which earned them the name Bibabikiyya, al-Daylami relates once again that many Yemeni Batiniyya communities have a "special night" of women-snatching, known as the "Night of the Ifada."[54] Accordingly, the Batiniyya, including the Qaramita, organized large-scale mingling of the sexes which disregarded the prohibitions on which the institutions of the family and society were founded. Such calumnious imputations were evidently intended to stir up hatred and contempt for the Batiniyya at large.[55]

While often the reference is to the Qaramita of Bahrain, "Qaramita" gradually became a flexible pejorative term that was used widely to refer to other groups of Batiniyya. The designations Batiniyya and Qaramita were often interchangeable. Hence, in the third/ninth-century Yamani work entitled *Kitab sirat al-hadi ila al-haqq,* the author uses the term "Qaramita" when he is really talking about another Batini group whom he accuses of authorizing incest. The esoteric nature of these groups, the lack of factual knowledge about their beliefs and doctrines, and the inability to fit them into the norm allowed the propagation of a particular stereotyped gender discourse. Sunnis accused them of engaging in sexual relations with their mothers, sisters, and daughters. *Kitab sirat al-hadi ila al-haqq* discusses the Isma'ilis' having sexual relations with their mothers and sisters. On Fridays, all the men and women intermingled: "Mothers have sexual relations with their sons, sisters with their brothers . . . whoever refrained from this, was killed."[56] Accounts such as these aroused offense and incited hostility. It was the offense to purity, abstention, and devotion that provided enough justification for the Sunnis to defend their values and to confirm them within the boundaries they were striving to erect.

Qadi 'Abd al-Jabbar, whose *Tathbit* reflects the position of *ahl al-sunna* toward the Isma'ilis and Fatimids, represents an advanced stage of the anti-Isma'ili Sunni awakening in the fifth/eleventh century. He writes about the admissibility for the Isma'ilis in general of sexual intercourse with female kin and the sharing of wives.[57] The author of *Al-Farq bayn al-firaq* states that "the Batiniyya reinterpreted the principles of religion *(usul al-din)* as well as the principles of the law *(usul al-sha'ria)* for the purpose of eliminating them," and that this is demonstrated in their sexual behavior.[58] This insistence on incestuous practices is reiterated in an early anti-Isma'ili pamphlet that purports to be reproducing the Isma'ilis' line of reasoning: "Is there anything more strange than the behavior of certain people who claim to be possessed of intelligence and of religion? If they have a beautiful sister or beautiful daughter, far exceeding the beauty of their own wives, they will deem it unlawful to marry them . . . and will give them away to a stranger, considering him as having a better title to those women than they themselves! Do not the fools realize that they have a much better right to their own sisters and daughters than a stranger? Look at the ancient Zoroastrians; did they consider such marriages as unlawful?"[59] Indeed, the pamphlet attempts to justify such conduct and suggests that the Isma'ili initiates have dissociated themselves from sharia altogether—that when a believer reaches the highest degree of the faith, he is relieved from religious practice, and nothing previously forbidden will be prohibited for him now.[60]

Al-Nuwayri summarizes the extreme state that the Qaramita as a community had reached, discharged of religious duties and held to no obligations.[61] 'Abd al-Jabbar makes a similar if not more damning list: the Qarmati men are not forbidden from anything, neither from their mother, daughter, or sister; nor from pork, adultery, or sodomy *(liwat)*, nothing at all.[62] The accusation of sexual deviancy included that of sodomy. 'Abd al-Jabbar, in relating the episode of al-Isfahani, stated that he called for sodomy to be permitted and that generally the Batiniyya allowed sodomy; al-Baghdadi also states that the ruler of Bahrain ordered sodomy and that a *ghulam* (slave youth) who refused would be killed.[63] Sodomy, as another form of sexual deviance in the Abbasid era, served as a further cultural backlash against the Qaramita and was represented in the sources as another offense against order and modesty.

Sexualizing Heresy

The information in our texts regarding the immorality of the Qaramita was part of the temporal discourse about civilization and religion and helped develop it, and as such functioned as a cultural marker, a sign, about the place of the Qaramita in Islamic society. The manipulation of the categories of women, gender, and sexuality played an important role in the construction of orthodoxy and the categorization of those who represented deviation from the cultural norms of Islam; orthodoxy was defined, in part, to stand in contrast to the Qaramita notions of these categories. The negative connotations implied that religious deviance entailed immoral behavior and that the religiously deviant were uncivilized and wicked. Indeed, the effect of such stories was to barbarize the Qaramita—as the story of near-cannibalism had barbarized Hind and what and whom she represented—and to put them outside the pale of civilization. In the words of the judge 'Abd al-Jabbar: "And once the swords were all raised against Islam, *zandaqa*, *ilhad* and *ghuluww* took the upper hand, and so they reverted to *jahiliyya*. Don't you see that the Qaramita and Batiniyya in al-Ahsa', once they were victorious, . . . cursed the prophets, discontinued the laws *(shara'i')*, killed the Muslim pilgrims . . . and . . . brought in Dhakira al-Isfahani and said: this in truth is the Lord, and they worshipped him."[64]

Their reversion to *jahiliyya* is patent in the actions of Zaynab bint Sa'id, wife of Zurqan: Dhakira had killed her husband and son, and so once he was himself killed, in a salient imitation of Hind bint 'Utba, "Zaynab came, she slit his abdomen, removed his liver and ate it. It was a great scandal."[65] The underlying message of these accusations was that the Qaramita were people who had distanced themselves, in a fundamental way, from their general cultural context. The threat they represented led them to be ejected beyond the scope of the possible, the tolerable, the thinkable, lying there quite close, but being impossible to assimilate.[66]

Such hostile stereotyping was also engaged in against the Mazdakites/ Khurramis, who were accused of indulging in any and every unnatural and illicit pleasurable inclination, including intercourse with close relatives. Such stereotyping is malicious in the way in which it bundles together various acts and customs, taken out of context to portray the actors as barbaric, with no concern for civilized behavior or self-control. Patricia Crone has detected a pattern to the charges: the targets are invariably secretive sectarians of a spiritualist, Gnostic, and/or antinomian kind. Their beliefs diverge widely from those of their neighbors, and their failure to live by the religious law of the majority is equated with libertinism.[67]

All the wild stories about the Qaramita were meant to characterize the movement as disorderly and rebellious, turning the Qaramita into a danger to society because they subverted household loyalties and the sexual social order through their orgiastic, incestuous, and homosexual practices. This perception expresses the threatening image of a community with uncontrolled moral boundaries. Was this symbolic functioning of sexuality emerging at the time when the Sunni community was becoming more concerned with defining itself as an orthodoxy, constantly guarding against the attacks of heretical opponents? In any event, there is no doubt that incompatible boundaries were at issue and that the treatment of Qarmati women helped define the edges and, in so doing, to structure the inner workings of true orthodoxy as, at least in part, a reaction to Qaramita practice.

Neguin Yavari has pointed out that the fifth/eleventh-century *Siyar al-Muluk* by the Seljuk vizier Nizam al-Mulk (d. 485/1092) accuses the Qaramita of practicing community of wives and adhering to the abolition of private property. Like other Sunni works, the anti-Isma'ili anecdotes in *Siyar al-Muluk* serve to formulate orthodoxy and to outline the instability of the world Nizam al-Mulk was living in, notably the weakening of centralized rule, the emergence of autonomous dynasties, economic collapse, and a general lack of order, where good religion is under threat and women do not remain in their prescribed roles of purity and piety. *Siyar al-Muluk* readily uses women and heresy as "rhetorical devices to warn of political and social unease."[68]

In identifying the politics of gender as they are inscribed in textual production, Leila Ahmed singled out the Qaramita as a group that posed a very different interpretation of gender relations. They were presented as having departed from the prescriptions in orthodox Islamic society pertaining to women and to the proper relations between men and women.[69] However, as Marshall Hodgson suggests, "it is easy to draw a picture of general licentiousness out of a difference in principle on where to draw the line in eliminating a set of prescriptions."[70] The accusers were, rather, filling a lacuna in their knowledge of Qaramita beliefs and practices, the defamation relying less on what was known than on what was left to be imagined. As mentioned earlier, accusations of incest and immorality had been leveled against pagan and Christian sects who were condemned to a clandestine existence.

The Qaramita, in their early stages, were a diffuse category, but they were crucial in shaping the processes that went into the definitions of religious identities during this period. Accusations of heresy became valuable rhetorical tools for the Sunnis during times of political upheaval. The Qaramita represented one of the gravest threats to the stability of Islam and the Abbasid caliphate; war against them was, hence, a means of assisting the Abbasid state to confirm its legitimacy and its credentials as the defender of Islam. The Qaramita were invested with dreadful images which inspire hatred and fear and consequently inflame persecution.

The heresiographical schemas reflect the concerns of orthodox scholars who were trying to shape the community in which they lived. According to Paul Freedman, historians offer two main explanations for the increased climate of intolerance in medieval Europe, one focusing on irrational fears with respect to certain groups, and another on the growth of an official apparatus of taxonomy and control.[71] In the same vein, the Qaramita were unsettling the border, complicating and blurring the binary divide, providing moments in which the borders of supposedly established, socially accepted categories were transgressed. Defining the Qaramita as a sectarian category was meant to order the world and set and impose meaning on early Islamic society. This is a function of power. It was only after proponents of a popular, or accepted, set of beliefs gained enough clout to impose their views on others that heterodoxy could become heresy.[72]

The Qaramita represented in the Islamic tradition what the Sunni majority came to reject morally, politically, socially, and theologically. Their image, which was the result of a Sunni-controlled vision, was meant to teach lessons that would naturally come at the expense of the Qaramita. Jeffrey Kenney has stated that the Khawarij sect came to be seen as an example of what Islam was not: the Khawarij were cast as "rebels against the established order not because they were inherently evil or anti-Islamic but because they lost out in the historical competition to determine what the Islamic order would be."[73] Likewise, Sunni historians and theologians used the Qaramita as a social policing mechanism to define and defend the borders of Islam. They manipulated the perceived gender roles and sexual mores of the Qaramita to prevent them and others like them from infringing on the Islamic community's social, religious, and political space.

Heresiology insists on a discourse of the pure, a discourse that requires the hybrid as its opposite.[74] The dominant culture was not open to syncretism and would not accept anything but uniformity in dogma and in religious practice. This explains, according to Abdelmajid Charfi, the polemicists' obstinacy in protecting Islam from all types of "contaminations" as well as hardening the lines of partition.[75] Orthodoxy, even if elusive, provided the norms of the true and universal standards of civilization. Orgiastic behavior, incest, and sodomy were markers of cultural distance, of barbarity. However, unlike the barbarity of *jahiliyya* or of outsiders, the enemy within was much more dangerous, because cultural distance was, in this case, not correlated with either temporal or geographical distance. The Sunnis saw the Qaramita as related to perversion, especially since they were presumed neither to give up nor to assume a prohibition, a rule, or a law; rather, the reigning orthodox body turned the Qaramita aside, misrepresenting their beliefs and actions, taking advantage of them, the better to deny them. It is this ambiguity that deeply disturbs identity, system, and order; and this is especially so when the subject finds the "impossible within."[76] Hence, what we have is a discourse about internal divisions, in which the lines between "them" and "us" were drawn between neighbors. Damning the Qaramita was important in the effort to neutralize them and to exert authority over them and the threat they posed, especially in times of disturbance, when pressure rose to redefine relations among the various emerging communities. Women were used instrumentally, in this context, to regulate the boundaries, inventing symbolic overlap between "the woman as other and the other as women."[77]

Analyzing the images, ideas, and stories assembled in the mainstream narratives reveals the way in which the Qaramita as a phenomenon were imagined and interpreted by non-Qaramita Muslims. The world of the Qaramita was invented to resemble, in some sense, that of *jahiliyya*. It was a world in which distrust and fear ruled, in which the norm was a state of all-against-all warfare and, even worse, in which lasting bonds of family, community, peace, and prosperity would be unknown. It is a *jahili* world reborn in the horrific excesses of the Qaramita phenomenon whose violent character transgressed all limits. In addition to the story of Zaynab (wife of Zurqan) related earlier, this willingness to transgress all is equally reflected in a tale related by a pious mother who searched the desert camps to reclaim her son, who had joined the rebels: "I found him in a Qarmati army. . . . He asked me: what is your religion? I said, it is Islam, my son, as you know. He answered: mother, leave this religion and join me." As she tried to run away from her son, he followed her and, striking her with his sword, wounded her shoulder.[78] The mother told the story, horrified at the defiant atmosphere of the camps, whose converts rejected the ethics, moralities, and laws of established society. Her zealous and emancipated son was tough and cruel, showing no acknowledgment of a mother's dignity.

The Qaramita withdrew from the community of ordinary Muslims, as they considered themselves to be the only true Muslims, determined to reproduce the Prophet's exemplary migration *(hijra)*. This is why they moved to the desert or lived on the periphery of the Muslim world, alone in their camps. They believed they were being confronted not by Muslims of lesser quality but by unbelievers. It is this perspective that makes the anecdote just related understandable. However, for the Muslims, the Qaramita reflected a total rejection of the most basic of social bonds and the most instinctive of loyalties.

The Abbasid sources reinforced the preconceptions and constructed a stereotypical description of these heretics and of their heretical behavior. While such stories do not prove that anything of the sort took place, they do suggest that the mainstream culture was ready to believe the worst about those it marginalized or excluded. It is as if the establishment did not want to comprehend any inclination or reflex to diverge from the norm as anything but perverse, which in turn reproduced the image of heresy that those recording it already entertained.[79] The formidable portrait painted of the Qaramita in the surviving literature was part and parcel of the thread of accusations of sexual license routinely attributed to deviant groups. Indeed, heretical ideologies were seen not only as antagonistic to the regime, but also as dissenting from Islam.[80] Tales of women naturally found their way into descriptions of heretical debauchery. In their diatribes, the Sunni writers ascribed to them sexual promiscuities and transgressions. In such a historical vision, the Qaramita emerged as a main foil to Islam's essential (hetero) normativity. By mobilizing public opinion, by spreading rumors that cast aspersions on the private activities of the Qaramita, those in authority were trying to undermine any legitimacy the Qaramita may have had. In any case, it was not necessary to know anything about the Qaramita other than that it was a community that had parted from the practices of society and was inducing secession in others.

Hodgson emphasizes that one should not rule out the possibility of the elimination of many sexual taboos in a movement of revolt.[81] The Qaramita women were not veiled, men and women intermingled, and monogamy was practiced. The fact that the rank and file of the group consisted of Bedouins and peasants goes a long way toward explaining their relative freedom compared with the more restricted movements of the female urban middle and upper classes. This urban/rural distinction and the Qaramita's alternative value system regarding gender relations may have appeared to their Sunni contemporaries as nothing less than debauchery. Were the Qaramita spawning new models of different Muslims, men and women, no longer completely following the same norms, imperatives, and logic? As Ann Brenon states, "whoever controls women ... holds the key to the hearts, to the engagements, and to the intimate and profound choices. If a society trips, it is because its women, at the least, have given the nods."[82] The Qaramita established their own subculture, creating a religious hierarchy, rites, and beliefs. While distortions of elements of actual practices attached to the Iranian Mazdakites and Khurramis could have influenced them, as the connection with the Persian Mahdi might indicate, Qaramita women seem to have actively participated, at least from a social and economic standpoint, in sustaining the movement, as is evident from their financial contribution as spinners and weavers. Perhaps this meant that they played a more dynamic role than was generally assigned to women in urban settings. It is as if the Qaramita were themselves prompting the development of new definitions of authority and gender as well as challenging preexisting ones.

The Qaramita women—symbolizing the threatening forces of sexuality, social chaos, and false belief—represented the fears of men who long for an articulation of precise group boundaries and individual relationships in a world where everything seemed muddled. Indeed, the threat presented by the heretics was prevalent and contagious, especially so in the sexual menace it contained. The "threat" was packaged in a repulsive reaction of fear—a fear of social change. That the Sunnis protected their social boundaries by eliminating "sexual pollution" may suggest that "the boundaries which the prohibitions in question protect are threatened, or thought to be."[83]

The primary evidence for the Qaramita comes from a body of texts that do not view them in a favorable light. The unequal distribution of political power in Abbasid society gave more authority to the predominant, Sunni, segment of society *(ahl al-sunna)*, privileging their narratives, interpretations, and understanding.[84] The production of the Qaramita women was a discursive one, focusing on a particular mode of appropriation, codification, and knowledge about women, with the implicit assumption of mainstream Islam as the primary referent in theory and praxis. Establishing an authoritarian discourse is an important technique in demonizing one's opponents. Sharp definitions of opposites, coupled with a clear, orthodox view of history, enabled contemporaries to create for themselves an imagined world of certainty, consisting of firm moral boundaries. A preoccupation with the definition and place of ethical borders reflected the anxiety of Muslims who feared the disintegration of traditional social structures and thus engaged in reinforcing such structures. The emerging discourse of heresiology acted as a catalyst to redefine the parameters of its imagined community, guarding its borders, delineating for itself who is inside and who is not. Standing on the fault line, the Qaramita projected the unresolved issues created by the hegemonic ideology.

4

Beyond Borders

Gender and the Byzantines

WHILE THE EARLY MUSLIMS assumed a reformist and punitive approach to the pagan or "unorthodox" groups, they approached their main imperial rival—Byzantium—in a more nuanced manner, albeit still offering judgment, and a misconstrual of Byzantine reality, in their own texts. Medieval Muslim thought distinguishes between *dar al-islam,* territory under Muslim political authority, and *dar al-harb,* the world outside Muslim territory. Within *dar al-islam,* another distinction is made between Muslims and non-Muslims, and within the general classification of non-Muslims, two separate identities are recognized: the *dhimmi*s, believers of recognized religions—notably Jews, Christians, Zoroastrians, and Sabians—on the one hand, and polytheists on the other. In medieval Muslim understanding, Christianity was an incomplete and imperfect revelation, one that had been superseded and perfected by Islam, the final revelation. Muslim polemical literature accused the Christians of having deviated from true Christianity and of having corrupted the Christian scriptures *(tahrif),* with the Qur'an itself stating that Jewish and Christian scriptures have been tampered with. Medieval Muslims felt, therefore, a religious superiority over Christians, and this vision helped to define the Christian Byzantines in ways that reinforced the gulf between Byzantium and the Islamic establishment.[1]

From the very beginning of the Arabic Islamic historical consciousness, Byzantium served as one of the primary sites of "otherness" in contrast to which it constituted itself. The early conflict between the two powers, Byzantium and the Islamic state, directed the orientation of the medieval Arabic Islamic sources, in many instances giving military and political affairs a predominant place in the major chronicles and historical works. However, a permanent state of war did not discourage cooperative contacts, which arose in a variety of contexts—through continuous commercial relations; exchange of embassies; internment and ransom of prisoners of war; deportation of conquered urban populations; movements of traitors and exiles; and containment of Byzantine women as harem slaves. The frontier was a barrier, but also a point of contact as a semiporous border that permitted the exchange of ideas and standards, manners and customs, languages and literatures. Byzantium was not, therefore, an exotic, impenetrable land. It was relatively well known, leaving limited room for speculation.[2] The one main exception, however, was in the Islamic representation of Byzantine women and gender relations, which served as a polemical focus for the belittlement of Byzantine culture. Byzantium was similar to the new Islamic order because of its shared monotheism and geographical closeness, while, conversely, its gender and sexual systems were radically different: Byzantium was hence characterized by moral licentiousness, permissiveness, and decadence, whereas the Islamic social system reflected modesty, female seclusion, and monogamy. Byzantine women's threatening sexuality was one of the well-known axes along which identity and alterity were constructed as a response to exposure to the ominous contiguous neighbor. It was a trope that played a central and polyvalent role in the textual production of the Abbasids, particularly since its image presented a portentous picture of what Muslim women would become if they were to test the bounds set for them by their orthodox Islamic culture.

The Imperial Byzantine Female Figure

The alternative moral standard of the Byzantines was most perceptible in Byzantine empresses, who could play a variety of roles, notably, participating in imperial ceremonies, dispensing patronage, becoming regents, and legitimizing a new reign. Byzantine imperial women were, moreover, depicted on coins and in statuary and other official art, and were addressed with titles such as *augousta* (majesty) and *despoina* (mistress, lady).[3] By contrast, wives and mothers of caliphs were secluded at the caliphal court, were not depicted on coins or other pictorial manifestations, and were not granted any titles. They managed to obtain power only once their son or husband succeeded to the caliphate, and even then only through the private exercise of influence.

The Arabic Islamic texts expose an awareness of this significant differ-ence, as they include information about some Byzantine empresses, notably Irene (AD 797–802), an empress and regent for her son Constantine VI. The sources tell of the battles in which Irene confronted Harun, son of Caliph al-Mahdi (158–169/775–785), and the subsequent peace treaty by which she promised to pay a rich tribute to the Abbasid state. Irene continued to send gifts to the caliph until her son Constantine came of age and began to wreak havoc. Constantine reportedly violated the agreement, and his in-justice, tyranny, and vice became obvious to his subjects. Consequently, Irene ordered that Constantine's eyes be exposed to a heated mirror, and in this way he was blinded.[4] The blinding of Constantine VI was explained by the Arab authors in terms of Arab-Byzantine relations. Irene's act was not seen as indicative of her own political ambitions; rather, it was the act of an able stateswoman who placed the interest of the Byzantine Empire above everything else, even her own son. The Arab authors do not condemn the cruel act of blinding. In fact, they seem to condone it in light of the great trouble that Constantine's policies had caused the Abbasid state.[5] These actions of Irene's show the potential agency of the imperial Byzan-tine female, but of special significance here is the very fact of a female ruler. Al-Tabari states that the "sovereign (*sahib* in masculine form) of the Byzantines was Augusta, wife of Leon, because her son was a minor at the death of his father."[6] This use of the masculine form of *sahib* calls to mind the fact that when Irene took power she did so as an honorary man, using male titles to denote her status and projecting herself into male rit-uals and male definitions of imperial majesty.[7]

Generally, in Byzantium the personality of the imperial female was al-most exclusively private and social in nature, reflecting the temporal view of women as passive, peripheral figures and the expectation that they would fill a companionable, decorative role. However, as the last example suggests, their position could extend to the political sphere and, on rare occasions, endow them with agency and influence. While Irene's rule was rather excep-tional, the general visibility of Byzantine empresses was manifested in their participation in court ceremonials. The empress and her entourage were required to balance the male hierarchy attending on the emperor, as well as to receive the wives of dignitaries and to provide a female counterpart to the imperial ceremonies. The role of the empress as leader of the court women is confirmed in an anecdote about the long-term widower Emperor Michael II, whereby the men of his court complained because there was no empress to lead their wives in the court of women.[8] This is attested also on the occasion of the visit of Princess Olga of Kiev to Constantinople in 957, when Empress Helen and her attendants prepared an elaborate series of receptions and banquets, along with introductions, obeisances, and exchanges of gifts: "Upon the arrival of Elga the Princess of Rus', a reception was held . . . the princess entered with her noble (female) relations and the elite of her female attendants. They all stood in front of the Emperor."[9]

This unique case of the reception of a female head of state reveals the involvement of women in the palace as well as of all the imperial family in such official formalities. The empresses' ceremonials, however, were not confined to the palace, but on special occasions took place in the public arena: we know of religious and civil commemorations from the fourth/tenth-century *Book of Ceremonies,* a manual compiled at the order of the Byzantine emperor Constantine VII.[10] The *Book of Ceremonies* records that during the Pentecostal liturgy the empress sat in the gallery of Haghia Sophia and granted an audience to the wives of imperial dignitaries, offering each of them the kiss of peace. On Palm Sunday, the empress received church officials. Byzantine empresses thus presided over their own court and ceremonial sphere and were involved in a calendar of rites and ceremonies.[11] This role of reception reinforced the stately image of the court, reflecting its grandeur and majesty as well as its sense of beauty and structure.

Muslim authors were aware of the Byzantine empresses' participation in public events. Muhammad al-Marwazi (d. 334/945) wrote that the queen was seated next to the king on the royal throne, partaking in his decisions, politics, and other business. He was called *basilus* (king or sovereign), and she was referred to as *dizbuna (despoina).*[12] Al-Marwazi was amazed that the Byzantine empress accompanied the emperor on campaigns and attended particular games in the hippodrome. On such occasions, "the king comes with his intimates and servants. . . . He sits on an eminence overlooking the place and there appears his wife called *dizbuna* with her servants and intimates . . . and she sits in a place opposite the king."[13] This account illustrates not only the visibility of the imperial Byzantine female, but also her potential for agency, as demonstrated in her ability to participate in important public events during which she could offer advice and judgment on political matters to the king.

A famous encounter between an Arab ambassador and a Byzantine empress is reported by al-Maqqari (d. 1040/1631); he mentions the poet Yahya b. al-Hakam al-Ghazal, who was a member of the diplomatic mission that the Andalusi ruler 'Abd al-Rahman II sent to Constantinople in the third/ninth century. Al-Ghazal was then very old. Some episodes mention his meeting with the Byzantine empress Theodora: "He was one day sitting in an audience with the emperor when his wife appeared in her great attire. She was as beautiful as the rising sun." Al-Ghazal could not remove his eyes from her. Her presence distracted him from the conversation with the emperor. When prompted by the latter, he confessed the matter to him through his translator: "Inform him that the beauty of this queen has dazzled me to the point of distracting me from his conversation for I have never seen the likes of her."[14] The captivating beauty of the empress and the poet's reactant distraction reveal in part the imperial female's symbolism as decorative and sexual. Presumably adorned with jewels, fine clothing, and provocative makeup and hair, she represents a fanciful view of an ideal female, as passively attractive and sexually open, as well as an expression of male sexuality and desire.

Such visibility and the interaction of Byzantine empresses with high officials were unthinkable for the Muslim authors of Islamic texts. Exposure to the imperial Byzantine female presented a stark contrast to the atmosphere at the Abbasid court. Women of the caliphal family were never introduced to officials or courtiers, and at no time did they play a role in court ceremonies, either inside or outside the palace. Even the most important feminine presence at the Abbasid court, namely, the mother of the caliph, was not connected to any ceremonial. In the Abbasid context, the segregation of the sexes was especially enforced among the higher strata of society. In the Abbasid view, women represented reserve and modesty, as reflected in their religious practice as well as their lifestyle: seclusion was considered a form of modesty and would encourage the female culture of demureness to which early Islam aspired. The only class of women who might have escaped this rigid system to some extent were the slave concubines.

The *Rumiyya*

The Arabs knew Byzantine women mostly through the institution of concubinage. As enslavement of Muslims was forbidden, concubines often came from outside the Islamic lands and were generally either taken as war booty or purchased from slave traders. These concubines brought with them the manners and customs of their countries, cultures, and religions, as well as stories of their homelands. There were manuals and epistles designed to assist merchants and connoisseurs in the purchase of female slaves by listing the characteristics specific to women of different origins. For instance, a passage in the epistle of Ibn Butlan (d. 458/1066) states, "It is said that whoever wants a slave-girl for pleasure should take in a Berber; if he wants her to tend precious things, he should take in a Byzantine; for bearing children, a Persian; for nursing, a Frank; for hard work, a black; for war and courage, a Turk or a Slav."[15] This passage not only evidences the acceptability of concubinage in Abbasid society, but also further illustrates the distanced, stereotyped views that Muslims had of women of the various races and geographical entities.

The Abbasid caliphs gave concubinage respectability as a means of royal reproduction, as foreign concubines often mothered Muslim heirs to the caliphate and thus served an integral role in perpetuating Muslim "nobility." In the third/ninth and fourth/tenth centuries, it was above all Greek women from the Byzantine Empire who formed the aristocracy of the caliphal harem, and it was their sons who became caliphs. The mothers of the Abbasid Caliphs al-Muntasir (247–248/861–862), al-Muhtadi (255–256/869–870), al-Mu'tadid (279–289/892–902), and al-Muqtadir (295–320/908–932) were all concubines of Byzantine origin.[16] That the only "real" knowledge of Byzantine women Islamic authors may have had derived from their encounters with Byzantine concubines constitutes a significant factor that influenced their perception.

Byzantine concubines and Byzantines in general were considered beautiful.[17] One reference to the beauty and seductiveness of Byzantine women is contained in the biography of the Prophet, which states that during one of the incursions led by the Prophet Muhammad, he asked Jadd b. Qays, of the Banu Salima, whether he would like to fight the Byzantines. Jadd replied, "Will you allow me to stay behind so as not to be tempted, for everyone knows that I am deeply attracted to women and I am afraid that if I see the Byzantine women, I shall not be able to control myself." It was likely in connection with this incident that the Qur'anic verse (9:49) descended: "Some of them there are that say, 'Give me leave and do not tempt me.'"[18] These examples serve to teach us of Islam's acknowledgment of men's innate desire and its aim to tame that appetite not only in favor of self-control but also through principled action.

The allure of Byzantine women is also stressed in the story of the Abbasid caliph Harun al-Rashid (170/786–193/809), who took captive the daughter of the patrician overseeing the fortress of Heraclea. She was beautiful and he loved her, building for her a fortress on the Euphrates which he called Heraclea to remind her of her own home in *bilad al-Rum* (the Byzantine Empire).[19] This belief is reiterated in a poem in *Siyar al-Thughur* when the poet turns our attention to the Byzantine women captured by the raiders and describes their physical beauty and sexual attraction:

> In transparent clothing, they are driven like sheep,
> Seized and defended with spears and missiles
> As flocks are guarded by herdsmen in the desert.
> Among them are many a slow-stepping gazelle,
> Who cannot walk, so fat are their thighs,

And so heavy her sloping, even buttocks!
She is flirtatious and diffident: were a stylite to see her, he would descend.
Were a priest to see her he would not be able to resist
Kissing her feet and making excuses.
She weeps with an eye flirtatious and black
And strikes a face as luminous as the moon.
It is white, overlaid with a color like wine.
On her right breast, she tempts [you]
With slapping and scratching and plucking
Of the long hair that hangs to her waist.
Every part of her you can see is tasty
And any man who attains her might rest easy.[20]

The importance of Byzantine women's physical appearance is reflected in these references. Such glowing reports of the beauty of the Byzantine female also tend to belittle Muslim women, as emphasis on the attractions of Byzantine women implies that local beauty was no match for them.[21] Yet the very presence of this allure on the other side of the frontier—and thus relatively close by—had the potential to threaten the harmony of the Islamic male-centered universe, as it was believed that Islamic men would be tempted by Byzantine attractiveness and sexuality. Indeed, the Prophet states in al-Bukhari's *Sahih* that there will be no "*fitna* more harmful to men than women." In its broadest meaning, *fitna* is any test put before humans, but it is often used to describe women's function as moral and spiritual tests, "female beauty" as a "bait that leads to perdition, to damnation."[22] *Fitna* is a key concept in defining the dangers that women and, more particularly, their bodies, were capable of provoking in the mental universe of men. *Fitna* in the sense of disorder and chaos refers also to the beautiful femme fatale who makes men lose their self-control. Women's beauty is *fitna*. And so is their disruptive influence. Women as a source of *fitna*, as a source of temptation, are a constant theme of the Arabic Islamic literary tradition, and this is especially so in the case of Byzantine women.[23]

Byzantine Women's Sexuality and the Threat of *Fitna*

The fourth/tenth-century *Fihrist* of Ibn al-Nadim includes a provocative pre-Islamic story that tells of Byzantine women's influential capability. The protagonist of the vignette is the daughter of the Byzantine emperor Julian (361–363). The Persian king Sabur Dhu al-Aktaf (Shapur II, 310–379) was imprisoned in Julian's imperial palace, where the emperor's daughter met and fell in love with him, freeing him and endangering the empire as a consequence, for Persia was Byzantium's foremost enemy.[24] The Byzantine princess actively collaborated in the enemy's cause, conspiring against her own father: thus, she became dangerous to her own people. The Arab Muslim authors also mention another emperor's daughter who captured the heart of the sixth-century Arab poet Imru' al-Qays.[25] But, indirectly, she was to cause his death, since her father, in anger, sent Imru' al-Qays the gift of a poisoned shirt. Thus, the disruptive role universally ascribed to women—and especially to Byzantine women—in their interaction with men is reiterated and given a particularly perilous dimension, as their behavior may result in others' deaths or, even worse, in the defeat of a whole nation. This disruptive female role is found again and again in different contexts and ways, with varied outcomes, in the Arab Islamic sources. In general, the stories we read attribute a threatening, negative quality to the disorderly female role, as it incites lack of attention, abandonment of duty, or war and the death of men and others. This negative association casts the influential potential of females in an unfavorable light and further diminishes the character and quality of women, which these societies largely advocated to subdue. Moreover, this disruptive trait is hazardous to the sought-after religious order, which may explain Islamic prescriptions for a modest, passive role for women, to prevent any cause for such disruption.

The danger posed by *fitna* proceeds from female sexual allure and promiscuity, leading to the downfall of men and nations. However, *fitna* is not solely an attribute of Byzantine women: it is a marker for any woman who is given "too much" liberty—that is, the Islamic social expectation was that women should be highly regulated so as to prevent the disruptions associated with *fitna*. Islamic sources show not Byzantine women but the writers' image of these women, who served as symbols of the eternal female—constantly a potential threat, particularly given the blatant exaggerations of their sexual promiscuity. In Abbasid texts, Byzantine women are associated with sexual immorality, and that quality overshadows their other attributes and virtues—so much so that it is difficult to unearth historical evidence of their daily routines and individual achievements. The third/ninth-century prose writer al-Jahiz states that Byzantine women are not circumcised, and this is why they are among "the most shameless women in the whole world." Al-Jahiz also draws a direct connection between chastity and circumcision. Byzantine women were thought to have sharper passions because they were not subjected to circumcision. The "uncircumcised woman," he writes, "finds pleasure, which the circumcised woman does not." Because Byzantine women were thought to find sex more enjoyable, they were more prone to adultery. The judge 'Abd al-Jabbar confirms this opinion. However, he reports that married Byzantine women were usually chaste; it is the unmarried who were adulteresses, and they often started fornicating while still living in their parents' homes. He also mentions that Byzantine women were not veiled; even when married, they passed the people in the market with heads and faces uncovered, showing all their beauty.[26] That Byzantine women are unveiled illuminates the idea that they represent an ideal yet alluring female form, an expression of male desire; and the connotation of this passage suggests the irreverence and immodesty of their exposure and the reflexive repulsion of an Arabic Islamic readership.

However, these random references betray a strong inclination toward generalizations and stereotypes. While it is difficult to know the social reality of Byzantine women at any given time, the Byzantine sources are clear enough about the conventions of behavior and thought attributed to Byzantine women. In Byzantium, women were expected to be retiring, shy, and modest, and devoted to their families and to religious observances. The upbringing of middle- and upper-class daughters was expected to take place in the gynaeceum, the part of the house reserved for women, in virtual seclusion. Outside of the gynaeceum, women had little contact with men and were expected to wear a veil. Byzantine girls devoted most of their youth to learning domestic skills in preparation for married life and running a household. They would learn to spin, weave, and embroider at an early age. One of the few surviving descriptions of girlhood is found in the encomium written by the eleventh-century Byzantine intellectual and politician Michael Psellus for his daughter who died at the age of ten. He praises her piety, modesty, skill with the needle, and devotion to learning. She attended church services regularly and was engaged in charitable work. A portrait of the life of married women in eleventh-century Constantinople emerges in the funeral oration of Psellus for his mother, whom he presents as the model of a wife and a mother. A somewhat austere figure, she spent her days in the women's quarter, spinning and weaving. She was sober in her clothing, set great store in almsgiving, and was very pious. She did not concern herself with public affairs. After her daughter and her husband died, she never left the house again. However much idealized, this portrait must have seemed credible to Psellus's contemporaries. According to Angeliki Laiou, every normative statement on the subject of woman's place insisted that a good woman did not leave her house and that all women were to stay within that protected space.[27] This anecdotal evidence attests to the existence of demureness among Byzantine female society and counteracts the more salacious stereotype of the Byzantine female figure.

Accusations of *zina* (illegal intercourse) abound with respect to the Byzantines and are especially attributed to the alleged sexual promiscuity of

Byzantine women. 'Abd al-Jabbar states that *zina* was commonplace in the cities and markets of Byzantium. If a woman had no husband, chose not to marry, she was free to do what she pleased. There were, he claims, many markets for prostitutes, who possessed their own shops and sat in their doorways, uncovered and conspicuous. If one of them gave birth to a child, she could carry the baby to the patriarch, bishop, or priest and say, "I am giving this child so that he may become a servant of Christ." Inevitably, the response was that she was a "pure and blessed saint," accompanied by the promise of her requital for her good deeds. More provocative is the claim that the nuns from convents went out to offer themselves to monks, receiving thanks for such deeds.[28] In reality there was an absolute separation of the sexes in monastic life. But how can one account for such claims? Where do such stories originate?

Adab al-ghuraba' by Abu al-Faraj al-Isfahani (d. 356/967) includes anecdotes featuring monks and monasteries within the Islamic empire where high dignitaries would stop for refreshment during hunting trips or other journeys. Monasteries provided a special sort of shelter, a "kind of abroad," for notable Muslim and Christian men, who anticipated erotic adventures of a variety of types.[29] One story takes place in 355/965 in the monastery of al-Tha'alib:

> While we were walking around the monastery . . . we saw a woman with a face like an inscribed *dinar* . . . we went with her filled with pleasure in her and her grace and sweetness of diction that only God knows. She stayed with us for the rest of the day and I composed the following verses about her, which I recited to her and which pleased her:
>
> > A slender girl of bewitching looks passed by us [in the monastery]
> > Brought out from her seclusion by monks
> > To glorify the religion as living proof of it.[30]

Monasteries served as secluded sites for men to experience their desire and sexuality; the woman's face here is described as if inscribed on a *dinar*, or as exhibiting beauty comparable to female royalty. It demonstrates the appeal and captivation of the Christian female, whose looks and manners succeed in bewitching the visitor.

This collection also suggests that the monks were welcoming of homosexual lovers. 'Abdallah al-Wasiti tells in one story about having frequented a group of sophisticated young men who once invited him to visit the monastery in the city of Wasit: they traveled to the monastery and stayed for three days and were entertained with music and wine. Returning to the monastery a few months later, the priest informed them that a handsome young man had come in, accompanied by a good-looking boy whom he assumed was the young man's lover. They drank and became enraptured, continuing such behavior for three days.[31] He was later saddened to learn about their departure.

A third account in *Adab al-ghuraba'* has as its main character the third/ninth Abbasid caliph al-Mutawakkil, who visited a monastery in Hims, where he saw a beautiful girl. Al-Mutawakkil asked the monk about her, and the monk informed him that she was his daughter: "[Al-Mutawakkil's] admiration and desire for her grew . . . and [he] was enraptured and almost tore his shirt . . . she took us up to an upstairs room, overlooking the churches." He eventually married her after she converted to Islam.[32] In contrast to the anecdote about the monastery of al-Tha'alib, this story depicts the common qualities of distraction and undeniable desire: that the caliph had such a strong physical reaction to the Christian girl, and had her convert so that he could marry her, attests not only to her attractive features but to the consequential transformative trigger brought on by the female. In this light, she is perceived as a threat to the Islamic sense of order and self-control.

Elite members of the Abbasid Empire found the combination of beautiful natural surroundings, the availability of wine, and the prospect of amorous adventures irresistible; the image of the monastery as a pleasure ground might be surprising to many Christians, but it is the image al-Shabushti (d. 388/948) propagates in his book on monasteries. Al-Shabushti mentions a convent inhabited by nuns that attracted Muslims and Christians from the surrounding areas for nights of sexual abandon.[33] Such manuals of "spiritual geography" not only depict a total absence of piety in the Christian monasteries but portray the monasteries and convents as locations whose principal function was pleasure.[34]

The women featured in these stories are Christians and embody, as such, an alterity that prefigures and/or parallels the Byzantine women's otherness. According to Thomas Sizgorich, the women in the convent symbolize Christianity, as exotic representations of civilized and attractive difference, but also serve—as do Byzantine women—the function of sexual extravagance.[35] Hence the stories on Byzantine monasteries and the sexual transgressions of the monks and nuns belong to what seems to be a collection of vignettes, assigning transgressive behavior in Islamic lands and, by extension, Byzantine lands, to monks and monasteries. The pornographic allusion of this material is clear; but it is also indicative of attempts to denigrate and defame a rival culture by exaggerating the laxity with which Byzantine culture dealt with its women. Cultural fantasy represented at once a form of wish fulfillment, emanating from deep insecurity in the face of the alien and unpredictable, and a form of sheer pleasure, delighting in the exotic.[36] The Byzantines, both female and male, are omnisexual, and prone to engage in sexual relations with no restraint. Not even monks and nuns are spared these accusations, as this licentiousness was a facet of a general pattern of moral shortcomings.

Men and Eunuchs, Marriage and Celibacy

Marital practices, notably issues of polygamy versus monogamy as well as divorce and celibacy, were also major markers of difference between the gender systems of the Byzantine and Islamic societies. Each of the two empires had its own conceptions of social and familial life, and, perhaps inevitably, the Arabic Islamic texts criticize Byzantine concepts of celibacy, marriage—including monogamy—and divorce. In Islam, the question of celibacy versus marriage is resolved largely in favor of the latter. The centrality of marriage in Islam is best captured by a tradition of the Prophet: "There shall be no monkery in Islam." The clear example of the Prophet established marriage, and more generally legal sexual intercourse, as *sunna*. Since marriage is so firmly regarded as the norm, it is not surprising that al-Jahiz expresses amazement at the Christian ideal of continence and at the priests, monks, nuns, hermits, bishops, and archbishops who do not marry and do not have children.[37]

Linked to the issue of celibacy was the use of eunuchs, notably the Byzantine custom of castrating (young) boys, especially those destined to the service of the Church. Al-Jahiz writes, "The Byzantines are the originators of this custom which contradicts the spirit of kindness and mercy." The Byzantines, along with the Saqaliba (Slavs), were the only people to practice castration, which was thought by the Arabs to be a most odious crime and a sign of the Byzantines' pitiless natures and corrupt hearts. The Byzantines were accused of mutilating innocent and defenseless children and, still worse, of even castrating their own sons and selling them.[38] If they captured Muslims, they took the children and castrated many of the boys, a number of whom died as a result. They claimed to have compassion and mercy, yet castration was not even prescribed in canonical law or the Torah.[39] Al-Jahiz explains that the eunuchs in the Muslim empire held the Byzantines responsible for their mutilation, and this practice was offered as one reason why the Muslim eunuchs fought the Byzantines so fervently.[40]

Matrimonial practices of the Byzantines and medieval Christians in general were among the preferred themes that Arab Muslim writers routinely used to construct and consolidate their topoi of differences. Al-Jahiz states that the Christians could not divorce; only in the case of adultery could the husband initiate divorce. The Andalusi geographer Abu 'Ubayd al-Bakri (d. 487/1094), in relating an anecdote about Europe and the papacy, stressed that divorce was not allowed in their religion.[41] The strict monogamy prevailing in Christian communities represented a significant contrast, since for Muslim men divorce was relatively easily attainable.

The other peculiar feature of the Byzantine institution of marriage, from the perspective of the Arab Muslims, was monogamy. An anecdote about Jurjius b. Jibra'il, who specialized in medicine and helped cure Caliph al-Mansur (r. 136–158/754–775), highlights this practice. One biographical dictionary relates a conversation between the two in the year 151/768. The caliph asked him: "Who serves you? He answered, my students. The caliph told him: I heard that you do not have a woman/wife. He answered: I have a wife who is old and weak and cannot move from her place. . . . The caliph ordered his servant . . . to choose from among the *Rumi* female slaves three beautiful ones that would be carried to Jurjius together with three thousand *dinars*." Upon seeing them, Jurjius sent them away, explaining to the caliph that Christians practice monogamy and never marry another or remarry so long as their wives are still alive.[42] This anecdote demonstrates the difference of Christian monogamous practice, which must have seemed unusual, and certainly restrictive, to the elite Muslims.

Similarly, a Muslim text includes an anecdote that concerns a Muslim prisoner who converted to Christianity and married a "well-to-do, beautiful Byzantine woman." He lived happily with her until, one day, he was sent on a forty-day expedition; while absent, he was informed that his wife had remarried. When he returned, he did not go home. Soon his mother-in-law came to see him with a large escort of her female neighbors, all wearing expensive clothes and jewelry. His mother-in-law informed him that his wife had not remarried because as a *rumiyya,* a Byzantine, she could not have two husbands; she had simply taken a lover during his absence. The other women stood as witnesses to the fact that her lover was nothing more than that, for "this was not objectionable or shameful in their eyes." The mother-in-law urged him to return to her, and he did. The conclusion of the narrator is that "all who enter *bilad al-rum* lose their jealousy and passion, and allow their wives to take lovers."[43] The warning tone of this passage insinuates that Muslim Arabs who would venture into Byzantine lands had better brace themselves, as they would encounter fiery passions and strange sexual and marital practices.

This anecdote, moreover, hints at a particular feature attributed to Byzantine males. Competing nations often attribute "feminine" characteristics to their male rivals as a means of explaining dispositions that are unfamiliar and undesirable. Muslim perceptions of Byzantine men as lacking in pride

toward their womenfolk reinforced the values of serious piety and responsibility over family and possessions in Muslim society, as contrasted with
supposed Byzantine nonchalance. The cuckolded husband's absence of jealousy was an accusation leveled against Byzantine men, but also against the
Slavs and other Europeans and, later on, the Crusaders. Muslim men's jealousy, possessiveness, and protection regarding their wives or other female
relatives were indicators of proper Islamic practice and, in their view, set
them apart from other cultures who took these traits and characteristics
less seriously. Ibn Fadlan's account of the caliphal embassy from Baghdad
to the king of the Volga Bulgars in the early fourth/tenth century includes
passages that confirm this attitude by dwelling on sexual improprieties:
"Each of them has a couch on which he sits. They are accompanied by beautiful slave girls for trading. One man will have intercourse with his slave-girl
while his companions look on. Sometimes a group of them comes together
to do this, each in front of the other." Another passage states that on the
throne of the king of the Rus "there sit forty slave-girls who belong to his
bed. Sometimes he has coitus with one of them in the presence of those
companions whom we have mentioned." James Montgomery has confirmed
that Ibn Fadlan's account of the Rus does not balk at the opportunity to
affirm the cultural and religious superiority of Islam.[44] André Miquel also
points to the different register that one encounters in the passages pertaining
to some non-Muslim populations: the freedom of *moeurs*—real, imagined,
or exaggerated—that the Islamic world attributes to the women of the
North, Turks, Bulgars, or Slavs.[45] As Muslims hold themselves to an ethos
of duty and purity, a Muslim male figurehead's concern is to keep the family
and community intact—pure and without interference; this difference must
have been incredibly difficult for the early Muslims to comprehend, as pride
of virtue and devotion is a very fundamental element in Islamic faith. The
references, moreover, insist on the lack of jealousy shown by the men of these
cultures.

Such a laissez-faire attitude is well known in a later Muslim text that
dates to the Crusader period, namely, the autobiography of the fifth/twelfth-
century Usama b. Munqidh, where it is stated that the Franks have no hint
of jealousy—for example, that where one Frankish man walks along the
street with his wife and encounters a friend, the husband will allow or encourage his wife to talk to his friend while he stands aside, away from her
private conversation, and waits until she is done conversing. Another story
confirms this assessment, highlighting Frankish males' lack of marital jealousy as well as Frankish females' licentiousness. Here a Frank who finds a
man in bed with his wife reacts solely by telling him that if he finds him
there again he will take him to court, "and this was his only reaction, the

height of his outburst of jealousy."[46] The Muslim perception of the Franks as lacking marital jealousy and of Frankish women as sexually loose should be seen, according to Carole Hillenbrand, as reflective of widespread Muslim attitudes and prejudices about the Franks which were already deeply ingrained by Usama's own time.[47]

We also find such judgments in Andalusi accounts of their northern neighbors. The Andalusi Muslim writers dwell on the freedom of European (and other) women, finding the same irreverent aspects of absence of jealousy among men and sexual license of unmarried women.[48] The Byzantines are thus not the exclusive target of such allegations, but they receive a greater proportion of the charges simply because they loom much larger in the Arabic Islamic textual production than any of the other Europeans.

The disempowerment of the Byzantine male is brought up as well in narratives of conquests where the rhetorical struggle of the self and the other emphasizes the enslavement and consequent sexual defilement of Byzantine womenfolk as well as their presence in public; while Arab Islamic women were modest and confined in private settings. Ibn Hazm's verses stress this point:

> Of our women. You did not capture many.
> Whereas of yours we have as many as the drops of rain.
> Indeed, counting them is an endless task
> Like a man counting the pigeons' feathers.[49]

The tone of this poem reflects Arabs' pride in their women, whom they perceive as modest and whom they seek to protect. The victory ode of Abu Tammam (d. 231/845 or 232/846) on the conquest of Amorium, "The Sword Is More Veracious," illustrates the central role played by "the sexual gender-based imagery" in the description of Muslim military and political domination of the Byzantines. One of the most important poems of the Arabic language, the victory ode was presented to the caliph al-Mu'tasim (218–277/833–842) after his conquest of the Byzantine city of Amorium in 223/838. The poem uses concepts of gender, notably a dialectic of male domination and female submission, to convey the relationship of the triumphant Arab Muslims to the defeated Byzantine Christians. Suzanne Stetkevych explains how sexual domination in the form of the rape of the conquered Byzantine city operates as the prevailing metaphor for military and political control. The Muslim army is described in defensive, masculine terms, whereas Amorium, and Byzantium in general, assume female characteristics of passivity and allurement.[50] In the verses that tell of Muslim soldiers raping Byzantine women (lines 63–66), Abu Tammam uses the paired gender construct of male/female, aggressor/victim, and Muslim/infidel to consolidate Arab Islam as a masculine, thriving, and powerful body, and Byzantine Christianity as feminine, acquiescent, and submissive.[51]

This textual process of exposing Byzantine women carries with it religious/theological overtones of Byzantine inferiority and also allegorizes the Islamic masculinist power of possession. The justification of expansion could then be linked to issues of sexuality. Stetkevych notes that the image of sexually defiled womanhood is the customary means for expressing male dishonor and downfall.[52] Here again, reference to Usama b. Munqidh's text is relevant. He reports that Rafful, a Muslim Kurdish woman from Shayzar, was captured during an attack on the town in 1137. Her father almost lost his mind, roaming the streets and telling bystanders that Rafful had been captured. It was later found that Rafful had thrown herself from the horse of the Frank who had captured her, thus taking her own life to save her honor.[53] While in this and other Arab Muslim texts women's social and moral roles hinged on the concept of honor, the Byzantines and the Crusaders are belittled for lacking the most basic human sense of honor.

Byzantine Women and the Bounds for Muslim Women

The writings on which I have shed light had produced the Byzantine world for an Abbasid audience. These texts' emphasis on certain sexual tropes worked to construct Byzantium as a particular kind of location and helped solidify Islam's identity and sense of pride and belonging. Sexuality played a great role in mapping differences: the Arab Islamic "here" and the Byzantine "there" were distinguished by the imagined differences between the sexual practices of "us" and "them."[54] The established rules of sexual morality in a given society are commonly subjected to friendly or hostile—but rarely impartial—evaluation by that society itself and by other societies it encounters. Islamic authors' depictions mirrored their expectations. Their assessment of Byzantine women derived not entirely from their observations, but was rather determined by the values, standards, and prejudices of Abbasid society. Accounts of first- or secondhand experiences, absorbed within existing paradigms, were used to support rather than challenge contemporary social norms and practices. Indeed, for the Byzantine woman to be recognizable within an Islamic context, she had to reflect a series of preexisting stereotypes that Islamic society had adopted to strengthen its own sovereign base.[55]

The writings on Byzantine women seem to articulate Muslim fears of female excess, and especially uncontrolled sexual activity, which threatened to undermine Islamic feminine purity and the faith's gender hierarchy of propriety. This threat was not unrealistic, for although Islam officially tolerated only marriage and concubinage, it was difficult to prevent illicit sexual contact from occurring. Al-Tanukhi, writing in fourth/tenth-century Baghdad, relates a serious social condition when the daughters of important notables in Baghdad were reported, by the police, to have been caught participating in immoral acts:

> One of my neighbors was Abu 'Ubayda. . . . He used to be a companion *(nadim)* of Ishaq b. Ibrahim al-Mas'abi. He told me that one day Ishaq summoned him in the middle of the night. . . . He [Ishaq] threw at me [Abu 'Ubayda] papers that he was holding in his hands and said: read these. I read them all. They were the reports of the police chiefs . . . each one relating the day's events. All the reports mentioned raids undertaken against women who were found fornicating. They were the daughters of [high-ranking officials], viziers, *umara'* and notables who had died or who had lost their positions. . . . [Ishaq said] I am afraid lest a similar fate befalls my five daughters and I have gathered them in this room to kill them immediately and find rest.[56]

The passage informs us about raids undertaken by the police performed to enforce purity and propriety within society at the private level, and about the implication of free women of a certain standing in "immoral" activities. What connection does this story about fornication bear to reality? Does it indicate that debauchery among upper-class women was commonplace? While these questions are difficult to answer, what this story clearly implies is the belief that in the absence of constant vigilance, the natural depravity of women would inevitably lead to their downfall and the consequent dishonor of their families and community—and by extension that of the Islamic empire itself. Indeed, this anecdote presents in an almost obsessive way a testimony to the precariousness of the lives of all Arab Islamic women—even elite ones—and the profound fears of humiliation that their male relatives permanently harbored.

A similar story mentions the daughter of Ibn Abi 'Awf, a wealthy and influential man belonging to the close circle of 'Ubayd Allah, the vizier of both al-Mu'tamid (256/870–279/892) and al-Mu'tadid (279/892–289/902): "It was mentioned that the news spread in Baghdad that Ibn Abi 'Awf entered his home to find his daughter with a man who is not her *mahram*."[57] This text again suggests the possibility of illicit sexual contacts in fourth/ tenth-century Baghdad, implicating upper-class women. His daughter's act had significant repercussions on the powerful Ibn Abi 'Awf. In fact, his very downfall resulted from her actions. This anecdote, in conjunction with the earlier one, reveals the existence of a certain freedom from conventional moral behavior among the upper classes that is not described in legal and religious texts. Thus, while the early Muslims wrote derogatorily of

Byzantine licentiousness, the fact remains that such behavior also existed in the Islamic empire despite being viewed as unacceptable and punishable there.

There are also indications that prostitution prospered in various Islamic cities during certain periods. In Baghdad, the Hanbalites, known for their intransigent rigidity, rose up against this corruption of true Islamic moral standards, notably drinking wine, singing, and prostitution. In 323/935 they confiscated wine, harassed singing girls, organized raids on houses of ill-repute, destroyed musical instruments, and interrogated men accompanying women unrelated to them in the streets. In 327/939 the Hanbalites are said to have prevented performances by musicians and the sale of female slaves as prostitutes. In addition, under the Buyid 'Adud al-Dawla (d. 372/983) prostitution was officially taxed.[58] There was thus a real and constant fear of the degradation of Islamic mores that is represented in Islamic texts by a fear of uncontrolled sexuality. The views on Byzantine women were thus indicators of widespread internal concern.

Maria Rosa Menocal posits that what proves to be significant and influential in intercultural contacts are the perspectives generated between competing cultures and their views and judgments of each other—whether true or fictionalized. Indeed, scholars investigating the interactions between cultures must impart the reality of a culture, along with their impressions of what only appears to be reality to others.[59] Within their presentation of Byzantine women, what we have is an acute scenario of how women might be compromised if they were to go beyond the bounds set for them by their orthodox Muslim culture. The perception of Byzantine women as seen through the lens of the Arab Muslims' system of values and beliefs represents a reconfirmation of the "proper" Muslim way of life. The images permeating Islamic sources corroborate the Muslim attitude that sees the control of sexual morality and hence of women's behavior as a prerequisite for stable social organization. The texts reveal a complex relationship to gender: the Byzantine female and male are made sexually strange, acting as the site where gender distinctions are blurred, the threat of the feminine more explicitly acknowledged, and the relationship between the sexes redefined in looser terms.

Irvin C. Schick has postulated that sexuality plays an integral part in the creation of "spatial differentiation";[60] and according to Valerie Traub, as sexual definitions and theories/knowledge passed across empires and cultures, we realize that cultural understanding is highly politically and religiously charged.[61] Arabic Islamic authors projected a Byzantine value system through the use of sexual tropes in order to trigger a discourse of spatiality. Rather than comprising an expository explanation of Byzantium, the texts developed paradigms of oppositions, which reflected only temporal, culturally saturated ideals and perspectives of a collective Islam. Byzantium in these texts is feminized, transformed into a seductive and dangerous land whose sexual values are perceived only through a comparative lens. Gender and sexuality came to function as constitutive elements of Byzantine alterity in two respects: first, through a developed notion of a sexualized Byzantium; and, second, through depictions of the Byzantine male as effeminate, a judgment supported all the more by the strong presence of eunuchs in Byzantium. These revealing texts illustrate the extent to which gender and sexuality served as vectors within the discourse of Byzantine alterity, effectively used to draw boundaries and to imagine.[62] But describing the sexual difference of the Byzantines also served as a ploy in the construction of the Abbasid norm itself. Byzantium, the geographical elsewhere, will continue to play this dual role. Arab Muslim interest in Byzantine women did not stem from their importance or visibility, nor from anthropological or ethnographic concerns. Rather, Arab interest arose from a desire to show difference and to strengthen the idea that Arab Islam was the foremost culture of morality, propriety, and control—in particular, in the texts of authors who featured and contrasted the lax Byzantine attitude toward women and sexuality to the ordered perfection of Islamic civilization. Moreover, by insinuating that Byzantine (and also Slavic and Frankish) men did not feel jealous when their womenfolk engaged with other men, the texts were striking at the very masculinity—and, by extension, the moral order and authority—of their rivals.

Byzantium was posited as the locus of eroticism in a textual production constrained by a moralistic code. These representations are reminiscent of nineteenth-century depictions of the Oriental harem, which was an imagined image from which Europe's "sexual repressions, erotic fantasies and desire of domination" were produced.[63] Exploited as a means of evoking venues of erotic fantasy, Byzantium was, like the Orientalists' Orient, a scene of escapist sexual fantasy, a space of sexual promise and threat. The long-term consequence of this formulation of Byzantine eroticism was to degrade Byzantine sexuality, for it was thought to contain a mode of obscene decadence that set the Byzantines apart.

To tell about Byzantine women and gender relations was to enter into a well-understood narrative, part of an ongoing dialogue with which the audience was familiar. Rather than taking the discussion to be evidence of corroborative information, this iteration occurs because the stereotyped depiction agrees with the anticipated image.[64] It is noteworthy that these accounts were written by individuals who had not traveled to the countries they described. Their imaginative approach to other cultures helps explain how these authors could write with such confidence on the Byzantines when almost none of them had firsthand experience of the Byzantines and their empire. It is nevertheless crucial to remind the reader that "engaged representations" tend to rely on the imagination of the writer/compiler and his cultural and historical context rather than on any detached, scientific observation.[65] In the final analysis, looking toward Byzantium brought only counterexamples of accepted, appropriate behavior, and that helped the writers reaffirm their own identity.

The contentious nature of the relationship between Byzantium and Islam colored the discourse about Arab Islam's orthodox Christian rival. Moreover, the relationship between the two was not hierarchical or one of oppressor and oppressed. Arab Muslims did not see the Byzantine Empire and its history as barbaric, uncivilized, and inferior: the two rivals were equal, but different. The image of Byzantium is one of a civilization that possessed an admirable history and culture—although its more contestable aspects of intimate relations are presented as corrupt, degenerate, and irredeemable. Throughout, there is a clear and self-evident idea of "us" and "them," but behind this seemingly totalizing discourse exists a rich, diverse, and intricate image of Byzantium. The discourse is nuanced in ways that temper the extremes and admit common ground, which perhaps explains why the sexuality of the Byzantines seldom provokes any sodomitic readings. Their sexual excesses are almost always presented in a heteronormative mode, and whenever they are made to operate "against nature," they do so in ways that Muslims do, in excessive or illicit heterosexual activity.[66]

These Arab Islamic texts disclose an acute anxiety in their representations of Byzantine women. This apprehension emanates from the cultural difference of the foreign (Byzantine) women as well as from the moral expectations of their own local women. Byzantium was figured in Arabic Islamic lore as libidinously eroticized, becoming a "porno-tropics"[67] for the Muslim imagination onto which its forbidden sexual desires and fears were projected. Lack of control over passion characterized the Byzantines, who as such represented the antitype and constituted a warning of what the future might hold if Muslim society were to relax its morals and controls.

5

Fashioning a New Identity

Women Exemplars and the Search for Meaning

EARLY ISLAMIC DISCOURSES about women and gender intimate a desire to uphold and preserve communal religious and ethical boundaries in the face of their permeability. These perimeters were dependent upon observing one's place among other members of one's religious affiliation, and in relation to other religious communities, especially since one's position in society was to be ascribed within a matrix of identities, events, and beliefs.[1] The limits of these religio-ethical boundaries and the imperative for their protection were articulated in the sacred stories of the female exemplars who tested their limits and who, through their acts, helped refashion a new, accepted Muslim female identity; early Muslim female identity was, in fact, dependent upon the limits set by the exemplars' stories from the first/seventh century.

The events surrounding Islamic origins would have lasting consequences for Muslim self-identity. Muslim intellectuals articulated a metanarrative of the primordial Islamic past, centered on the events of the life of the Prophet Muhammad and those of the period immediately following his death. Muslim theologians chose to remain anchored to this inspired past, and specifically to the men and women who most exemplify pious attitudes and model behavior. Legitimacy and authority came to depend upon perceived imitation of the example set by Muhammad and the first members of his community. Thus the foundational principle of inclusion in the *umma* was, consequently, a "mimetic performance" through which Muslims sought to imitate the behavior of those men and women who were present at the founding of the religion and who observed for themselves and lived by the example of the Prophet.[2]

The primary female exemplars were the Qur'anic women—notably, Mary, mother of Jesus, and the women who have pride of place in the tradition of the Prophet, particularly his wives Khadija and 'A'isha and his daughter Fatima. However, there are dozens of other women, mentioned in both the Qur'an and the Prophet's tradition, who served as exemplars, defining by their behavior, in both actions and words, the bounds of acceptable Muslim identity. In his *Mu'jam a'lam al-nisa' fi al-qur'an al-karim,* 'Imad al-Hilali includes 114 women who are mentioned directly or indirectly in the Qur'an.[3] Some of these women are biblical figures who serve as models of virtue and devotion, while others, also biblical, epitomize the evil in women, like the wife of Noah and the wife of Lot. In *Surat al-tahrim* (Qur'an 66:9–12) the Qur'an singles out a few women as either poor or praiseworthy examples: "God has struck a similitude for the unbelievers, the wife of Noah and the wife of Lot; for they were under two of Our righteous servants, but they betrayed them. . . . God has struck a similitude for His believers, the wife of Pharaoh, when she said, 'My Lord, build for me a house in Paradise, in Thy presence, and deliver me from Pharaoh and his work.' . . . And Mary, Imran's daughter, who guarded her virginity, so We breathed into her Our Spirit, and she confirmed the Words of her Lord and His Books, and became one of the obedient." The prophetic message for female followers is to abandon one's aggressive, emotional, and heedless past and embrace a future of devotion, purity, and obedience.

A large number of verses target Muhammad's contemporaries, and in the featured female figures we encounter, the feminine model and antimodel coexist side by side. The Prophet's aunt by marriage and wife of Muhammad's enemy Abu Lahab, Umm Jamil, is specifically accursed in verses in the Qur'an (111:1, 4–5): "Perish the hands of Abu Lahab, and perish he! . . . and his wife, the carrier of the firewood, upon her neck a rope of palm-fibre." However, a large number of Qur'anic verses address the piety of the female companions of the Prophet, each of whom displays instances of exemplary behavior, such as patience, fidelity, and courage or other personified principles from which Muslim women could learn.

This "teaching" material is found in more copious form in the *Sira* and the tradition of the Prophet, as well as in the early biographical dictionaries that include information on female companions of the Prophet Muhammad (the Sahabiyyat) whose devotion, conduct, and actions led them to supreme esteem as moral exemplars and prescriptive models for later generations of Muslim women. If we can envision the formation of the Is-

lamic *sunna* against the background of *jahiliyya,* and in the face of the in-
difference of newly converted individuals, we can see, at least in part, why
we find in hadith descriptions of the early Islamic female elite idealized traits
and inspirational examples requiring mimesis.[4] The normative behavioral
precedents set by these women are exemplified, for instance, by Umm al-
Fadl Lubaba, whose biography served as a religious model and precedent
for later generations of Muslims. Umm al-Fadl Lubaba was the Prophet's
aunt by marriage and one of the earliest converts. Ibn Sa'd states that she
was the first woman, after Khadija, to become Muslim.[5] Upon Muhammad's migration to Medina, she remained unprotected in Mecca. A highly
reliable traditionalist, her piety was reflected in her fasting, and her devotion to Islam was proved when, wielding a tent pole, she attacked one of
Muhammad's leading opponents, Abu Lahab.[6] Early converts to Islam such
as Umm al-Fadl Lubaba and Khadija were above all challenged to remain
devoted to the new faith amid the enormous difficulties that the early
Muslim community faced.

Another exemplary female was Umm Kulthum bint 'Uqba, who accepted
Islam in Mecca before the *hijra* (the Prophet's migration to Medina in 1/622)
and was the first woman to migrate to Medina. As written by Ibn Sa'd, "We
know of no female Qurayshi other than Umm Kulthum bint 'Uqba who
left her parents as a Muslim woman, emigrating to God and his messenger."[7]
She arrived at Medina, and her two brothers, who opposed her conversion
and migration, arrived the next day and requested that the Prophet return
her to them in accordance with the terms of the Treaty of Hudaybiyya,
which had been agreed to between Muhammad and his opponents in
Mecca. Umm Kulthum pleaded not to be returned, explaining that she
might be tortured and forced to recant. A verse descended making room
for a special dispensation for the women refugees from Mecca (Qur'an
60:10): "O believers, when believing women come to you as emigrants,
test them. God knows very well their belief. Then if you know them to be
believers, return them not to the unbelievers." The Prophet, after testing
Umm Kulthum bint 'Uqba, determined that she had not left Mecca for any
monetary need or marital reason, but only because of her love for God,
Muhammad, and the religion.[8] The occasions of revelation surrounding this
verse emphasize Umm Kulthum's exemplary piety, selflessness, and courage.

Another such character is Umm 'Umara, who was present during the
early battles of Uhud, Khaybar, Hunayn, and al-Yamama and was celebrated
for her bravery. At Uhud, as a combatant, she is said to have sustained
twelve wounds to her body while defending the Prophet, who praised her
valor and stated that her performance on the battlefield was unsurpassed
by anyone else.[9] On the first day of the battle, in which her husband and

two sons participated, she set out with her water skin to quench the thirst of the wounded. She braved the battlefield until she reached the Prophet. As the tide of the battle began to turn against the Muslims, she began fighting with a sword as well as shooting a bow until she was wounded in the shoulder. According to al-Waqidi, she proved her valor at Uhud as the Prophet witnessed her fight a strong battle until she sustained thirteen injuries. Her fervor was such that the Prophet smiled "until his teeth showed. He said: You are zealous, O Umm 'Umara!" 'Abdallah b. 'Umar also said that he heard the messenger of God say on the day of Uhud, "I did not turn right or left but I saw her fight for me."[10] This element of female devotion, solidarity, and companionship is found repeatedly and serves as one of the first examples of the religio-ethical turn from selfishness to selflessness, from perfidy to loyalty.

At the battle of Uhud it was as though two temporalities were clashing in one moment: a pre-Islamic temporality of emotional and reactive extremes against that of a new era exemplified by the courageous albeit controlled behavior of the Sahabiyyat. On the battlefield, the women of the opposing camps are reported to have invested themselves in combat, albeit in different manners. The *jahili* women provided encouragement, bolstering energy and a wish for revenge, but they did not fight alongside their husbands, as Umm 'Umara reported: "In the name of God, I did not see a woman among them aim with an arrow or stone, but I saw them strike tambourines and drums and remind the people of the dead at Badr." Thus, women of the rival forces were thought not to have physically fought, but to have played a sentimental or emotional role by commemorating and mourning those who had died in the previous battle. Umm 'Umara refers specifically to Hind bint 'Utba, who, she says, "was a heavy woman for her frame, sitting with another woman, fearing the cavalry, and having no strength to walk."[11] As I mentioned in Chapter 1, Hind stood at the edge of the field, aggressively inciting the warriors into battle to the point where she was nearly killed. A more energetic stance was taken by 'Amra bint 'Alqama al-Harithiyya, who, when the standard of the Quraysh fell to the ground, took it and raised it up for the Quraysh to gather around. Her action was momentous, as reflected in the words of the poet Hassan b. Thabit: "Had not the Harithite woman seized the standard, they would have been sold in the market like chattels."[12]

While the *jahili* women's role was limited to acts of encouragement, some Sahabiyyat seem to have fought a hard battle, risking their lives and sustaining numerous wounds. These acts of bravery illustrate women's dedication to the new faith, merged with an instinctive resistance to adopting a more controlled nature during such intense war-filled moments of this transitional period. At no point, however, are Muslim women—in this battle or any other battle, for that matter—accused of mutilating their enemies' corpses. At the end of the battle, *jahili* women such as Hind bint 'Utba were the sole culprits in the atrocities perpetrated on the bodies of the fallen. While some women in battle may have vigorously or inspirationally provoked force, they strived to cultivate the new faith's requirement of patience and acceptance in the face of the death of loved ones. The Muslim women showed a pious resignation in relation to the fate of their relatives who fell in the course of the battle. The section in the *Sira* entitled "Verses Recited on the Battle of Uhud" includes only a handful of poems recited by women: verses by Safiyya crying over her brother Hamza; the verse of Nu'm, wife of Shammas, crying over her husband; and verses by Hind bint 'Utba.[13] Both Safiyya's and Nu'm's poetry show an acceptance of God's will. Safiyya recited:

> God the true, the Lord of the Throne, called him
> To live in paradise in joy. That is what we hoped and longed for.

The yearning for vengeance by the *jahili*s was, by contrast, unquenchable. Even after their victory at Uhud, the killings, and the mutilation of the corpses, Hind bint 'Utba, on her return to Mecca, is said to have recited:

> I came back my heart filled with sorrow,
> For some from whom I sought vengeance had escaped me,
> Men of Quraysh who were at Badr,
> Of Banu Hashim, and of Yathrib's people.
> I gained somewhat from the expedition
> But not all that I had hoped.[14]

Nothing could quench the *jahili* thirst for revenge. No act, no matter how atrocious or excessive, could alleviate the sorrow verging on despair at the death of their loved ones. The poetry selected in the *Sira* mirrored a new ethos and a certain psychology. The reckless but profound discontent exhibited by Hind, whose acts, words, and anger do nothing toward decreasing her feelings of apprehension and anxiety and, ultimately, her sense of defeat, is to be contrasted with the confidence of the Muslim Safiyya, tranquil and gratified in her belief in an afterlife and her acceptance of God's divine decree.

Khadija

This binary construction between *jahili* women and the Sahabiyyat was further elaborated in the typology of Khadija, the first wife of the Prophet and perhaps the foremost female exemplary in Islam. Ibn Sa'd states that before her marriage to Muhammad, Khadija experienced a miraculous occurrence during her participation in a pagan celebration with other Meccan women that centered on an idol in the shape of a man. This idol started to speak and predicted that a prophet by the name of Ahmad would be sent with God's message. The other women assailed the idol with stones, denouncing it, while Khadija instead paid attention to its words.[15]

Khadija is a primary player in the stories of attestation, recognition, and revelation. The *Sira* relates that when Muhammad was in Syria, Khadija had commissioned him for caravan work and had sent her servant Maysara to assist Muhammad; at that time, a hermit noticed Muhammad and told Maysara about him. Maysara communicated the information to Khadija, telling her about his honesty and his purity and what the People of the Book said about him. Khadija became aware of Muhammad's prophetic mission and consequently decided to marry him. Khadija was the first to be told about Muhammad's first revelation, and it was her cousin, Waraqa b. Nawfal, an Arabian Christian scholar with knowledge of the sacred scriptures, who confirmed that the first vision experienced by Muhammad was a genuine prophetic one.[16]

Khadija gave the disconcerted Muhammad moral assistance and assurance. The tradition relates that whenever Muhammad would hear a call addressing him as "O Muhammad!" he would return home and tell Khadija that he was losing his mind, and she would respond: "No, God will never do this to you. I know you as an honest person; you deliver whatever is put in your safekeeping, and you do good unto the kindred."[17] The *Sira* states that following her death and that of Muhammad's uncle Abu Talib, which occurred in the same year, a series of catastrophes befell the Prophet, as she had been a faithful vizier *(wazir sidq)* to him.[18]

Khadija is described as a merchant woman of wealth and honor within Meccan society. Due to her stature in the community, her conversion made a considerable impression on the Quraysh. The *Sira* states that she was the first person to become a Muslim.[19] She died in 619, departing at a critical juncture, before Muhammad's migration to Medina. Her legacy is founded on her presentation as an unfaltering supporter of Muhammad's mission at a time when he was rejected by his own tribe, by his own people. Her role is amplified by Muhammad's attachment to her memory, a matter reiterated by his later wife 'A'isha, who confessed, "I was not jealous of any of the wives of the Prophet except Khadija, even though I came after her death."[20] The memory of the calm and poised Khadija was so estimable that it had entered the realm of perfection and made other women feel jealous or less worthy, as they could not aspire to her venerable character.

Al-Bukhari's *Sahih* includes a tradition that confirms Khadija's special status in an answer by the Prophet to 'A'isha's complaint that it is as if "there has been no other woman on earth but Khadija." He replied: "She was, and it happened and she bore me a progeny."[21] Muhammad confirmed Khadija's irreproachable legacy, stating in a tradition preserved in the *Musnad* of Ibn Hanbal: "No indeed, Allah has not replaced her with a better [wife]. She believed in me when I was rejected. When they called me a liar, she proclaimed me truthful. When I was poor, she shared with me her wealth and Allah granted her children though withholding those of other women."[22] As Muhammad attested, Khadija was the ultimate female model—devoted, believing and supportive, nurturing, and endowed by God—an unmatched mimetic object.[23] Khadija, as Muhammad's pious wife, represents a marker for Muhammad: she is the archetypal woman and wife—and such first women and wives set an indelible precedent and leave a lasting impression. Further, she is a marker for Muslim women—the first woman to convert to Islam, the first woman to put her whole trust and devotion in the Prophet, and the first model of Islamic female behavior.

Both the hadith and the *Sira* praise Khadija as a woman and a wife, crediting her with insight into Muhammad's character as well as recognition of the initial signs of his prophetic call. Her wealth supported Muhammad in his spiritual endeavors, and her financial backing may have cost her her fortune during the period of the economic and social boycott proclaimed by major clans of the Quraysh, vis-à-vis the Prophet's clan, the Banu Hashim, in the hope of forcing them to withdraw their protection of Muhammad. Her constant devotion to Muhammad is reflected in the ways she comforted and counseled him, steadying him in his path. Her role is summarized in a passage from the *Sira:* "She strengthened him [the Prophet], lightened his burden, proclaimed his truth, and belittled men's opposition."[24] The hadith and the *Sira* touch upon the superiority of Khadija, highlighting her exclusive position among the wives of the Prophet, as the mother of his children, but also through his monogamous marriage to her as long as she lived. The parental and monogamous character of Muhammad's marriage with Khadija is significant, as this first marriage of his was the only monogamous one, during which he fathered a number of children and remained singularly committed to them all; these factors further mythologize the figure of Khadija and contribute to her veneration. A number of traditions, moreover, link Khadija to Qur'anic figures and show Khadija as an influence on or model for other premier Islamic female figures. In one hadith, for instance, the Prophet said, "The best of its women is Maryam bint 'Umran; the best of its women is Khadija."[25]

'A'isha

Unlike the later wives of Muhammad, Khadija lived most of her life in *jahiliyya,* and *jahiliyya* society had shaped her culture and environment, though she had adopted an Islamic lifestyle and piety upon conversion. She died before the *hijra,* that is, before the establishment of the first Muslim community in Medina, in which new types of relationships and new forms of behavior were born. It is the later wives of the Prophet who were required to abide by the tenets prescribed for them by Muhammad in Qur'anic verse. In particular, his wife 'A'isha, brought up in a Muslim household, lived at a moment of transition, and consequently her life reflects both *jahiliyya* and Islamic practices. Two major episodes reveal such ambivalence in her life as well as her potentially exemplary role.

One incident is the affair of the lie *(hadith al-ifk),* an accusation of adultery made against 'A'isha in 5/627. Ibn Hisham relates that 'A'isha had accompanied the Prophet during a raid and was inadvertently left behind to be rescued by a young Muslim man, Safwan. Upon her return, rumors claimed that she had betrayed Muhammad with Safwan. The Prophet was concerned about the personal and communal implications of the accusation and asked for the advice of his close companions, until he finally went to 'A'isha and asked her to repent. She narrates: "The Apostle came in to me. . . . He sat down and after praising God, he said: 'A'isha you know what people say about you and if you have done wrong as men say, then repent towards God."[26] 'A'isha's parents had been present, and she waited for them to reply, but they remained silent. She specifically requested first that her father and then her mother speak in her defense, but they each replied, "By God, I do not know what to say to the messenger of God."[27] It is at this point that 'A'isha realized that she was totally on her own and that she would have to defend herself, having lost the support of her parents and her husband; she tenaciously refused to admit guilt. She reports that as she heard the Prophet's words, "my tears ceased and I could not feel them."[28] She steadfastly asserted her innocence and finally could only utter in her defense a Qur'anic verse she had once heard (12:18): "But come sweet patience! And God's succor is ever there to seek against that you describe." 'A'isha verbally acknowledges that if she were to protest her innocence, she would not be believed, and that she knows of no better example for her case than that of the Prophet Yusuf's father's speech.[29]

By evoking the situation of Yusuf, 'A'isha supported her own innocence, placing herself within a Qur'anic story involving a prophet who had also been subjected to false accusations. Moreover, her representation evokes other women who were accused of cunning and seduction, as the episode of Yusuf with the wife of 'Aziz forms a major subplot of the Qur'anic *sura* of Yusuf. She was thus conjuring the larger subtext of an attractive woman accused of adultery in order to turn judgment of her accusation to her favor.[30] She was ultimately divinely vindicated by Qur'anic verses (24:11–20): "Those who came with the slander are a band of you ... Why when you heard it did the believing men and women not of their own account think good thoughts and say, 'This is a manifest calumny'? Why did they not bring four witnesses against it? But since they did not bring the witnesses, in God's sight they are the liars." While the revelation does not directly refer to 'A'isha, focusing rather on the punishment of those who spread slander, 'A'isha would, in Sunni sources, be given the epithet *al-mubarra'a* (the vindicated).

It is noteworthy that her story represents a striking similarity to the accusations leveled against Hind bint 'Utba, who, as mentioned earlier, was also accused of adultery, lost the support of her parents as her words failed to exonerate her, and was only vindicated in a supernatural way. Hind swore to her father "in the ways they used to swear in *jahiliyya*" that her husband was a liar, but to no avail, and it was ultimately a pre-Islamic priest in Yemen who was responsible for proclaiming her innocence.[31] Thus, the saving of Hind's honor was accomplished divinely, as was 'A'isha's reputation with the descent of Qur'anic verse. A main difference between 'A'isha and Hind, however, is that whereas the accusation against Hind reflected on her persona and her immediate family, the accusation against 'A'isha adversely affected her husband, Muhammad, and the entire *umma*.[32] 'A'isha, as a wife of the Prophet, was already a highly visible figure to whom many were expected to pay respect and from whom they would take their cue—any sign of moral mischoice or degradation would reflect poorly on her, the Prophet, and the faith, and could in a sense disenchant the public with them.

Another parallel between 'A'isha and Hind bint 'Utba is drawn between their public political involvement in the affairs of their communities. Arwa bint al-Harith had criticized Hind for stepping out of the traditional female role of *tahrid* (inciting male relatives to take blood vengeance), and instead taking matters into her own hands. This type of criticism is echoed in the Muslim sources with similar recriminations vis-à-vis 'A'isha, whose involvement in the politics of succession and in the civil war, following the murder of the third caliph, 'Uthman, was played out textually in Sunni and Shi'i sources. Denise Spellberg divides the earliest written responses to 'A'isha's role in the first civil war, or the first *fitna* between 'Ali and the Umayyads, into five general thematic categories—namely, slander, humor, regret, predictions of doom, and negative definitions of womanhood. Her actions on the battlefield are thus perceived as unholy, destructive, and unfeminine. Often in the same account 'A'isha is the object of both praise and blame—praise as the wife of the Prophet, and blame for her political actions as his widow. The divergent accounts about 'A'isha reveal that, in the process of writing about the first civil war, the Sunni and Shi'i communities formulated different strategies in their presentation of a shared past. While Shi'i Muslims cast 'A'isha as the persecutor of 'Ali, Sunni Muslims recognized the tension between 'A'isha's exemplary status as the Prophet's favorite wife and her public political actions as his widow. 'A'isha's defense did not focus on her participation in the confrontation but rather on reminding the blasphemers of her special status as the Prophet's beloved wife: "Silence your disgraceful clamor. Are you slandering the *habiba* (beloved) of the prophet of God? She is his wife in heaven."[33]

The Sunni defense of 'A'isha partially transferred her blame at the battle of the Camel to her companions during battle, Talha and al-Zubayr. Shi'is, however, continued to reproach 'A'isha for her role in that infamous battle. The sixth/twelfth-century Shi'i author Ibn Shahrasub condemned 'A'isha as a major player, as is shown in verses describing her march to Basra: "She came in a palanquin with the two villains; she pressed her army onto Basra; and it was as if she, in this action, was a cat who wanted to devour her male offspring."[34] This near-cannibalistic imagery reminds us, once again, of Hind bint 'Utba, as does al-Mas'udi's poem of lament by a woman who maintained that two sons, two brothers, and her husband were killed in the confrontation. The final line signifies a causal relationship between 'A'isha's transgression of the Qur'anic injunction and the human suffering occasioned by the battle.[35]

Commenting on the battle of the Camel, Tayeb El-Hibri states that 'A'isha is represented as a fickle personality, incoherent and ultimately harmful to the community; in a general sense, the message conveyed is about the detrimental role of women in politics. Conspicuously absent from this depiction is Mu'awiya, who is distanced from the scene, perhaps to let the discussion focus more on 'A'isha. It is 'A'isha who is placed in the ironic position of arguing against 'Ali in a way that facilitates the later rise of the Umayyad political claim.[36] What is perhaps obliquely suggested is that 'A'isha's participation and prominent featuring in the battle of the Camel potentially threatens to bring back *jahiliyya*. This is reflected in the adversarial exchange that took place between Umm Salama, the Prophet's wife and a staunch supporter of 'Ali, and 'A'isha. Like the exchange between Hind bint 'Utba and Hind bint Athatha, in which the latter attacked the former's role at the battle of Uhud, the sources highlight Umm Salama's reprimand as she reminds 'A'isha from the outset that if she sets out for Basra, she will be disobeying God's command, which in Qur'anic verse explicitly forbade the wives of the Prophet to leave the house (Qur'an 33:33). The opposition between Umm Salama and 'A'isha is inscribed in Ibn 'Abd Rabbih's *Al-'Iqd al-farid* in a series of communications in which Umm Salama's major argument is that women are not permitted to participate in battle. Umm Salama tells 'A'isha, "If the Prophet knew that women could sustain *jihad,* then he would have authorized you." 'A'isha defends herself, reminding Umm Salama that her involvement in the problems of the community is her own business: "If I stay it will not be because of any restrictions [on your part]. If I leave, it will be concerning something about which I need explain no further."[37] It is indeed 'A'isha's special status as Mother of the Believers that gives her the right to act in this way and to deliver a public speech. Almost as an apology for her behavior in these events, Ibn 'Abd Rabbih is careful to include in his text a litany of her qualities, including the fact that the Prophet died in her arms, that she is one of his wives in paradise, and that Qur'anic verses descended to exonerate her from the charge of adultery.[38]

Although praised by Sunnis, 'A'isha defies categorization as absolutely positive or negative in the Muslim search for her meaning. 'A'isha is the transitional woman; her actions suggest that the legacy of *jahiliyya* was not extinguished overnight. She would remain for the Sunnis, nonetheless, a model of intelligence and an example of one who transmitted Muhammad's traditions. Indeed, it is primarily through her role as transmitter of hadith that 'A'isha is rehabilitated. About three hundred hadith transmitted through her are included in the canonical collections of al-Bukhari and Muslim al-Naysaburi. In this guise, she becomes a main source of details about the Prophet's life. Her superior knowledge and reliability were consequently established in Ibn Sa'd's biography.[39] 'A'isha, however, engages not just in the transmission of Muhammad's sayings but also in shaping the meaning that Muhammad's practice would have for later generations. In al-Bukhari's chapter on exegesis in his *Sahih,* she emerges as an exegetical authority pronouncing authoritatively on theological and ritual matters of central concern to Sunni orthodox belief.[40]

The hadith collection of al-Bukhari, moreover, devotes a special section to the superiority *(fadl)* of 'A'isha. One hadith compares her with *tharid,* a dish said to have been Muhammad's favorite food: "There are many perfect men, but there are no perfect women except Maryam bint 'Imran and Asya, the wife of Pharaoh; and the superiority *(fadl)* of 'A'isha over other women is like the superiority of *tharid* over the rest of foods."[41] Here she is made to participate in a perfect triad composed of Maryam, Asya, and

'A'isha. Linking her to these Qur'anic figures, models of purity and belief, enhanced her prestige and indirectly suggested that 'A'isha was, like Maryam and Asya, a supreme female ideal.[42]

'A'isha's image was further sanitized through the depiction of a more mature version of herself, stricken with regret over her impulsive, aggressive, and wrongful public acts. The traditional Sunni sources refrain from having others censure 'A'isha for her role at the battle of the Camel and instead present her bitterly grieving her part in it. She is reported to have spent her final days in self-recrimination, sighing that she wished she had been "a grass, a leaf, a tree, a stone, a clump of mud . . . not a thing remembered."[43] This story is corroborated by Ibn Abi Tayfur, who elaborates on the context in which the statement by 'A'isha was uttered: he says that when 'A'isha' became anxious and remorseful, people asked why she felt and behaved so when she was the Prophet's wife and the Mother of Believers. She replied that the battle of the Camel still haunted her and made her "choke," and she repeated that she wished she had died before the battle or that she were a forgotten thing *(nasyan mansiyya)*.[44]

'A'isha's wanting to be unremembered, in a moment of despair, is related in a variety of traditions. One of them makes a clear reference to the words of Mary, mother of Jesus. 'A'isha, as she was replying to 'Abdallah b. 'Abbas, who had been praising her, said, "I wish I were a thing forgotten *(nasyan mansiyya)*."[45] This is a verbatim reference to the verse that Mary utters as she is giving birth under the palm tree (Qur'an 19:23): "Would I had died ere this, and become a thing forgotten *(nasyan mansiyya)*." Mary, who aims solely to please God with complete submission, is the one who asks for nothing at all except to be utterly forgotten; this wish to be forgotten is not only a verbal acknowledgment of suffering and shame, but a form of pleading to alleviate them or expunge them from one's history, to remove them from one's own and the world's memory.[46] Al-Tabari explains these words in his exegetical work as "something that is unknown and unmentioned," as if she was saying "I wish I were the thing that was thrown away, left and forgotten," or else "I wish I had never been born and were nothing at all."[47] The later exegete Fakhr al-Din al-Razi (d. 606/1209) explains that such words—that is, the wish for annihilation—are uttered by pious people whenever they are visited by affliction. He provides the examples of the Rashidun caliphs who, at various times, expressed their unworthiness in situations of distress. Caliph 'Umar b. al-Khattab took a straw from the ground and said, "I wish I were this straw, I wish I were nothing!" And 'Ali b. Abi Talib said concerning the Day of the Camel, "I wish I had died twenty years before this day!"[48] The culture of piety was profound, and any memory of disgrace—such as recalling 'A'isha's part in battle, or remem-

bering different traumatic and unholy moments—would cause an individual to want to withdraw the pain and torment caused, as if erasing a
major scar or flaw from an otherwise near-perfect order.

In hadith and Qur'anic exegesis, 'A'isha is often compared with Mary—not
in connection with Mary's divine selection, obedience, and chastity, but
rather with regard to both women's exoneration from the accusation of
adultery.[49] In this light, 'A'isha's likeness to Mary stands out. It is, however,
the mature 'A'isha and her later wish to be forgotten that brings her closest
to the model that Mary represented.

'A'isha's involvement in the battle of the Camel is said to have irked her
in the twilight of her life, especially since that battle came to be thought of
as the first *fitna*, encapsulating the negative forces working against the unity
of the Muslims. One detects a palpable tension between the picture of 'A'isha
as self-willed and independent and her representation as submissive, con-
forming to the private and socially confined role for virtuous women as it
emerged in early Islamic society. Therefore, 'A'isha's legacy remains complex. On the one hand, she was an exemplar, a beloved and favorite wife of
the Prophet, whose model was to be emulated by Muslim women; on the
other hand, major events in her life served textually as markers that would
trigger a rift between the diverging identities of the Sunnis and the Shi'is.

Fatima, Mary, and the Search for Meaning

'A'isha's life, intersected by dramatic events, occasioned strong, though
varied, reactions and contrasts with the tempered behavior of the Prophet's daughter Fatima, who is always presented in a state of demure piety.
Sunni and Shi'i depictions of her character praise her chastity, shyness, and
obedience to her father and her husband, as well as her work ethic and her
close relation to the Prophet.[50] One of the dominant themes of Fatima's
life is her experience of grief and affliction during her early years as a wife
and mother, which were characterized by physical, emotional, and financial hardships mostly resulting from living in poverty. Another main theme
is the intimacy of her relationship with Muhammad. As Muhammad's daughter, she hears the Prophet's teachings firsthand and with great devotion.
Al-Waqidi underscores this special relationship in an anecdote connected
to the battle of Uhud: "Fatima came out with the women. She saw what
was on the face of the Prophet, embraced him and began to wipe the blood
from his face."[51] Recurring traditions stress her physical and emotional
closeness to her father. Most women would not be permitted to come
close enough to the Prophet to touch him or wipe blood from his face;

Muhammad allows Fatima to do so, as he holds her in high regard and trusts her. Muhammad perceives of Fatima as so crucial to him and the faith that he sees her in himself; she reflects his vision for the faith back at him. Al-Bukhari's *Sahih,* for instance, includes a tradition by the Prophet that states, "Fatima is part of me; whoever angers her, angers me."[52]

Muhammad acknowledges Fatima not only as his kin, but as an esteemed woman with exemplary care and regard for him and others. Another tradition, repeated in the various hadith collections, in the *Tabaqat* of Ibn Sa'd, the history of al-Tabari, and *Al-'Iqd al-farid,* has it that Fatima visited her dying father, who whispered to her once, and she cried; and then whispered to her again, and she laughed. 'A'isha said to herself that she had thought Fatima had precedence over women, but Fatima showed herself to be one among women: after the Prophet died, 'A'isha asked Fatima about her reactions while the Prophet lay dying, and Fatima replied that Muhammad had whispered to her, and so she cried in her grief. When he whispered to her a second time, he told her she would be the first to follow him to the next world, and she laughed joyfully at the idea of it.[53]

Verena Klemm has posited that the early Sunni tradition does not provide a precise characterization of Fatima's virtues. In Prophetic tradition she is compared to Qur'anic female models and is recognized as the "mistress of all women of the world" *(sayyidat nisa' al-'alamin).*[54] Her life is normally divided into two parts—before and after the death of Muhammad—and it is the second part of her life that is depicted divergently in Sunni and Shi'i sources. In the Sunni representation, she is usually portrayed as an ordinary pious woman. Her ordinariness is reflected on one level in her marriage to 'Ali, which includes quarrels and misunderstandings. Her modesty and hard work are stressed, but it is her piety that elevates her, making her one of the four perfect women of the world, the other three being Mary, Asya, and Khadija.[55]

For the Shi'is, Fatima is venerated to such a level of perfection that it becomes impossible for other Muslim women to emulate her. The Shi'i theologian and devotional writer of the fourth/tenth century Ibn Babawayh al-Qummi played a central role in the formation of the Fatima legend by turning her into the paradigm of the Islamic woman par excellence. Shi'i sources catalogue the injustices visited on Fatima, emphasizing her status as victim and her patience and endurance through suffering. In these texts she is portrayed as an archetype of the sorrowful mother present on the battlefield of Karbala' to support her soon-to-be-martyred son; as a companion to her daughters when they were in captivity; and as the perpetually present participant in every *majlis* that commemorates Husayn.[56] She epitomizes not so much a victim who endures and mourns, but rather the reliable attendant to her family and other members of her community; she represents the Islamic belief in understanding the value of forbearance and withstanding life's hardships.

In the Shi'i tradition the comparisons between Mary and Fatima as "the mistress of all women" occur ever more frequently. Both Fatima and Mary are conceived and born in a miraculous way; both are suffering mothers who experience, actually or proleptically, the violence inflicted on their sons; both are heralded as "virgins"; to both is attributed the quality of purity—that is, freedom from menstruation and bleeding at childbirth; and both have sons who are martyred and whose deaths have a cosmic meaning and bring grief and lament to their sorrowful mothers. Among the names of honor given to Fatima in later times is the Greater Mary (Maryam al-Kubra). Fatima's preeminence is, however, unchallenged: Mary is "the mistress of all women in this life"; Fatima is "the mistress in this life and the hereafter."[57] The Shi'i narrative on Fatima established countless connections between her and Mary, as they share a significant number of similarities. Mary and Fatima possess qualities that other Muslim women can never achieve, such as their positions as first among the women of the world and of paradise, and their quality of eternal purity. However, while Fatima was revered as perfect—in such a way that she could not really be considered a mimetic object—Muslim women could still aspire to Mary's ideal of purity and to Mary's embodiment of perfect obedience.[58]

By the third/ninth century, Khadija, Fatima, and 'A'isha had come to represent a distinct, exemplary vision of women. While both Sunni and Shi'i believers chose Khadija as a figure of special reverence, the most bitter divide came over the place of Fatima and 'A'isha in Islam. And while the idealization of Khadija and Fatima glorified—and hence dehumanized—them, making emulation difficult, 'A'isha's life, with its turbulence and complexity, would continue to require defense.

Sunni and Shi'i assessments of 'A'isha and Fatima reflect several divergences; they agree, however, in their appraisal of Mary. Mary is the only female identified by name in the Qur'an, as if by this unique designation she is meant to encapsulate all women. The Qur'an celebrates Mary as an example of believers (Qur'an 66:12): "And Mary, 'Imran's daughter, who guarded her virginity, so We breathed into her Our Spirit, and she confirmed the Words of her Lord and His Books, and became one of the obedient." Despite the notoriety of Khadija, 'A'isha, and Fatima in prophetic tradition, the most prominent female in the Qur'an is Mary, who stands as the primary exemplar of obedience and piety.

Religious authorities have attempted to define the facets of Mary's premier status among Muslim women. Mary's admirable qualities include self-isolation and quiet domesticity, modest comportment and near invisibility, ascetic frugality and devout obedience to God; and these are the feminine attributes that Muslim women are meant to emulate.[59] Further, Michel Dousse argues that one of the primary characteristics of the Qur'anic image of Mary is her silence. The first time she speaks, she addresses not fellow human beings but angels (Qur'an 3:47), and even when she is challenged by her people—as when she is accused of adultery—she remains silent, pointing to the child in the cradle who speaks for her, a miraculous sign signaling his mother's blamelessness.[60] Mary, as the utmost female exemplar, is hence the idolized silent and forgotten one *(nasyan mansiyya)*, the one not known and not mentioned, the one without a voice, as she herself states in the Qur'an (19:26): "I have vowed to the All-merciful a fast, and today I will not speak to any man." Thus, the Muslim female ideal is self-denial with the ultimate purpose of sacrificing one's desires for faith in God.

The mainstream Sunni sources established the centrality of Khadija, Fatima, and 'A'isha as Islamic models. The need for female religious models united them in early Muslim discussions of their superiority, but in due course distinguished them as representatives of divergent political and confessional loyalties. It is ultimately through their comparison with Mary that Khadija, 'A'isha, and Fatima were confirmed as exemplars in Islam. But taken together, one realizes that these latter three female personalities reflect an attempt to find meaning in the process of fashioning a new Muslim female identity—one that separates them from Mary, who, while exemplary, predated Muhammad's Islam.

Defining the Bounds of Early Muslim Womanhood and Beyond

Descriptions of Khadija, 'A'isha, and Fatima evolved into a Sunni-Shi'i sectarian debate about which of the three exemplifies the most esteemed woman among the first Muslims. Their representations strive to create distance from the dismal days of *jahiliyya* in which life had been immoral in its excesses and passions. As such they stand together (with the early women companions) at the point of demarcation, defining the borderlines in a transitional age. Aziz al-Azmeh attests that Islamic history occurs at two levels—that of the pious Islamic self and that of its debasement by "otherness," meaning non-Islamic peoples, heresies, and a multitude of enemies. In his understanding, time is split between origins and corruptions, leading

to a "parallel register of examples and anti-examples," perfection and debauchery, rights and wrongs, each originating from the primitive ideals of
virtue and sin.[61] In Islamic thought there exists a temporality which acknowledges the contamination of the past *(jahiliyya)* and the radical nature of change—of a new Islamic ethos carried within a new exemplary
faith, wherein a set of female archetypes from the Qur'an and the hadith
became constitutive of the utopian past order.[62]

Early Islamic discourse urged the establishment of an orderly universe
that included "anxiety-provoking issues of gender."[63] The temporal anxiety
about gender identities and relations was such that it found its way into
apocalyptic material. The canonical books of Sunni hadith contain a chapter
on *fitan* (sing. *fitna*), apocalyptic material devoted to relating prophecies
and warnings about the events that would precede the end of the world.
Fitna, a multivalent word that encapsulates negative forces at work against
the unity of Muslims, came to be intimately woven with women who were
seen as one of its major sources; *fitna,* in fact, came to signify women's destructive influence on the social order and to implicate them in the apocalyptic horror. It is noteworthy that the earliest association between women
and *fitna* occurred around the events of the battle of the Camel because of
the pivotal role 'A'isha played. In this regard, the Prophet's companion
'Ammar b. Yasir stated, "By God, she ['A'isha] is the wife of your Prophet in
this world and in the coming world; yet God has tested you with her *(ibtal-
akum biha)* so as to know whom you will obey, Him or her."[64] Thus, 'A'isha
was perceived as the first evidence of the presence of *fitna* in the female and
in the universe at large; 'A'isha, as arguably the most "human" among these
prominent female figures, served a dual role as perfect/favorite companion
and a reminder of the trials that humans have to endure.

'A'isha's part in the battle of the Camel would never be erased from Islamic memory, as that battle witnessed a rupture that ended the notion of
a unified Muslim community. That moment was seen as the first *fitna* in a
series of *fitan* that would culminate in the coming of the Hour. 'A'isha's role
in the battle of the Camel thus ensured that women were participants in
the events that would result in the Day of Judgment. Walid Saleh posits that
apocalyptic discourse was a tool that societies used to reinforce power structures and to warn of changes to the social order. In this vein, containing or
regulating women was not considered lightly; it was a matter of "cosmic
magnitude."[65]

The early Islamic sources, both religious and secular, agree on women's
place and role in society, and consequently also on women's nature. The female models in the Qur'an symbolized facets of the Islamic order and represented a means toward its preservation.[66] Ibn Shahrasub incorporates a list

of characteristics of the thirteen women that God mentioned in the Qur'an, including Eve's repentance, Asya's yearning (for a house in paradise), Sara's hospitality, Balqis's intelligence, Moses's wife's bashfulness, Khadija's beneficence, 'A'isha's advice, and Fatima's sinlessness. Another list registers the ten things that God gave to ten women: repentance to Eve, beauty to Sara, protection to Rahima (wife of Ayub), sanctity to Asya, wisdom to Zulaykha, intelligence to Balqis, patience to Burhana (mother of Moses), choice position to Maryam, contentment to Khadija, and learning to Fatima.[67] This catalogue of virtues provided an inventory of qualities that Muslim women would be expected to draw on and adopt in casting their own identities.

In addition to the Qur'anic female figures, the women who are particularly favored by God are the Prophet's wives. As the most influential women of early Islam, they were elevated as unrivaled models for Muslims. Their special status is revealed in Qur'anic legislation—in the rights, privileges, duties, and limitations imposed upon them—and they, in fact, served as the foundation for later sharia legal structures. In hadith, they are made to represent a cultural model for Muslim female morality—they are righteous, moral Muslim women of indispensable religious knowledge but who are thus "not like any other women" (Qur'an 33:32). Their actions illustrate their dedication to establishing God's order on earth by personal example. Their roles as the Prophet's helpmates and supporters in his mission, in addition to their intimate involvement with him, gained them a high level of prestige. These figures' biographies were sketched in a rhetoric of exemplarity that recorded their merits, rendering the writing not as merely regressive or historical in character, but as currently relevant and future-oriented. Their special status expanded gradually as Muslim piety came to view them as models to emulate. With time, their behavior, as recorded in the tradition, was recognized as _sunna_ that provided criteria of what was lawful or forbidden for Muslims, especially Muslim women. These traditions of the Prophet's wives (and daughter) are also read as explanations to legitimate the status quo or establish the validity of a new religio-ethical paradigm. Hadith material on their personal comportment, dress code, and performance of ritual and worship was intended to be normative or prescriptive, not merely descriptive. According to Barbara Stowasser, each recorded quality symbolizes an element of the "_sunna_-in-the-making," and taken together they embody the corpus of the female ethos developed in early Islamic law and thought.[68]

The early Muslims were required to interpret textual Islamic examples and create their new pious selves, to build and strengthen the new Islamic world. A growing body of research has suggested that people undertake such identity transformations in accordance with narratives in which they imagine themselves "emplotted": creating one's identity occurs with an individual locating oneself within a narrative—that is, seeing oneself as part of a context or story—and envisioning oneself emplotted as such. And thus individuals are driven to behave based on the memory and imagined view of themselves within that limited narrative.[69] The early Islamic women were expected to re-create themselves within the new religious order and its acceptable limits, bringing out clear distinctions between the old order and the new. They would imagine themselves in the parables of the archetypal women featured in the new Islamic scripture in order to recast their identities as compatible with their evolving context. The past would be recalled in accordance with a common repertoire of narratives that emplotted not only women exemplars but their rivals as well, for the two are inextricably entwined.

The formulation of a new order and a new identity was achieved through a demonstration of ethical opposites: of Islamic virtues that would allow the world to prosper, and the *jahiliyya* or non-Islamic principles that would lead to its destruction. As the former prevailed through the power of its persuasion, the new order would define what it meant to be a "true" Muslim. An ideal type of Muslim womanhood was constructed to symbolize key aspects of the Islamic struggle for the maintenance of the boundaries of Muslim identity. This was necessary given that human nature is always in danger of being overtaken by the primitive elements within it—in other words, reverting to *jahiliyya*. This is why the past *(jahiliyya)* needs to be constantly remembered. *Jahiliyya* is recalled, for instance, by Fatima in her one defying moment, when she requested her inheritance from the first caliph, Abu Bakr. On that singular occasion Fatima addressed Abu Bakr in the mosque while he was surrounded by the Muhajirun and the Ansar and reminded them all of the *jahiliyya* condition from which they were saved by her father, Muhammad. She quoted the Qur'anic verse (3:103): "You were upon the brink of a pit of fire and he delivered you from it."[70] Therefore, we may gather that it is up to Muslims themselves to live by this example and deliver themselves from such evil, and to incessantly discipline and transform any regressive elements. Women, hence, must continually strive against any *jahiliyya* or primal tendencies and combat any inclinations by emulating the companions of the Prophet, including the women exemplars.

The ever-present danger of backsliding to *jahiliyya* was offset by incredible success stories that served to promote and emphasize the strength of the new order; if one had faith and lived a pious life, that counteracted the *jahiliyya* in one's nature. For in spite of looming dangers, all is not hopeless, since Islam alters people. Even the relentless al-Khansa', with her persistent elegizing of her fallen brothers, was transformed. The sources state that she accompanied her four sons in the campaigns of the Muslim conquests, inciting them and reminding them of the glories that awaited them and of the heavenly reward of those martyred in religiously motivated combat:

> You may know what God has prepared for Muslims,
> A gracious reward for warring against infidels.
> Know that the everlasting abode is better than the abode that passes away.

Each of her sons advanced into the battle, uttering a few lines of poetry in response to their mother's speech, only to die one after the other. Al-Khansa's reaction to the news of their deaths reflected her conversion: she thanked God for their honorable end and asked that she be able to join them in his abiding mercy.[71]

Such narratives celebrated a massive transformation by which the pre-Islamic past, *jahiliyya,* flowed into a triumphant Muslim present. The conversion of Hind bint 'Utba, in particular, amounted to a declaration of total victory. According to Muhammad Brayghash, it is impossible for some to see the one who chewed on Hamza's liver as a truthful believer. Her tale is, however, significant, for if she manages to follow the straight path it is because Islam succeeds in enlightening the heart and the mind, and in teaching maturity, understanding, and wisdom.[72] Hind thus is the exemplar who was transformed by Islam. She is perhaps the only model of a woman who changed her position so completely. Ultimately, she herself becomes an archetype for Muslim women.

Authoritative narratives of the sacred women of the Islamic past helped Muslims to imagine their origins and to affirm their understanding of crucial moments in their past, which have helped guide their identities. Qur'an and hadith female models are not only central to religious discourse on women. Mary, Khadija, 'A'isha, and Fatima became symbols of Islamic identity in dialectic with proximate communities, including the *jahili* Arabs, the Byzantine Christians, and the sectarian Qaramita. The Qur'anic women, the Prophet's wives and other female companions, became models for emulation, their lives constituting powerful teaching devices for the faithful. They were and continue to be particularly important as models for Islamic formulations of self-identity, their meaning extending beyond Islam's origins into an eternal present.

Conclusion

IDENTITY FORMATION is integrally linked to gender relations, sexuality, and representations of women; widespread identity transformation is most prominent during historical shifts and periods of upheaval. During the early Islamic and Abbasid periods, women's identities were challenged and diverged most between religious groupings—the *jahili*s, early Muslims, Qaramita, and Byzantines—though with increasing conversions to Islam, hybrids between these communities emerged, a reflexive way of shedding one's old identity for the new. The violence, emotional temperament, and exposed sexuality of these hybrids, as well as the more unadulterated female forms of the non-Muslim communities, posed a threat to the new order, and the early *umma* sought to create—through scripture, law, and other stories and texts—a widespread narrative that served to persuade women, and the community at large, of their proper pious roles. The different female personalities and groups I have featured serve as markers of changing ideological boundaries of the Islamic "us" and the non-Muslim "them," as well as historical time posts in Muslim women's evolution.

The evolving metanarrative of the advent and victory of a distinctively Arab Islam cast the dreadful conditions of life in Arabia during *jahiliyya* in stark contrast to the civilized environment of the Islamic Empire.[1] The very continued presence of *jahiliyya* was itself instrumental in constructing, buttressing, and sharpening the social boundaries of Islam. The writings of Abbasid authors assumed the contemporaneity of *jahiliyya* along the same line that the influential twentieth-century Islamist thinker Sayyid Qutb posited, that the world he lived in was in a state of *jahiliyya*. *Jahiliyya* in this sense can be understood as an atemporal notion, as it does not refer to a past era or to a specific geographical location, but is rather a cultural, social, and spiritual condition that can exist at any time and any place. Indeed, as propounded by its modern advocate, there are only two kinds of cultures in the world: the Islamic culture and the *jahili* culture; and between them there is constant struggle, one that is ultimately between belief and unbelief, between Islamic devotion to God and *jahili* adoration of the self and bodily needs.[2] Consequently, *jahili*s are in some sense our contemporaries, the ever-present adversaries of true Muslims, who are perpetually poised between sin and salvation. *Jahiliyya* lingers and must linger, if only as that which exists as the limit line to the practices and discourses that define Islam.[3] *Jahiliyya* was a focus of Islamic ideology from the onset, acquiring new layers of meaning but remaining a main foil against which Islam and Muslims define themselves. And it was Hind bint ʿUtba, the transgressive woman whose savage excesses verged on cannibalism, who was its ultimate embodiment.

The Muslim community, in this period of great historical transition, strove to establish a new order that would realize its religio-ethical vision, replacing kinship and the power of blood relations with the principles of the new *umma*. The excessiveness of the *jahili* female lamenters would be contrasted to the controlled, quietist attitude that the women of the new faith were to follow upon the death of their loved ones. Mourning rituals served as markers in the articulation of religious identities and the evolving conceptions of Islam in its early centuries. While Muslim women were to lament their dead with controlled dignity, wailing for the dead persisted and continued to be a female occupation throughout the Abbasid and Mamluk periods; we read of professional women mourners all the way down to modern times. Hilma Granqvist collected death and burial songs in the early 1930s in Palestinian-Jordanian villages and included a statement by a dying man, Khalil, in which he said: "I forbid their women mourners coming and their lamentations. The sin is on your neck if you let them mourn me."[4] In a more recent anthropological study, Lila Abu Lughod describes a funeral in which women go to "cry with" somebody, as they perceive it as a shared experience. Crying by women, accordingly, remains the quintessential act of ritual mourning, and it "involves much more than weeping; it is a chanted lament."[5] It is in this respect that women were seen as borderline, to be controlled, where emotional impulses must be subdued or swept away by the "steady hand" of male rationality.[6]

Any narrative is built on selection and exclusion. The main difficulty in understanding the Qaramita movement lies in the scarcity of sources bearing witness to their creed and their historical origins and development; this is further problematized by the fact that historians have to rely on the views of their opponents. The story of the Qaramita was that of those marginalized and even rejected by the metanarrative in the process of creating the mainstream imagined community. This has raised a series of questions: Whose story is told? From whose perspective? Who is being silenced in order to tell it? How does one write the histories of suppressed groups? The narrative that is our only source of knowledge is one that has "imperialistically" filtered the utterances of the marginalized Qaramita, a matter that compels us to think about the nature of historical representation and the pervasive influence of the dominant epistemological framework.[7]

The Qaramita were the difference that threatened to become the same: they were hybrid figures, too close to the new order, who consequently needed to be rejected all the more strongly. This perilous and subversive blurring of boundaries provoked deep fears and anxieties, and the Qaramita had to be cast in dark contrast to make orthodoxy appear all the clearer and more attractive and to maintain the coherence of the metanarrative. Producing an orthodoxy was a main discursive formation around which early Muslim strategies of self-definition coalesced. It is noteworthy, however, that while gender and sexual symbolism are extensive in these anti-Qaramita narratives, Qaramita women as individuals are conspicuously absent. If it is the historian's task, as Gyanendra Pandey posits, "to struggle to recover 'marginal' voices and memories, forgotten dreams and signs of resistance if history is to be anything more than a celebratory account of the march of certain victorious concepts of power,"[8] then the story of the Qaramita women that we have represents a massive failure in this respect.

In trying to demarcate the world our mainstream authors inhabited, women of other cultures were also recalled and brought to bear on the Muslim male's own self-definition, as well as on the gender system he sought to protect. Byzantines represented proximate alterities within Islamic culture, as well as a historical Christian presence of which Muslims were aware and with which they interacted. For Muslim men, Byzantine women represented an inferior, erotic, and pride-wounding form of alterity, but still symbolized an enticing, attractive difference, as their beauty was superior and held the power of distraction. The Arab Muslims saw Byzantine women through a lens blurred by misinformation, misconceptions, and stereotypes. "Engaged representations" rely more significantly on the imagination of the writer and his cultural and historical context than on any detached, objective observation.[9] This imaginative approach to other cultures explains how Islamic authors could write with such confidence on the Byzantines even though almost none of them had firsthand experience of the Byzantines and their empire; and even when they did go to Byzantine lands, they drew conclusions that focused on and reinforced their own culture. These authors found Byzantium as they wanted it to be; they knew, a priori, what they would discover about it. Such preconceived "discoveries" have been brought up in connection with, among others, the nineteenth-century Egyptian work *Takhlis al-Ibriz fi Talkhis Baris* (Trip to Paris in 1827), in which Rifa'a al-Tahtawi does not present an accurate geography of Paris but one whose comparison draws on the geography of Alexandria or Cairo. Al-Tahtawi's depiction was merely an occasion to emphasize the self; more importantly, it is al-Tahtawi's trip to Paris that drives him to return home.[10]

The Islamic writers return to uphold their most prominent female figures as powerful feminine prototypes who remain crucial for contemporary Muslim practice and politics. Crafting women as exemplars, in Islam's formative phase, also served to focus the debate and determine the nuances of Islamic identity. The female companions of the Prophet enjoy the position of *al-salaf al-salih* (the pious predecessors) and have been regarded as moral exemplars of the *umma*. Details of the lives of these women remain centrally constitutive both to traditionalist discourse and to contemporary Muslim women who revisit them in their search for empowering models and alternative ideas of gender roles.[11]

My study has examined how female identities were represented and constructed in the Abbasid sources that sought to depict and direct them. The historical communities—*jahili,* Islamic, Qaramita, and Byzantine—that I have highlighted in this inquiry are not entities, but rather collectivities that come into being through the very narratives that seek to invoke them. The formation of communal memory is a "reconfiguration" reflecting shared and present experiences and future expectations of a particular group. Thus, "remembering" is not a matter of recall, but a retrospective reconstruction of traditions so that the present can be better understood in light of its past and so that a sense of continuity between the present and the past can thus be achieved.[12]

The gender-based representations of groups and identities that we encounter in the Abbasid texts constitute a master narrative that seeks to discipline and assimilate difference. Creating a dominantly negative image of other groups in compelling textual form was an effective way of shaping Muslim collective identity(ies). The texts reflected a prevailing ideology and contributed to the dominant discourse by shaping, selecting, and confirming cultural constructs governing mental and social life through limited representations of women, gender, and sexuality. But the lesson of examining the narratives on early Muslim women and those of the surrounding communities is clear: the process of deconstructing identity formation, particularly during an intense transitional period of history, reveals the insight that the metanarrative of an emerging or existent faith or society seeks to define the limits of both ideological affiliations and identities and is also, in part, redefined and reformed by an evolving social context and temporal ethos.

Notes

Introduction

1. Muhammad b. Habib, *Kitab al-muhabbar* (Haydarabad, 1942), 184–188; translation and discussion of this passage in A. F. L. Beeston, "The So-Called Harlots of Hadramaut," *Oriens* 5 (1952): 16–22. Dates are provided in both forms, the Muslim date preceding the Common Era date.
2. G. R. Hawting, *The Idea of Idolatry and the Emergence of Islam: From Polemic to History* (Cambridge, 1999), 99–100. Peter Webb has identified four archetypal topoi that are emblematic of pre-Islamic Arabian society: idol worship, tyranny/injustice, ritual killing of infant girls, and the violence of tribal antagonisms. In "*Al-Jahiliyya*: Uncertain Times of Uncertain Meanings," *Der Islam* 9 (2014): 69–94.
3. Michael Cook, *Forbidding Wrong in Islam: An Introduction* (Cambridge, 2003), 3; see also Thomas Sizgorich, "Your Brothers, the Romans: Early Islamic History as a Turn of the Classical Page in Early Muslim Thought and Literature," in *The Rhetoric of Power in Late Antiquity: Religion and Politics in Byzantium, Europe and the Early Islamic World,*" ed. Robert M. Frakes et al. (London, 2010), 101–123. Translations of Qur'anic verses are, throughout this book, by Arthur J. Arberry, *The Koran Interpreted* (Oxford, 1983).
4. 'Abdallah al-Azdi al-Basri, *Futuh al-Sham,* ed. W. N. Lees (Calcutta, 1854), 182–183.
5. Chase F. Robinson, "The Rise of Islam, 600–705," in *The New Cambridge History of Islam,* vol. 1, *The Formation of the Islamic World, Sixth to Eleventh Centuries,* ed. Chase F. Robinson (Cambridge, 2011), 171–225.
6. Roy Mottahedeh, *Loyalty and Leadership in an Early Islamic Society* (London, 2001), 7–16.

7. Farhad Daftary, "Diversity in Islam," in *Isma'ilis in Medieval Muslim Societies* (London, 2005), 1–26.

8. Tayeb El-Hibri, *Reinterpreting Islamic Historiography: Harun al-Rashid and the Narrative of the Abbasid Caliphate* (Cambridge, 1999), 1.

9. Tayeb El-Hibri, "The Empire in Iraq, 763–861," in *New Cambridge History of Islam,* 1:269–304.

10. Judith Tucker, "Gender and Islamic History," in *Islamic and European Expansion: The Forging of a Global Order,* ed. Michael Adas (Philadelphia, 1993), 37–73. See also Elizabeth Thompson, "The Gendered Edge of Islam," in *Views from the Edge: Essays in Honor of Richard W. Bulliet,* ed. Neguin Yavari, Lawrence G. Potter, and Jean-Marc Ran Oppenheim (New York, 2004), 304–321; and Amira El-Azhary Sonbol, "Rethinking Women and Islam," in *Daughters of Abraham: Feminist Thought in Judaism, Christianity, and Islam,* ed. Yvonne Yazbeck Haddad and John L. Esposito (Gainesville, FL, 2001), 108–146.

11. Abdelwahab Bouhdiba, *La sexualité en Islam* (Paris, 1986), 131; Leila Ahmed, *Women and Gender in Islam: Historical Roots of a Modern Debate* (New Haven, CT, 1992); Julia Bray, "Men, Women and Slaves in Abbasid Society," in *Gender in the Early Medieval World, East and West,* ed. Leslie Brubaker and Julia M. H. Smith (Cambridge, 2004), 121–146; and Ira M. Lapidus, *Islamic Societies to the Nineteenth Century: A Global History* (Cambridge, 2012), 181–192. Kecia Ali contends that the use of analogy between marriage and slavery is key to understanding Muslim marriage law; Ali, *Marriage and Slavery in Early Islam* (Cambridge, MA, 2010).

12. In imitation of Alexander Kazhdan's "Homo Byzantinus." See A. P. Kazhdan and Giles Constable, *People and Power in Byzantium: An Introduction to Modern Byzantine Studies* (Washington, DC, 1982).

13. Abu al-Faraj al-Isfahani, *Al-Diyarat,* ed. Jalil al-'Atiyya (London, 1991), 48–52. This work belongs to the genre of *diyarat* (monasteries), a literary genre that narrates meetings between Muslims and Christians within the confines of Christian monasteries populated by desirable women, and whose seduction by Muslim men provides the exoticizing tendencies of these texts. See Thomas Sizgorich, "Monks and Their Daughters: Monasteries as Muslim Christian Boundaries," in *Muslims and Others in Sacred Space,* ed. Margaret Cormack (Oxford, 2013), 193–211.

14. See Tamara L. Hunt, introduction to *Women and the Colonial Gaze,* ed. Tamara L. Hunt and Micheline R. Lessard (New York, 2002), 1–14; Kathleen Davis, "Time behind the Veil: The Media, the Middle Ages, and Orientalism," in *The Postcolonial Middle Ages,* ed. Jeffrey Jerome Cohen (New York, 2000), 105–122; Tamar Mayer, *Gender Ironies of Nationalism: Sexing the Nation,* ed. Tamar Mayer (London, 2000), 1–22.

15. Manuela Marin, "Women, Gender and Sexuality," in *The New Cambridge History of Islam,* vol. 4, *Islamic Cultures and Societies to the End of the Eighteenth Century,* ed. Robert Irwin (Cambridge, 2010), 355–377.

16. In addition to Bouhdiba, *La sexualité,* see Bassim Musallam, *Sex and Society in Islam: Birth Control before the Nineteenth Century* (Cambridge, 1986);

Sahar Amer, "Medieval Arab Lesbians and Lesbian-Like Women," *Journal of the History of Sexuality* 18 (2009): 215–236; Sara Omar, "From Semantics to Normative Law: Perceptions of *Liwat* (Sodomy) and *Sihaq* (Tribadism) in Islamic Jurisprudence (8th–15th Century CE)," *Islamic Law and Society* 19 (2012): 222–256. On homoeroticism, see Everett K. Rowson, "The Traffic in Boys: Slavery and Homoerotic Liaisons in Elite Abbasid Society," *Middle Eastern Literatures* 11 (2008): 193–204.

17. Kathryn Babayan and Afsaneh Najmabadi, eds., *Islamicate Sexualities: Translations across Temporal Geographies of Desire* (Cambridge, MA, 2008); Afsaneh Najmabadi, *Women with Mustaches and Men without Beards: Gender and Sexual Anxieties of Iranian Modernity* (Berkeley, 2005). See also Dror Ze'evi, *Producing Desire: Changing Sexual Discourse in the Ottoman Middle East* (Berkeley, 2006).

18. Marin, "Women, Gender and Sexuality"; Marilyn Booth, "New Directions in Middle East Women's and Gender History," *Journal of Colonialism and Colonial History* 4, no. 1 (2003), http://muse.jhu.edu/journals/journal_of_colonialism _and_colonial_history/v004/4.1booth.html; Margaret L. Meriwether and Judith Tucker, introduction to *Social History of Women and Gender in the Modern Middle East* (Oxford, 1999), 1–24.

19. Julie Scott Meisami, "Writing Medieval Women: Representations and Misrepresentations," in *Writing and Representation in Medieval Islam: Muslim Horizons*, ed. Julia Bray (London, 2006), 47–87. For the use of literary critical methods in the study of medieval Islamic historiography, see also her "Mas'udi and the Reign of al-Amin: Narrative and Meaning in Medieval Muslim Historiography," in *On Fiction and Adab in Medieval Arabic Literature*, ed. Philip Kennedy (Wiesbaden, 2005), 149–176.

20. Jo Ann McNamara, "*De quibusdam mulieribus*: Reading Women's History from Hostile Sources," in *Medieval Women and the Sources of Medieval History*, ed. Joel T. Rosenthal (Athens, GA, 1990), 239. See also Janet Nelson, "Family, Gender and Sexuality in the Middle Ages," in *Companion to Historiography*, ed. Michael Bentley (London, 1997), 153–176.

21. Albrecht Classen, "Introduction: The Self, the Other, and Everything in Between: Xenological Phenomenology of the Middle Ages," in *Meeting the Foreign in the Middle Ages*, ed. Albrecht Classen (London, 2002), xvi.

22. Thomas Sizgorich, *Violence and Belief in Late Antiquity: Militant Devotion in Christianity and Islam* (Philadelphia, 2009), 241; see also Fred Donner, *Narratives of Islamic Origins: The Beginnings of Islamic Historical Writing* (Princeton, NJ, 1998), 112–118.

23. R. Stephen Humphreys, *Mu'awiya ibn Abi Sufyan: From Arabia to Empire* (Oxford, 2006), 17–18.

24. Marlé Hammond, *Beyond Elegy: Classical Arabic Women's Poetry in Context* (Oxford, 2010), 10; Antoine Borrut, *Entre mémoire et pouvoir: L'espace syrien sous les derniers Omeyyades et premiers Abbasides (v. 72–193/692–809)* (Leiden, 2011), 3–4.

25. Donner, *Narratives,* 125.

26. Sizgorich, *Violence and Belief,* 165.

27. Antoine Borrut, "Vanishing Syria: Periodization and Power in Early Islam," *Der Islam* 91 (2014): 37–68.

28. This is visible in El-Hibri's analysis of the history of the Rashidun, where he shows that the Abbasid texts addressed political, moralistic, religious, and legalistic themes that mattered above all to Abbasid society in the first half of the third/ninth century. Tayeb El-Hibri, *Parable and Politics in Early Islamic History* (New York, 2010), x, 18–23.

29. Richard Miles, "Introduction: Constructing Identities in Late Antiquity," in *Constructing Identities in Late Antiquity,* ed. Richard Miles (London, 1999), 1–15.

30. Sheila Fisher and Janet E. Halley, "The Lady Vanishes: The Problem of Women's Absence in Late Medieval and Renaissance Texts," in *Seeking the Woman in Late Medieval and Renaissance Writings: Essays in Feminist Contextual Criticism,* ed. Sheila Fisher and Janet E. Halley (Knoxville, TN, 1989), 1–17; Tova Rosen, *Unveiling Eve: Reading Gender in Medieval Hebrew Literature* (Philadelphia, 2003), 21.

31. The material of early hadith included individual reports on legal injunctions, ethical conduct, eschatology, rituals, the virtues of individual tribes, biographical fragments, the Prophet's expeditions, correct manners, admonitions, and homilies. Tarif Khalidi discusses the origins, mode of transmission, and authenticity of hadith in *Arabic Historical Thought in the Classical Period* (Cambridge, 1994), 17–28. See also Michael Cooperson and Shawkat M. Toorawa, introduction to *Dictionary of Literary Biography,* vol. 311, *Arabic Literary Culture, 500–925,* ed. Michael Cooperson and Shawkat Toorawa (Detroit, 2005), xvii–xxiv.

32. Chase Robinson, *Islamic Historiography* (Cambridge, 2003), 35–36; and more recently, Chase Robinson, "Islamic Historical Writing, Eighth through the Tenth Centuries," in *The Oxford History of Historical Writing,* vol. 2, *400–1400,* ed. Sarah Foot and Chase Robinson (Oxford, 2012), 238–266. See also Donner, *Narratives,* 130.

33. Muhammad Qasim Zaman, *Religion and Politics under the Abbasids: The Emergence of the Proto-Sunni Elite* (Leiden, 1997), 20.

34. Gabriel Said Reynolds, "'Abd al-Jabbar," in *Christian-Muslim Relations: A Bibliographical History,* 6 vols., ed. David Thomas and Alex Mallett (Leiden, 2010), 2:604–609.

35. S. A. Bonebakker, "Adab and the Concept of Belles-Lettres," in *The Cambridge History of Arabic Literature: Abbasid Belles-Lettres,* ed. Julia Ashtiani et al. (Cambridge, 1990), 16–30. Julia Bray states that *adab* represents "the link between literature and living"; Bray, "Arabic Literature," in *New Cambridge History of Islam,* 4:383–412. Bilal Orfali has opined that while *adab* is a term that resists precise definition, there seems to be a general agreement that "moral and social upbringing, intellectual education, and entertainment are key ingredients of *adab*"; Orfali, "A Sketch Map of Arabic Poetry Anthologies up to the Fall of Baghdad," *Journal of Arabic Literature* 43 (2012): 29–59.

36. Jacqueline de Weever, *Sheba's Daughters: Whitening and Demonizing the Saracen Woman in Medieval French Epic* (New York, 1998), xvii.

37. Louise Mirrer, *Women, Jews, and Muslims in the Texts of Reconquest Castille* (Ann Arbor, 1996), 2.

1. Hind bint ʿUtba

1. Jacqueline Chabbi, "La representation du passé aux premiers âges de l'historiographie caliphale: Problèmes de lecture et de méthode," in *Intinéraires d'Orient: Hommages à Claude Cahen,* ed. Raoul Curiel and Rika Gyselen (Bures-sur-Yvette, 1995), 21–47.

2. El-Hibri, *Reinterpreting Islamic Historiography,* 13; and El-Hibri, *Parable and Politics,* 22, 43.

3. Hawting, *Idea of Idolatry,* 2.

4. Chase F. Robinson, "Reconstructing Early Islam: Truth and Consequences," in *Method and Theory in the Study of Islamic Origins,* ed. Herbert Berg (Leiden, 2003), 101–134.

5. Andrew Rippin, *Muslims: Their Religious Beliefs and Practices* (London, 2005), 18.

6. John Dagenais and Margaret R. Greer, "Decolonizing the Middle Ages: Introduction," *Journal of Medieval and Early Modern Studies* 30 (2000): 431–448.

7. Edward Said, *Orientalism* (New York, 1978), 55.

8. Henri Lammens, *L'Arabie occidentale avant l'hégire* (Beirut, 1928), 124.

9. William Muir, *The Caliphate: Its Rise, Decline and Fall* (London, 1891), reprinted in *Orientalism: Early Sources,* 12 vols., ed. Bryan S. Turner (London, 2000), 3:165.

10. Abu Jaʿfar al-Tabari, *Tarik al-rusul wa al-muluk,* 8 vols., ed. M. J. de Goeje (Leiden, 1964), first series, 3:1348–1349; W. Montgomery Watt and M. V. McDonald, trans., *The History of al-Tabari: The Foundation of the Community,* 40 vols. (Albany, 1987–2007), 7:75.

11. Al-Waqidi, *Kitab al-maghazi,* 3 vols., ed. Marsden Jones (Oxford, 1966), 1:121, 124. See also Fr. Buhl, "Hind Bint ʿUtba b. Rabiʿa," *Encyclopaedia of Islam,* 2nd ed.

12. In Mohamed Abdesselem, *Le thème de la mort dans la poésie arabe des origines à la fin du III/IX siècle* (Tunis, 1977), 220.

13. Ibn Hisham, *Al-Sira al-nabawiyya,* 4 vols., ed. Mustafa al-Saqqa, Ibrahim al-Abyari, and ʿAbd al-Hafiz Shalabi (Beirut, n.d.), 3–4:39, translation from A. Guillaume, *The Life of Muhammad* (London, 1955), 358. See also Abu al-Faraj al-Isfahani, *Kitab al-aghani,* 20 vols. (Bulaq, 1868–1869), 4:34–35.

14. The poetic genre of *marathi* subsumes the overwhelming majority of women's compositions preserved in the classical canon of Arabic literary heritage. See Clarissa C. Burt, "Al-Khansaʾ," *Dictionary of Literary Biography,* 311:256–261. According to Alan Jones, there were many women who turned to poetry to express their feelings at the death of a loved one although they had never ventured to try to compose poetry before; Jones, *Early Arabic Poetry,* 2 vols. (Oxford, 1992–1996), 1:51.

15. Suzanne P. Stetkevych, "The Generous Eye/I and the Poetics of Redemption: An Elegy by al-Fariʿah b. Shaddad al-Murriyah," in *Literary Heritage of Classical*

Islam: Arabic and Islamic Studies in Honor of James Bellamy, ed. Mustansir Mir (Princeton, NJ, 1993), 85–105.

16. The women listed in al-Tabari are Hind bint 'Utba, Umm Hakim bint al-Harith, Fatima bint al-Walid, Rayth bint Munnabih, Sulafa bint Sa'd, Khunas bint Malik, and 'Amra bint 'Alqama. Al-Tabari, *Tarikh,* first series, 3:1385–1386; Ibn Hisham, *Al-Sira,* 3–4:62.

17. Al-Tabari, *Tarikh,* first series, 3:1400; translation from Watt and McDonald, *History of al-Tabari,* 7:118. Ibn Hisham, *Al-Sira,* 3–4:68.

18. Ibn Hisham, *Al-Sira,* 3–4:61–62.

19. Ibid., 3–4:69.

20. Ibid., 3–4:91, translation from Guillaume, *Life of Muhammad,* 385. Ibn Sa'd, *Al-Tabaqat al-Kubra,* 8 vols. (Beirut: Dar Sader, n.d.), 3:10; al-Tabari, *Tarikh,* first series, 3:1415; Ahmad al-Ya'qubi, *Tarikh,* 2 vols. (Beirut, 1980), 2:47. According to Maxime Rodinson, the Arabs regarded the liver as an especially precious part of the body. To chew the liver of an enemy would seem to mean annihilation or the highest curse; Rodinson, "Kabid," *Encyclopaedia of Islam,* 2nd ed.

21. Al-Tabari, *Tarikh,* first series, 3:1415–1416.

22. Ibn Hisham, *Al-Sira,* 3–4:91–92, translation from Guillaume, *Life of Muhammad,* 385.

23. Ibn Hisham, *Al-Sira,* 3–4:92, translation from Guillaume, *Life of Muhammad,* 386.

24. Al-Tabari, *Tarikh,* first series, 3:1416–1417; translation from Watt and McDonald, *History of al-Tabari,* 7:130. Ibn Hisham, *Al-Sira,* 3–4:92–93. *Kitab al-aghani* reproduces the events at Uhud and Hind's role in them in volume 14, pages 11–25.

25. Ibn Sa'd, *Tabaqat,* 8:237.

26. Al-Ya'qubi, *Tarikh,* 2:59–60; Ibn Sa'd, *Tabaqat,* 2:136.

27. *Encyclopaedia of Islam,* 2nd ed., s.v. "Djahiliyya."

28. Sayed Khatab states that the concept of *jahiliyya* has been the subject of controversy centering on two issues, namely, its meaning and its referent. See Khatab, *The Political Thought of Sayyid Qutb: The Theory of Jahiliyyah* (London, 2006), 10.

29. S. Pines, "Jahiliyya and 'Ilm," *Jerusalem Studies in Arabic and Islam* 13 (1990): 175–194. See also Frank Rosenthal, *Knowledge Triumphant: The Concept of Knowledge in Medieval Islam* (Leiden, 1970), 33, where he states that "there is nothing to indicate in the Qur'anic passages that *jahiliyyah* signifies . . . a definite 'period of ignorance' or a well-defined 'paganism.' All they say is that there is or was *jahiliyyah,* meaning, perhaps[,] 'ignorant persons' who spoke and acted contrary to what Muhammad considered the right way of thinking and behavior." Paul Webb also confirms that the Qur'an's *jahiliyya* is a moral state of being without a specific temporal aspect, the citations conveying the disquiet and ignorance of nonbelievers in contrast with the repose of the believers; Webb, "*Al-Jahiliyya:* Uncertain Times of Uncertain Meanings."

30. Webb, "*Al-Jahiliyya:* Uncertain Times of Uncertain Meanings."

31. Ibn Manzur, *Lisan al-'arab,* 6 vols. (Beirut, n.d.), 5:130.

32. Khatab, *Political Thought of Sayyid Qutb,* 26.

33. Charles Pellat, "Concept of *Hilm* in Islamic Ethics," in *Etudes sur l'histoire socio-culturelle de l'islam (VII–XVe s.)* (London, 1976), ix.

34. Khatab, *Political Thought of Sayyid Qutb,* 22.

35. Ignaz Goldziher, "What Is Meant by al-Jahiliyya," in *Muslim Studies,* ed. S. M. Stern, trans. C. R. Barker and S. M. Stern (New Brunswick, NJ, 2006), 201–208. Toshihiko Izutsu has likewise proposed that *jahiliyya* meant "the keenest sense of tribal honor, the unyielding spirit of rivalry and arrogance, and all the rough and rude practices coming from an extremely passionate temper"; Izutsu, *Ethico-religious Concepts in the Qur'an* (Montreal, 2002), 29.

36. Izutsu, *Ethico-religious Concepts in the Qur'an,* 29.

37. Ibn Hisham, *Al-Sira,* 1–2:336; translation from Guillaume, *Life of Muhammad,* 151.

38. Ibn Hisham, *Al-Sira,* 1–2:336; translation from Guillaume, *Life of Muhammad,* 151. The companion of the Prophet, al-Mughira b. Shu'ba, describes their pre-Islamic condition in the following way: "We used to eat carcasses, lizards, hedgehogs and the like . . . we did not know the permissible and we did not reject the unlawful until God almighty sent us our Prophet Muhammad . . . through whom he made us aware of *jahala.*" In Ibn A'tham al-Kufi, *Kitab al-futuh,* 8 vols., ed. Muhammad Khan (Hyderabad, 1968), 1:199.

39. Geraldine Heng, "Cannibalism, the First Crusade, and the Genesis of Medieval Romance," *Differences* 19 (1998): 98–174.

40. Khalidi, *Arabic Historical Thought,* 88, 97.

41. Sizgorich, "Your Brothers, the Romans."

42. Rina Drory, "The Abbasid Construction of the Jahiliyya: Cultural Authority in the Making," *Studia Islamica* 83 (1996): 22–49.

43. Robert Hoyland, *Arabia and the Arabs: From the Bronze Age to the Coming of Islam* (London, 2001), 10–13, 32, 245–246.

44. Drory, "Abbasid Construction of the Jahiliyya."

45. Leor Halevi, *Muhammad's Grave: Death Rites and the Making of Islamic Society* (New York, 2007), 125.

46. Maqbul al-Ni'ma, *Al-Marathi al-shi'riyya fi sadr al-islam* (Beirut, 1997), 30. See also Alford T. Welch, "Death and Dying in the Qur'an," in *Religious Encounters with Death,* ed. Frank E. Reynolds and Earle H. Waugh (London, 1973), 183–199.

47. Muhammad al-Azraqi, *Akhbar Makka,* 4 vols., ed. Ferdinand Wustenfeld (Beirut, 1964), 1:481.

48. Suzanne Stetkevych, *The Mute Immortals Speak: Pre-Islamic Poetry and the Poetics of Ritual* (Ithaca, NY, 1993), 202.

49. Ibn Hisham, *Al-Sira,* 3–4:91; translation from Guillaume, *Life of Muhammad,* 385. These verses are attributed in Ibn Abi Tahir Tayfur to Arwa bint al-Harith. Abu al-Fadl Ahmad b. Abi Tahir Tayfur, *Kitab balaghat al-nisa',* ed. Barakat Habbud (Sayda, 2000), 46. See also Nancy N. Roberts, "Voice and Gender in Classical Arabic Adab: Three Passages from Ahmad Tayfur's 'Instances of the Eloquence of Women,'" *Al-'Arabiyya* 25 (1992): 51–72; and Stetkevych, *Mute Immortals Speak,* 202–205.

50. Ibn Hisham, *Al-Sira,* 3–4:971; translation from Guillaume, *Life of Muhammad,* 387.

51. Al-Tabari, *Tarikh,* first series, 3:1420–1421.

52. Ibid., 3:1421. While al-Tabari, in his exegetical work, does not mention Hind bint 'Utba in his commentary of this verse, the Shi'i scholar al-Tabarsi refers to her and to her actions: "She took his liver and chewed on it." Abu 'Ali al-Fadl al-Tabarsi, *Majma' al-bayan li usul al-qur'an,* 10 vols. (Cairo, 1972), 6:243.

53. Ruth Morse, *Truth and Convention in the Middle Ages: Rhetoric, Representation, and Reality* (Cambridge, 1991), 17. Heretics in the Latin West in the eleventh and twelfth centuries were accused of cannibalism. See De Weever, *Sheba's Daughters,* 68–69.

54. Ibn Sa'd, *Tabaqat,* 3:12–13.

55. Johannes Fabian, *Time and the Other: How Anthropology Makes Its Object* (New York, 1983), 75.

56. Bettina Bildhauer and Robert Mills, "Introduction: Conceptualizing the Monstrous," in *The Monstrous Middle Ages* (Cardiff, 2003), 1–27; Ian N. Wood, "Where the Wild Things Are," in *Visions of Community in the Post-Roman World: The West, Byzantium and the Islamic World, 300–1100,* ed. Walter Pohl, Clemens Gantner, and Richard Payne (Burlington, VT, 2012), 531–542. The region holding back Gog and Magog, at the edge of the Abbasid state, represented in later geographical writings a liminal space, on the frontiers of the marvelous and the apocalyptic. See Travis Zadeh, *Mapping Frontiers across Medieval Islam: Geography, Translation, and the Abbasid Empire* (London, 2011), 70.

57. Sizgorich, *Violence and Belief,* 129.

58. J. Rives develops this analysis by categorizing Christians and pagans in "Human Sacrifice among Pagans and Christians," *Journal of Roman Studies* 85 (1995): 65–85.

59. G. R. Hawting, *The First Dynasty of Islam* (Carbondale, IL, 1987), 17. According to Patricia Crone, the hostility of the sources against the Umayyads reflects Abbasid prejudice. However, the denunciation of the Umayyads as mere kings—and not caliphs—began perhaps in Iraq in the mid-Umayyad period when Umayyad government became openly authoritarian and when scholars hostile to the regime emerged. Crone, *God's Rule: Government in Islam* (New York, 2004), 44.

60. Antoine Borrut, "La 'memoria' Omeyyade: Les Omeyyades entre souvenir et oubli dans les sources narratives islamiques," in *Umayyad Legacies,* ed. Paul Cobb and Antoine Borrut (Leiden, 2010), 26–61; Borrut, *Entre mémoire et pouvoir,* 79, 98.

61. Hawting, *First Dynasty of Islam,* 11.

62. Humphreys, *Mu'awiya ibn Abi Sufyan,* 1–3; see also Aram Shahin, "In Defense of Mu'awiya ibn Abi Sufyan: Treatises and Monographs on Mu'awiya from the Eighth to the Nineteenth Centuries," in *The Lineaments of Islam: Studies in Honor of Fred Donner,* ed. Paul M. Cobb (Leiden, 2012), 177–208.

63. Al-Tabari, *Tarikh,* first series, 3:1418.

64. Ibn Sa'd, *Tabaqat,* 2:135.

65. R. Stephen Humphreys, "Qur'anic Myth and Narrative Structure in Early Islamic Historiography," in *Tradition and Innovation in Late Antiquity,* ed. F. M. Clover and R. S. Humphreys (Madison, WI, 1989), 271–280; al-Tabari, *Tarikh,* first series, 3:2166–2177; translation from Franz Rosenthal, *The History of al-Tabari: The Return of the Caliphate to Baghdad,* 40 vols. (Albany, 1987–2007), 38:48–63.

66. Humphreys, *Mu'awiya ibn Abi Sufyan,* 3–4.

67. 'Ali b. al-Husayn al-Mas'udi, *Muruj al-dhahab wa ma'adin al-jawhar,* 7 vols., ed. Charles Pellat (Beirut, 1965–1979), 3:171.

68. Ibn Sa'd, *Tabaqat,* 8:40. Umama was the daughter of the Prophet's daughter Zaynab.

69. Wilfred Madelung, "The Sufyani between Tradition and History," *Studia Islamica* 63 (1984): 5–48.

70. Ibn 'Abd Rabbih, *Al-'Iqd al-Farid,* 7 vols., ed. Ahmad Amin, Ahmad al-Zayn, and Ibrahim al-Abiyari (Cairo, 1940–1953), 4:16–17.

71. Ibn Sa'd, *Tabaqat,* 8:249–255. The Prophet instructed Asma' to receive her mother and accept her gift, and a verse descended on this occasion. See also 'Ali al-Ghazzawi, *Marwiyyat Asma' bint Abi Bakr fi al-kutub al-tis'a* (Beirut, 2011); and Uri Bitan, "Asma' Dhat al-Nitaqayn and the Politics of Mythical Motherhood," *Jerusalem Studies in Arabic and Islam* 35 (2008): 141–166. Asma' was the mother of the late first/seventh-century anti-caliph 'Abdallah b. al-Zubayr, and her image is also manipulated in ways to build the image of her son.

72. Citation and translation in Wilfred Madelung, *The Succession to Muhammad: A Study of the Early Caliphate* (Cambridge, 1997), 184.

73. Ibn 'Abd Rabbih, *Al-'Iqd,* 2:287. Anecdote also in Ibn Abi Tahir Tayfur, *Kitab balaghat al-nisa',* 167–168.

74. Ibn 'Abd Rabbih, *Al-'Iqd,* 1:14.

75. Ibn Sa'd, *Tabaqat,* 8:237.

76. Borrut, "La 'memoria' Omeyyade"; and Khalidi, *Arabic Historical Thought,* 111.

77. Tayeb El-Hibri, "The Redemption of Umayyad Memory by the Abbasids," *Journal of Near Eastern Studies* 61 (2002): 241–265; Syafiq Mughni, "Hanbali Movements in Baghdad from Abu Muhammad al-Barbahari (d. 329/941) to Abu Ja'far al-Hashimi (d. 470/1077)" (PhD diss., University of California, Los Angeles, 1990), 219; and Henri Laoust, *La profession de foi d'Ibn Batta: Traditioniste et jurisconsulte musulman d'école hanbalite* (Damascus, 1958), 66.

78. Al-Tabari, *Tarikh,* first series, 3:418; translation from Watt and McDonald, *History of al-Tabari,* 7:131.

79. Al-Waqidi, *Kitab al-maghazi,* 1:297; translation from Rizwi Faizer, ed. and trans., *The Life of Muhammad: Al-Waqidi's "Kitab al-Maghazi"* (London, 2011), 144.

80. See Nadia Maria El Cheikh, "Muhammad and Heraclius: A Study in Legitimacy," *Studia Islamica* 89 (1999): 5–21.

81. Ibn Sa'd, *Tabaqat,* 8:235–236; Ibn 'Abd Rabbih, *Al-'Iqd,* 6:87–88. Christian Decobert emphasizes that the tradition outlines a subtle description of Abu

Sufyan, representing him as a man of reason, a leader who succeeds in negotiating a peaceful capitulation of Mecca to the forces of the Prophet Muhammad
with the consequent rewards for his realistic policies. Christian Decobert,
"Notule sur le patrimonialisme Omeyade," in Cobb and Borrut, *Umayyad
Legacies,* 213–252.

82. Ibn Saʻd, *Tabaqat,* 8:99. See Nabia Abbott, "Women and the State in Early
Islam," *Journal of Near Eastern Studies* 1 (1942): 106–126; and Nabia Abbott, *Aishah, the Beloved of Muhammad* (London, 1985), 39–40.

83. Ibn ʻAsakir, *Tarikh Dimashq al-kabir,* 72 vols., ed. ʻAli al-Janubi (Beirut, 2001),
61:45. See Humphreys, *Muʻawiya ibn Abi Sufyan,* 40.

84. Ibn Saʻd, *Tabaqat,* 8:236–237.

85. Ibn ʻAsakir, *Tarikh Dimashq,* 73:132.

86. Muhammad al-Bukhari, *Sahih,* ed. Mahmud Muhammad Nassar (Beirut,
2009), #3,825.

87. Ibid. Also in al-Baladhuri, *Futuh al-buldan,* ed. ʻAbdallah Anis al-Tabbaʻ and
ʻUmar Anis al-Tabbaʻ(Beirut, 1957), 184.

88. Pellat, "Concept of *Hilm* in Islamic Ethics."

89. Humphreys, *Muʻawiya ibn Abi Sufyan,* 10, 19, 130–131. Maya Yazigi has stated
that, in the process of extolling his *hilm,* the accounts of the women delegates
to Muʻawiya were used as historiographical tools to stress the wisdom of
Muʻawiya and further reinforce the topos about him; Yazigi, "Some Accounts
of Women Delegates to Caliph Muʻawiya: Political Significance," *Arabica* 52
(2005): 437–449.

90. Pseudo-Jahiz, *Al-Mahasin wa al-addad* (Beirut, n. d.), 322.

91. Ibn ʻAbd Rabbih, *Al-ʻIqd,* 6:87; Pseudo-Jahiz, *Al-Mahasin wa al-addad,* 223;
al-Isfahani, *Kitab al-aghani,* 8:50–51.

92. The community recorded the incident as an ex post facto divine triumph, and
in Sunni sources ʻAʼisha retained the epithet *al-mubarraʼa,* the vindicated. The
story of Susanna in the Old Testament similarly focuses on a woman falsely
accused of adultery who is saved by Daniel with the help of God. D. A. Spellberg, *Politics, Gender, and the Islamic Past: The Legacy of ʻAʼisha bint Abi Bakr*
(New York, 1994), 64, 74–75.

93. Renate Jacobi, "Udhri," *Encyclopaedia of Islam,* 2nd ed.

94. Al-Isfahani, *Kitab al-aghani,* 8:48–50 and 19:104–105; Renate Jacobi, "Portät
einer unsympatischen Frau: Hind bint ʻUtba, die Feindin Mohammeds,"
Wiener Zeitschrift fur die Kunde des Morgenlandes 89 (1999): 85–107.

95. Sizgorich, "Your Brothers, the Romans."

96. Antoine Borrut and Paul M. Cobb, "Introduction: Towards a History of
Umayyad Legacies," in Cobb and Borrut, *Umayyad Legacies,* 1–22. Paul Cobb
has mentioned that Syrian sympathy with the Umayyad house was remark-
ably tenacious in the Abbasid period and that for many Syrians the Umayyad
past was a golden age; Cobb, *White Banners: Contention in Abbasid Syria,
750–880* (Albany, 2001), 51–52.

97. The terms "too much" and "too-muchness" are borrowed from Mohja Kahf,
*Western Representations of the Muslim Woman: From Termagant to Odal-
isque* (Austin, TX, 1999), 52.

98. 'Ali b. Yahya b. al-Munajjim, *Une correspondance islamochretienne entre Ibn al-Munajjim, Hunayn ibn Ishaq, et Qusta Ibn Luqa* (Turnhout, 1981), 571; English translation in Sizgorich, "Your Brothers, the Romans."

99. Muslim al-Naysaburi, *Sahih* (Beirut, 2010), #934; Halevi, *Muhammad's Grave*, 136.

100. Ibn Hisham, *Al-Sira*, 1–2:430.

101. El-Hibri, *Parable and Politics*, 158, 208.

102. See the role that Judas Kyriakos plays in Christian imperial narratives in Andrew S. Jacobs, "The Remains of the Jew: Imperial Christian Identity in the Late Ancient Holy Land," *Journal of Medieval and Early Modern Studies* 33 (2003): 23–45.

103. Borrut, *Entre mémoire et pouvoir*, 60–61, 98.

104. Ibn Abi Tahir Tayfur, *Kitab balaghat al-nisa'*, 188.

105. El-Hibri, *Reinterpreting Islamic Historiography*, 94.

106. Roy Mottahedeh, "Some Islamic Views of the Pre-Islamic Past," *Harvard Middle Eastern and Islamic Review* 1 (1994): 17–25.

107. David B. Leshock, "Religious Geography: Designating Jews and Muslims as Foreigners in Medieval England," in *Meeting the Foreign in the Middle Ages*, ed. Albrecht Classen (London, 2002), 202–225; Dagenais and Greer, "Decolonizing the Middle Ages." James Montgomery has talked of the semantic emptiness of the pre- and early Islamic Hijaz, "effected by the Qur'anic event," and which led to the obliteration of anything extra-Islamic except for "the pre-Islamic *qasida*." Montgomery, "The Empty Hijaz," in *Arabic Theology, Arabic Philosophy: From the Many to the One; Essays in Celebration of Richard M. Frank*, ed. James E. Montgomery (Leuven, 2006), 37–97.

108. Uri Rubin, "Prophets and Caliphs: The Biblical Foundations of the Umayyad Authority," in Berg, *Method and Theory in the Study of Islamic Origins*, 73–99; Camilla Adang, "Islam as the Inborn Religion of Mankind: The Concept of *Fitra* in the Works of Ibn Hazm," *Al-Qantara* 21 (2000): 391–410.

2. Women's Lamentation and Death Rituals in Early Islam

1. Georgina L. Jardim, *Recovering the Female Voice in Islamic Scripture* (Burlington, VT, 2014), 46, 153.

2. Fred Astren, "Depaganizing Death: Aspects of Mourning in Rabbinic Judaism and Early Islam," in *Bible and Qur'an: Essays in Scriptural Intertextuality*, ed. John C. Reeves (Leiden, 2004), 183–199.

3. Carlos M. N. Eire, *From Madrid to Purgatory: The Art and Craft of Dying in Sixteenth-Century Spain* (Cambridge, 1995), 5.

4. Sizgorich, *Violence and Belief*, 258.

5. Leor Halevi, "Wailing for the Dead: The Role of Women in Early Islamic Funerals," *Past and Present* 183 (2004): 3–39.

6. See Leanne Groeneveld, "Mourning, Heresy and Resurrection in the York Corpus Christi Cycle," in *Response to Death: The Literary Work of Mourning*, ed. Christian Riegel (Edmonton, 2005), 1–21. The sole exception was the Mater Dolorosa, in which "Mary assumed in silence the posture of pagan lament

while articulating an exemplary Christian message of patience and hope." James S. Amelang, "Mourning Becomes Eclectic: Ritual Lament and the Problem of Continuity," *Past and Present* 187 (2005): 3–31.

7. Amelang, "Mourning Becomes Eclectic."

8. Jenny Hockey, "Women in Grief: Cultural Representation and Social Practice," in *Death, Gender, and Ethnicity*, ed. David Field, Jenny Hockey, and Neil Small (London, 1997), 89–107.

9. Phyllis Palgi and Henry Abramovitch, "Death: A Cross-Cultural Perspective," *Annual Review of Anthropology* 13 (1984): 385–417.

10. Ibn 'Abd Rabbih, *Al-'Iqd*, 3:234–235. For a detailed analysis of this section in *Al-'Iqd*, see Nadia Maria El Cheikh, "Gendering Death in *Kitab al-'Iqd al-Farid*," *Al-Qantara* 31 (2010): 411–436.

11. Alford T. Welch, "Death and Dying in the Qur'an," in *Religious Encounters with Death*, ed. Frank E. Reynolds and Earle H. Waugh (London, 1973), 183–199.

12. Ira Lapidus, "The Meaning of Death in Islam," in *Facing Death: Where Culture, Religion, and Medicine Meet*, ed. Howard M. Spiro, Mary G. McCrea Curnen, and Lee Palmer Wandel (New Haven, CT, 1996), 149–159.

13. Jacques Waardenburg, "Death and the Dead," *Encyclopedia of the Qur'an*; Edhem Eldem, *Death in Istanbul: Death and Its Rituals in Ottoman-Islamic Culture* (Istanbul, 2005), 44; Lapidus, "Meaning of Death in Islam"; Abdesselem, *Le thème de la mort dans la poésie arabe*, 164.

14. Halevi, "Wailing for the Dead."

15. Avner Giladi, *Children of Islam: Concepts of Childhood in Muslim Society* (New York, 1992), 87–98; and Astren, "Depaganizing Death."

16. A longer list of such terms occurs in G. H. A. Juynboll, *Muslim Tradition* (Cambridge, 1983), 99.

17. See, for instance, al-Tabarsi, *Majma' al-bayan*, 9:512, and *Qurrat al-'ayn 'ala tafsir al-jallalayn*, ed. Muhammad Kan'an (Beirut, 1999), 737.

18. Ibn Sa'd, *Tabaqat*, 8:7–9.

19. Muslim, *Sahih*, #934.

20. Ibn Sa'd, *Tabaqat*, 1:138. Another story also relates that when Ruqayya (the daughter of the Prophet and wife of 'Uthman b. 'Affan) died, the women cried over her. 'Umar b. al-Khattab beat them with his whip until the Prophet held his hand and told him, "Leave them to cry O 'Umar." Ibid., 8:37.

21. Muslim, *Sahih*, #923.

22. Abu Dawud, *Musnad* (Heyderabad, 1321), 169, 1221.

23. Abu 'Abdallah Muhammad b. al-Hajj, *al-Madkhal*, 3 vols. (Beirut, 1972), 3:245.

24. Al-Bukhari, *Sahih*, #1,294, #1,297, and #1,298.

25. Muhammad al-Mubarrad, *Kitab al-ta'azi*, ed. Muhammad al-Dibaji (Beirut, 1992), 107.

26. This is one of the explanations that Ibn Manzur provides for the word *saqaba*. In *Lisan al-'Arab*, 1:468–469.

27. Al-Mubarrad, *Kitab al-ta'azi*, 279–280.

28. Hammond, *Beyond Elegy*, 2.

29. Ibn Hisham, *Al-Sira*, 3–4:151–152; translation from Guillaume, *Life of Muhammad*, 417.

30. Ibn Hisham, *Al-Sira*, 1–2:169–173; translation from Guillaume, *Life of Muhammad*, 73–76.

31. K. A. Fariq, "Al-Khansa' and Her Poetry," *Islamic Culture* 37 (1957): 209–219.

32. Ibn 'Abd Rabbih, *Al-'Iqd*, 3:48–49, 266–267.

33. Al-Mubarrad, *Kitab al-ta'azi*, 49.

34. Burt, "Al-Khansa'."

35. A. Bellamy, "Some Observations on the Arabic *Ritha'* in the Jahiliyya and Islam," *Jerusalem Studies in Arabic and Islam* 13 (1990): 44–61.

36. Amelang, "Mourning Becomes Eclectic."

37. Labid, *Diwan*, ed. Ihsan 'Abbas (Kuwait, 1962), 213.

38. Ibn Hisham, *Al-Sira*, 3–4:336; translation from Guillaume, *Life of Muhammad*, 515.

39. Al-Waqidi, *Kitab al-maghazi*, 2:860; translation from Faizer, *Life of Muhammad: Al-Waqidi's "Kitab al-maghazi,"* 423. Al-Baladhuri, *Ansab al-ashraf*, 13 vols., ed. Yusuf al-Mir'ashli (Beirut, 2008), vol. 1, pt. 1, p. 900.

40. Al-Raghib al-Isfahani, *Muhadarat al-udaba'*, 4 vols. (Beirut, 1961–1965), 4:494, 506.

41. Al-Bukhari, *Sahih*, #1,296. See also Abu Yahya al-Khazraji, *Fath al-'allam fi sharh al-islam bi ahadith al-ahkam*, ed. 'Ali 'Awad and 'Adil 'Abd al-Majid (Beirut, 2000), 315.

42. Ibn al-Jawzi, *Kitab ahkam al-nisa'*, ed. Ziyad Hamdan (Beirut, 1989), 203. Ibn al-Hajj, *Al-Madkhal*, 3:245.

43. Ibn al-Hajj, *Al-Madkhal*, 3:245.

44. Lapidus, "Meaning of Death in Islam."

45. James M. Wilce, *Crying Shame: Metaculture, Modernity, and the Exaggerated Death of Lament* (Chichester, 2009), 25, 48–51. One of the very few articles dealing with emotions in the medieval Islamic context is Zouhair Ghazzal, "From Anger on Behalf of God to Forbearance in Islamic Medieval Literature," in *Anger's Past: The Social Uses of an Emotion in the Middle Ages*, ed. Barbara H. Rosenwein (Ithaca, NY, 1998), 203–230.

46. Shakespeare, *Richard III*, act 4, scene 4, lines 35–36.

47. Ibid., lines 61, 77–78. References in Gail Holst-Warhaft, *The Cue for Passion: Grief and Its Political Uses* (Cambridge, MA, 2000), 2–25, 198.

48. Alfons Teipen, "Jahilite and Muslim Women: Questions of Continuity and Communal Identity," *Muslim World* 92 (2002): 437–459. Yahya al-Jabburi points out that at the battle of Uhud the poetry of the Quraysh reflected *jahiliyya* values with its stress on *fakhr* (self-praise), *zahu* (boasting), and calls for revenge; al-Jabburi, *Shi'r al-mukhadramin wa athar al-islam fihi* (Baghdad, 1964), 276.

49. Helen P. Foley, *Female Acts in Greek Tragedy* (Princeton, NJ, 2001), 35.

50. Moneera al-Ghadeer, *Bedouin Women's Poetry in Saudi Arabia* (London, 2009), 67.

51. Ibn Hisham, *Al-Sira*, 3–4:97; translation from Guillaume, *Life of Muhammad*, 389.

52. Ibn Hisham, *Al-Sira*, 3–4:167; translation from Guillaume, *Life of Muhammad*, 425.

53. Ibn Sa'd, *Tabaqat*, 2:311. See also Muslim, *Sahih*, #2,454.

54. Al-Mubarrad, *Kitab al-ta'azi*, 11. Similarly, the daughter of the Prophet, Fatima, stood at her father's tomb and recited, "Our loss is like the earth's loss of its rain; since you left we have been deprived of revelation and books"; Ibn 'Abd Rabbih, *Al-'Iqd*, 3:238.

55. Leslie C. Dunn and Nancy A. Jones, introduction to *Embodied Voices: Representing Female Vocality in Western Culture*, ed. Leslie C. Dunn and Nancy A. Jones (Cambridge, 1994), 1–13; Nicole Loraux, *The Invention of Athens: The Funeral Oration in the Classical City* (Cambridge, MA, 1986), 45.

56. Teipen, "Jahilite and Muslim Women."

57. Ibn Sa'd, *Tabaqat*, 2:319–326.

58. James T. Monroe, "The Poetry of the Sirah Literature," in *Arabic Literature to the End of the Umayyad Period* (Cambridge, 1983), 368–373.

59. Olga Taxidou, *Tragedy, Modernity and Mourning* (Edinburgh, 2004), 8–9; Nicole Loraux, *Mothers in Mourning*, trans. Corinne Pache (Ithaca, NY, 1998), 19.

60. Gillian Rose, *Mourning Becomes the Law: Philosophy and Representation* (Cambridge, 1996), 35.

61. Ibn Hisham, *Al-Sira*, 3–4:167–168; translation from Guillaume, *Life of Muhammad*, 425.

62. Al-Mubarrad, *Kitab al-ta'azi*, 53.

63. Ibn Hisham, *Al-Sira*, 3–4:98; translation from Guillaume, *Life of Muhammad*, 389. Also in Ibn Sa'd, *Tabaqat*, 8:241.

64. Muslim, *Sahih*, #935.

65. Al-Waqidi, *Kitab al-maghazi*, 2:766; translation from Faizer, *Life of Muhammad: Al-Waqidi's "Kitab al-maghazi,"* 377.

66. Ibn Hanbal, *Al-Musnad*, 10 vols., ed. Hamza A. al-Zayn (Cairo, n.d.), vol. 18, #558.

67. Ibn Sa'd, *Tabaqat*, 3:17–18.

68. Muslim, *Sahih*, #936.

69. Ibn Sa'd, *Tabaqat*, 2:312.

70. Al-Ya'qubi, *Tarikh*, 2:244.

71. Ignaz Goldziher, "On the Veneration of the Dead in Paganism and Islam," in *Muslim Studies*, ed. S. M. Stern, trans. C. R. Barker and S. M. Stern (New Brunswick, NJ, 2006), 209–238.

72. P. K. Hitti, *An Arab-Syrian Gentleman and Warrior in the Period of the Crusades: Memoirs of Usama ibn Munqidh* (London, 1987), 145.

73. In her study on medieval Syria, Daniella Talmon Heller concludes that "the 'ulama's long struggle against what they regarded as excessive expression of grief in the face of death was never successful"; Heller, *Islamic Piety in Medieval Syria: Mosques, Cemeteries and Sermons under the Zangids and the Ayyubids (1146–1260)* (Leiden, 2007), 168, 172.

74. Ahmad b. ʿAli al-Maqrizi, *Kitab al-suluk li maʿrifat duwal al-muluk,* 2 vols., ed. Muhammad M. Ziyadah (Cairo, 1939), 1:796.

75. Ibn al-Hajj, *Al-Madkhal,* 3:233.

76. Ibid., 3:245; Huda Lutfi, "Manners and Customs of Fourteenth-Century Cairene Women: Female Anarchy versus Male Sharʿi Order in Muslim Prescriptive Treatises," in *Women in Middle Eastern History: Shifting Boundaries in Sex and Gender,* ed. Nikki Keddie and Beth Baron (New Haven, CT, 1991), 99–121.

77. Ibn al-Hajj, *Al-Madkhal,* 3:246.

78. Halevi, *Muhammad's Grave,* 136.

79. Halevi, "Wailing for the Dead."

80. Al-Tabari, *Tarikh,* second series, 1:369–370.

81. Ibn Aʿtham al-Kufi, *Kitab al-Futuh,* 5:224–225; see also Raidh Ahmad, "Al-Husayn Ibn ʿAli: A Study of His Uprising and Death Based on Classical Arabic Sources (3rd and 4th Century A.H./9th and 10th Century A.D.)" (Ph.D. diss., McGill University, 2007), 207–208.

82. Al-Muhassin b. Ali al-Tanukhi, *Nishwar al-muhadara wa akhbar al-mudhakara,* 8 vols., ed. ʿAbbud al-Shalji (Beirut, 1971–1973), 2:233.

83. Mahmoud Ayoub, *Redemptive Suffering in Islam: A Study of the Devotional Aspects of ʿAshura' in Twelver Shiʿism* (The Hague, 1978), 143–148.

84. Karen Stears, "Death Becomes Her: Gender and Athenian Death Ritual," in *Lament: Studies in the Ancient Mediterranean and Beyond,* ed. Ann Suter (Oxford, 2008), 139–155.

85. Muhammad Umar Memon, *Ibn Taimiya's Struggle against Popular Religion: With an Annotated Translation of His "Kitab iqtida' as-sirat al-mustaquim mukhalafat ashab al-jahim"* (The Hague, 1976), 144–146.

86. Astren, "Depaganizing Death."

87. Teipen, "Jahilite and Muslim Women."

88. Halevi, *Muhammad's Grave,* 124.

89. Jacques Derrrida, *Aporias,* trans. Thomas Dutoit (Stanford, 1993), 61; Michael Naas, "History's Remains: Of Memory, Mourning and the Event," *Research in Phenomenology* 33 (2003): 75–96.

90. Halevi, *Muhammad's Grave,* 142.

91. Pierre Nora, "Between Memory and History, *les lieux de mémoire,*" *Representations* 26 (1989): 7–24. See also Angelika Hartmann, "Rethinking Memory and Remaking History: Methodological Approaches to 'lieux de mémoire' in Muslim Societies," *Culture e contatti nell'area del Mediterraneo: Il ruolo dell'Islam: Atti 21. Congresso UEAI* (Palermo, 2002), 51–61.

92. Juan Eduardo Campo, "Muslim Ways of Death: Between the Prescribed and the Performed," in *Death and Religion in a Changing World,* ed. Kathleen Garces-Foley (London, 2006), 147–177.

93. Elisheva Baumgarten, "A Separate People? Some Directions for Comparative Research on Medieval Women," *Journal of Medieval History* 34 (2008): 212–228.

94. Lila Abu-Lughod, "Islam and the Gendered Discourse of Death," *International Journal of Middle Eastern Studies* 25 (1993): 187–205.

95. Homi Bhabba, *The Location of Culture* (London, 1994), 2; Holst-Warhaft, *The Cue for Passion,* 31.

96. Clifford Geertz, "Religion as a Cultural System," in *Anthropological Approaches to the Study of Religion,* ed. Michael Banton (London, 1966), 3. See also Paul Connerton, *How Societies Remember* (Cambridge, 1994), 44–45.

3. The Heretical Within

1. R. I. Moore, *The Formation of a Persecuting Society: Power and Deviance in Western Europe, 950–1250* (Oxford, 1994), 71, 90.

2. Elspeth Whitney, "The Witch: 'She'/the Historian 'He': Gender and Historiography of the European Witch Hunts," *Journal of Women's History* 7 (1995): 77–101. Other notable outsiders were Jews and lepers.

3. Jeffrey Richards, *Sex Dissidence and Damnation: Minority Groups in the Middle Ages* (London, 1990), 59–60; and Evelyne Patlagean, "Byzance, le barbare, l'hérétique et la loi universelle," *Ni Juif ni Grec: Entretiens sur le racisme; Actes du colloque tenu du 16 au 20 Juin 1975 au centre culturel international de Cerisy-la-Salle,* ed. Leon Poliakov (Paris: Mouton, 1978), 81–90.

4. Virginia Burrus, "The Heretical Woman as Symbol in Alexander, Athanasius, Epipahnius, and Jerome," *Harvard Theological Review* 84 (1991): 229–248.

5. Kimberly B. Stratton, "The Rhetoric of 'Magic' in Early Christian Discourse: Gender, Power and the Construction of 'Heresy,' " in *Mapping Gender in Ancient Religious Discourses,* ed. Tod Penner and Caroline Vander Stichele (Leiden, 2007), 89–114.

6. Steven C. Judd, "Ghaylan al-Dimashqi: The Isolation of a Heretic in Islamic Historiography," *International Journal of Middle Eastern Studies* 31 (1999): 161–184.

7. Devin J. Stewart has clarified that while Islam does not have an ecclesiastical hierarchy, the jurists have tended to act as religious authorities during one historical and geographical context or another; Stewart, *Islamic Legal Orthodoxy: Twelver Shiite Responses to the Sunni Legal System* (Salt Lake City, 1998), 25, 45. Alexander Knysh has, however, cautioned against borrowing European categories to interpret aspects of Islamic civilization and religion, notably the binary opposition of "orthodoxy" and "heresy," which is not "entirely germane to the religious situation in the Muslim societies"; Knysh, " 'Orthodoxy' and 'Heresy' in Medieval Islam: An Essay in Reassessment," *The Muslim World* 83 (1993): 48–67.

8. Ahmed El Shamsy, "The Social Construction of Orthodoxy," in *The Cambridge Companion to Classical Islamic Theology,* ed. Tim Winter (Cambridge, 2008), 97–117.

9. Hamid Dabashi, *Authority in Islam: From the Rise of Muhammad to the Establishment of the Umayyads* (New Brunswick, NJ, 1989), 71. Heresy can be defined only when the central orthodoxy is capable of being formulated; to denounce heresy was to control the definition of orthodoxy. See Virginia Burrus, *The Making of a Heretic: Gender, Authority, and the Priscillianist Controversy* (Berkeley, 1995), 160.

10. Joseph van Ess, *The Flowering of Muslim Theology,* trans. Jane Marie Todd (Cambridge, MA, 2006), 27–28.

11. Bernard Lewis, "Some Observations on the Significance of Heresy in the History of Islam," *Studia Islamica* 1 (1953): 43–63. *Zandaqa* was a charged but ill-defined term that could denote many things, although it seems to have originally signified an adherence to Manichaeism. See M. Chokr, *Zandaqa et zindiqs en Islam au second siècle de l'hégire* (Damascus, 1993). Sarah Stroumsa states that in Islamic heresiographical literature, all types of heretics were labeled as *zanadiqa*, a term that could refer to dualists as well as to audacious philosophers or theologians whose doctrines bothered their mainstream Muslim adversaries; Stroumsa, *Freethinkers of Medieval Islam: Ibn al-Rawandi, Abu Bakr al-Razi, and Their Impact on Islamic Thought* (Leiden, 1999), 5.

12. W. Madelung, "Mulhid," *Encyclopaedia of Islam,* 2nd ed.; Mohammed Ali Amir-Moezzi, "Heresy," *Encyclopedia of the Qur'an;* Ahmad Atif Ahmad, "Al-Ghazali's Contribution to the Sunni Juristic Discourses on Apostasy," *Journal of Arabic and Islamic Studies* 7 (2007): 50–73. Another related term is *bid'a* (innovation), which can be defined as a belief or practice for which there is no precedent in the Prophet's lifetime. It is used as the opposite of *sunna* but should be distinguished from heresy, since *bid'a* does not originate with rebelling but rather arises through some kind of confusion, and its practitioners often remain within the bounds of the *jama'a*. See J. Robson, "Bid'a," *Encyclopaedia of Islam,* 2nd ed.

13. Marina Rustow, *Heresy and the Politics of Community: The Jews of the Fatimid Caliphate* (Ithaca, NY, 2008), 254, 347–348.

14. Sherman A. Jackson, *On the Boundaries of Theological Tolerance in Islam: Abu Hamid al-Ghazali's Faysal al-Tafriqa Bayna al-Islam Wa al-Zandaqa* (Oxford, 2003), 30; and Knysh, "'Orthodoxy' and 'Heresy.'" Judd also talks about the difficulty involved in defining the concepts of heresy and orthodoxy, suggesting that "heretics are simply those whom the dominant religious authority deems to be outside the bounds of orthodoxy"; Judd, "Ghaylan al-Dimashqi."

15. Van Ess, *Flowering of Muslim Theology,* 34.

16. Daniel Boyarin, *Border Lines: The Partition of Judaeo-Christianity* (Philadelphia, 2004), 2–3, 29.

17. Peter Brown, *Authority and the Sacred: Aspects of the Christianization of the Roman World* (Cambridge, 1995), 16–17.

18. Jeffrey T. Kenney, *Muslim Rebels: Kharijites and the Politics of Extremism in Egypt* (Oxford, 2006), 25.

19. Sean W. Anthony, *The Caliph and the Heretic: Ibn Saba' and the Origins of Shi'ism* (Leiden, 2012), 141.

20. Farouk Mitha has detected three main themes, namely, the organized conspiracy with the aim of domination; theological deviance in the interpretations of basic Islamic doctrines; and the antinomianism of the movement (symbolized by the Qaramita); Mitha, *Al-Ghazali and the Isma'ilis: A Debate on Reason and Authority in Medieval Islam* (London, 2001), 35–38.

21. W. Montgomery Watt, "The Great Community of the Sects," in *Theology and Law in Islam,* ed. G. E. von Grunebaum (Wiesbaden, 1971), 25–36; Richard

Lim, "Christian Triumph and Controversy," in *Late Antiquity: A Guide to the Postclassical World,* ed. G. W. Bowersock, Peter Brown, and Oleg Grabar (Cambridge, MA, 2000), 196–218.

22. Henri Laoust, "La classification des sectes dans le *farq* d'al-Baghdadi," *Revue des études islamiques* 29 (1961): 19–59. In another prominent *firaq* work of the fifth/twelfth century, Muhammad al-Shahrastani states that "the Isma'iliyya are most commonly known as the Batiniyya," a name given to them because they believe that "for every 'exoteric' there is an 'esoteric.'" Al-Shahrastani adds that "they are known by many other names," including Batiniyya, Qaramita, and Mazdakites. In Muhammad b. 'Abd al-Karim Shahratani (d. 1153), *Muslim Sects and Divisions: The Section on Muslim Sects in Kitab al-milal wa'l-nihal,* trans. A. K. Kazi and J. G. Flynn (London, 1984), 165.

23. Farhad Daftary, "The Earliest Isma'ilis," *Arabica* 38 (1991): 214–245.

24. Wilfred Madelung, "The Fatimids and the Qarmatis of Bahrayn," in *Medieval Isma'ili History and Thought,* ed. Farhad Daftary (Cambridge, 1996), 21–72.

25. Hugh Kennedy, "The Desert and the Sown in Eastern Arabian History," in *Arabia and the Gulf: From Traditional Society to Modern States,* ed. Ian Richard Netton (London, 1986), 18–27. According to Farhad Daftary, early Isma'ilism seems to have mainly addressed itself to and relied upon the support of the peasants and Bedouins. Both Marshall Hodgson and M. A. Shaban believe that support for the Qaramita came mainly from the Bedouins. See Farhad Daftary, *The Isma'ilis: Their History and Doctrines* (Cambridge, 1990), 124; Marshall G. S. Hodgson, *The Venture of Islam: The Classical Age of Islam,* 3 vols. (Chicago, 1974), 1:490; and M. A. Shaban, *Islamic History: A New Interpretation,* 2 vols. (Cambridge, 1981), 2:131.

26. Patricia Crone, *God's Rule: Government and Islam* (New York, 2004), 202.

27. Shihab al-Din al-Nuwayri, *Nihayat al-arab fi funun al-adab,* 33 vols., ed. Muhammad Jabir al-Husayni (Cairo, 1984), 25:194. This information is also found in a more condensed form in Abu Bakr al-Dawadari, *Kanz al-durar wa jami' al-ghurar,* 9 vols., ed. Salah al-Din al-Munajjid (Cairo, 1960–1982), 6:49.

28. Kennedy, "The Desert and the Sown in Eastern Arabian History."

29. Madelung, "The Fatimids and the Qarmatis of Bahrayn."

30. Crone, *God's Rule,* 202. According to Madelung, it was the episode of the Isfahani that gave rise to the charges that at the core of the secret Isma'ili doctrine lay a dualist atheism. Wilfred Madelung, *Religious Trends in Early Islamic Iran* (Albany, 1985), 98.

31. Naser-e Khosraw, *Book of Travels,* translated from Persian by W. M. Thackston Jr. (Albany, 1986), 87.

32. 'Abd al-Jabbar al-Hamadhani, *Tathbit dala'il a-nubuwwa,* 2 vols., ed. 'Abdul-Karim 'Uthman (Beirut, 1967), 2:608.

33. Daniel Boyarin and Virginia Burrus, "Hybridity as Subversion of Orthodoxy? Jews and Christians in Late Antiquity," *Social Compass* 52 (2005): 431–441.

34. J. L. Kraemer, "Heresy versus the State in Medieval Islam," in *Studies in Judaica, Karaitica, and Islamica,* ed. Sheldon R. Brunswick (Bar Ilan, 1982), 167–180.

35. 'Abd al-Qahir al-Baghdadi, *Al-Farq bayn al-firaq* (Beirut, n. d.), 213. Included in his list of Batiniyya are the Qaramita. According to Jackson, al-Baghdadi's work exerted great influence even though he was a fanatic who charged almost everyone with unbelief; Jackson, *On the Boundaries,* 41.

36. Fakhr al-Din al-Razi, *I'tiqadat firaq al-muslimin wa al-mushrikin,* ed. Sami al-Nashshar (Cairo, 1938), 76.

37. Yaron Friedman, "Ibn Taymiyya's Fatwa against the Nusayri-Alawi Sect," *Der Islam* 82 (2005): 349–363.

38. Madelung, "The Fatimids and the Qarmatis of Bahrayn" and "The Account of the Isma'ilis in *Firaq al-Shi'a*: Note by W. Madelung," in S. M. Stern, *Studies in Early Isma'ilism* (Leiden, 1983), 49.

39. Daftary, "Diversity in Islam"; and Farhad Daftary, "Isma'ili Studies: Medieval Antecedents and Modern Developments," in *Isma'ili Literature: A Bibliography of Sources and Studies* (London, 2004), 84–103.

40. S. M. Stern, "The 'Book of the Highest Initiation' and Other Anti-Isma'ili Travesties," in Stern, *Studies in Early Isma'ilism,* 56–80.

41. M. J. Edwards, "Some Early Christian Immoralities," *Ancient Society* 23 (1992): 71–82.

42. Robert Grant, "Charges of 'Immorality' against Various Religious Groups in Antiquity," in *Studies in Gnosticism and Hellenistic Religion: Presented to Gilles Quispel on the Occasion of His 65th Birthday,* ed. R. van den Broek and M. J. Vermaseren (Leiden, 1981), 161–170.

43. Stephen Benko, *Pagan Rome and the Early Christians* (Bloomington, IN, 1984), 65.

44. Gillian Clark, *Christianity and Roman Society* (Cambridge, 2004), 20, 31.

45. Georges Duby, *Le chevalier, la femme et le prêtre: Le mariage dans la France féodale* (Paris, 1981), 119. According to Anne Brenon, the mere presence of women in the ranks of the Cathars led to accusations of sexual debauchery although the essence of their divergence from Catholic Rome was their ideal of asceticism and purity; Brenon, *Les femmes cathares* (Paris, 2004), 84.

46. 'Abd al-Jabbar, *Tathbit,* 2:596.

47. Thabit b. Sinan al-Sabi', *Tarikh akhbar al-qaramita,* ed. Suhayl Zakkar (Beirut, 1971), 14.

48. 'Abd al-Jabbar, *Tathbit,* 2:379.

49. Muhammad b. Malik al Hammadi al-Yamani, *Kashf asrar al-batiniyya wa akhbar al-qaramita,* ed. Muhammad al-Kawthari (Cairo, 1939), 15. The author states that in disbelief of what he had heard of actions that neither Arabs nor 'Ajam would possibly do, he infiltrated the Sulayhids of Yaman in order to check the veracity of this information.

50. Abu Hamid al-Ghazali, *Fada'ih al-batiniyya,* ed. 'Abd al-Rahman Badawi (Cairo, 1964), 46.

51. Al-Nuwayri, *Nihayat al-arab,* 25:195.

52. Muhammad b. Hasan al-Daylami, *Bayan madhhab al-batiniyya wa bitlanih, manqul min kitab qawa'id 'aqa'id Al Muhammad,* ed. R. Strothmann (Istanbul, 1939), 10, 88.

53. Ibid., 21, 24.

54. Ibid., 25.
55. Thierry Bianquis, "The Family in Arab Islam," in *A History of the Family*, 2 vols., ed. Andre Burguière et al. (Cambridge, 1996), 1:601–647.
56. 'Ali b. Muhammad Abu 'Ubaydallah al-'Abbasi al-'Alawi, "Kitab sirat al-hadi-ila al-haqq Yahya b. al-Husayn," in *Akhbar al-qaramita fi al-Ahsa', al-Sham, al-'Iraq, al-Yaman,* ed. Suhayl Zakkar (Damascus, 1980), 96–97.
57. 'Abd al-Jabbar, *Tathbit,* 2:596.
58. Al-Baghdadi, *Al-Farq bayn al-firaq,* 216.
59. Stern, "The 'Book of the Highest Initiation,'" 56–80. According to Stern, the earliest writer to quote the treatise was Akhu Muhsin, a chief protagonist of the anti-Fatimid literary campaign.
60. Ibid.
61. Al-Nuwayri, *Nihayat al-arab,* 25:195.
62. 'Abd al-Jabbar, *Tathbit,* 2:596.
63. Ibid.; Al-Baghdadi, *Al-farq bayn al-firaq,* 216. See also Abu al-Rihan al-Biruni, *Al-Athar al-baqiya fi al-qurun al-khaliya,* ed. C. Eduard Sachau (Leipzig, 1878), 213, and Abu al-Husayn Muhammad al-Malati, *Al-Tanbih wa al-radd 'ala ahl al-ahwa' wa al-bida'* (N.p., 1949), 28.
64. 'Abd al-Jabbar, *Tathbit,* 1:106.
65. Ibid.; also 2:387–388.
66. Julia Kristeva, *Powers of Horror: An Essay on Abjection,* trans. Leon S. Roudiez (New York, 1982), 1.
67. Patricia Crone, *The Nativist Prophets of Early Islamic Iran: Rural Revolt and Local Zoroastrianism* (Cambridge, 2012), 391, 437.
68. Neguin Yavari, "Polysemous Texts and Reductionist Readings: Women and Heresy in the *Siyar al-Muluk*," in Yavari, *Views from the Edge,* 322–346.
69. Ahmed, *Women and Gender in Islam,* 82–98.
70. Marshall Hodgson, "Al-Darazi and Hamza in the Origin of the Druze Religion," *Journal of the American Oriental Society* 82 (1962): 6–20.
71. Paul Freedman, "The Medieval Other: The Middle Ages as Other," in *Marvels, Monsters, and Miracles: Studies in the Medieval and Early Modern Imagination,* ed. Timothy S. Jomnes and David A. Sprunger (Kalamazoo, MI, 2002), 1–4.
72. Judd, "Ghaylan al-Dimashqi."
73. Jeffrey Thomas Kenney, "Heterodoxy and Culture: The Legacy of the Khawarij in Islamic History" (PhD diss., University of California, Santa Barbara, 1991), 3, 5, 234.
74. Daniel Boyarin, "The Christian Invention of Judaism: The Theodosian Empire and the Rabbinic Refusal of Religion," *Representations* 85 (2004): 21–57.
75. Abdelmajid Charfi, "La fonction historique de la polémique islamochretienne à l'époque Abbasside," in *Christian Arabic Apologetics during the Abbasid Period,* ed. Samir Khalil Samir and Jorgen S. Nielsen (Leiden, 1994), 44–56.
76. Kristeva, *Powers of Horror,* 4–5, 15.
77. Joshua Levinson, "Bodies and Bo(a)rders: Emerging Fictions of Identity in Late Antiquity," *Harvard Theological Review* 39 (2000): 343–372.

78. Thabit b. Sinan, *Tarikh akhbar al-qaramita,* 21–22.

79. Steven Justice, "Inquisition, Speech, and Writing: A Case from Late Medieval Norwich," in *Criticism and Dissent in the Middle Ages,* ed. Rita Copeland (Cambridge, 1996), 289–321.

80. Kraemer, "Heresy versus the State in Medieval Islam."

81. Hodgson, "Al-Darazi and Hamza."

82. Brenon, *Les femmes cathares,* 60.

83. Moore, *Formation of a Persecuting Society,* 100–101.

84. Asma Afsarrudin, "Constructing Narratives of Monition and Guile: The Politics of Interpretation," *Arabica* 48 (2001): 315–351.

4. Beyond Borders

1. Jacques Waardenburg, "Muslim Studies of Other Religions: The Medieval Period," in *Muslims and Others in Early Islamic Society,* ed. Robert Hoyland (Burlington, VT, 2004), 211–239. See also 'Abdallah Ibrahim, *'Alam al-qurun al-wusta fi a'yun al-muslimin* (Beirut, 2007), 9–12, and Carole Hillenbrand, *The Crusades: Islamic Perspectives* (Edinburgh, 1999), 267, 282.

2. See introduction in Nadia Maria El Cheikh, *Byzantium Viewed by the Arabs* (Cambridge, MA, 2004).

3. Barbara Hill, Liz James, and Dion Smythe, "Zoe: The Rhythm Method of Imperial Renewal," in *New Constantines: The Rhythms of Imperial Renewal in Byzantium, 4th–13th Centuries,* ed. Paul Magdalino (Aldershot, 1994), 215–229; Barbara Hill, *Imperial Women in Byzantium, 1025–1204: Power, Patronage and Ideology* (Harlow, 1999), 102–103.

4. Al-Tabari, *Tarik al-rusul,* third series, 3:504; and Abu al-Hasan al-Mas'udi, *Kitab al-tanbih wa al-ishraf,* ed. M. J. De Goeje (Leiden, 1967), 167.

5. See, for instance, Hadi Eid, *Lettre du calife Harun al-Rashid à l'empereur Constantin VI* (Paris, 1992), 181–183.

6. Al-Tabari, *Tarik al-rusul,* 3rd series, 3:504. See also al-Mas'udi, *Kitab al-tanbih,* 166.

7. Liz James, *Empresses and Power in Early Byzantium* (London, 2001), 12, 54. Empresses ruling in their own right could adopt the masculine title *basileus* or *autokrator.* See Lynda Garland, *Byzantine Empresses: Women and Power in Byzantium, AD 527–1204* (London, 1999), 2, 87.

8. Kathryn Ringrose, "Women and Power at the Byzantine Court," in *Servants of the Dynasty: Palace Women in World History,* ed. Anne Walthall (Berkeley, 2008), 65–80.

9. Jeffrey Featherstone, "Olga's Visit to Constantinople," *Harvard Ukraininian Studies* 14 (1990): 293–312; Constantin Zuckerman, "Le voyage d'Olga et la premiere ambassade espagnole à Constantinople en 946," *Travaux et Mémoires* 13 (2000): 647–672; Carolyn L. Connor, *Women of Byzantium* (New Haven, CT, 2004), 214.

10. A. Cameron, "The Construction of Court Ritual: The Byzantine *Book of Ceremonies,*" in *Rituals of Royalty: Power and Ceremonial in Traditional Societies,* ed. D. Cannadine and A. W. Price (Cambridge, 1987), 106–136.

11. A. Vogt, ed., *Le livre des ceremonies,* 2 vols. (Paris, 1935–1940), 1:61–64. See James, *Empresses and Power in Early Byzantium,* 52–58, and Lynda Garland, "Imperial Women and Entertainment at the Middle Byzantine Court," in *Byzantine Women: Varieties of Experience, 800–1200,* ed. Lynda Garland (London, 2006), 177–191.

12. Vladimir Minorski, "Marvazi on the Byzantines," in *Medieval Iran and Its Neighbours* (London, 1982), #8, at 459–460.

13. Ibid., #8, at 461.

14. Ahmad al-Maqqari, *Nafh al-tib min ghusn al-andalus al-ratib,* 8 vols., ed. Ihsan 'Abbas (Beirut, 1988), 2:258–259. See also E. Levi-Provencal, "Un échange d'ambassade entre Cordoue et Byzance au IXè siècle," *Byzantion* 12 (1937): 1–24.

15. Ibn Butlan, "Risala jami'a li funun nafi'a fi shira' al-raqiq," in *Nawadir al-makhtutat,* ed. 'Abd al-Salam Harun, vol. 4 (Cairo, 1951).

16. Al-Mas'udi, *Muruj al-dhahab,* 5:46, 92, 137.

17. M. Tahar Mansouri, "Les femmes d'origine Byzantines/les roumiyyat sous les abbasides: Une approche onomastique," *Journal of Oriental and African Studies* 11 (2000–2002): 169–186. Beauty is a quality that the Arab Muslims assigned to the Byzantines in general, to the extent that Byzantine beauty became proverbial in Arabic literature. Sa'id al-Andalusi states, for instance, that the Byzantines have the most beautiful faces, well-proportioned physiques, and vigorous constitutions. Sa'id al-Andalusi, *Tabaqat al-umam* (al-Najaf, 1967), 13.

18. Ibn Hisham, *Al-Sira,* 3–4:516; translation from Guillaume, *Life of Muhammad,* 603. Reference to the occasion of revelation in Ibn al-Athir, *Al-Kamil fi al-tarikh,* 13 vols., ed. C. J. Tornberg (Beirut, 1979), 2:277.

19. Al-Mas'udi, *Muruj,* 2:58.

20. 'Uthman b. 'Abdallah al-Tarsusi, *Baqaya kitab siyar al-thughur min khilal makhtutat bughyat al-talab li Ibn al-'Adim,* ed. Shakir Mustafa (Damascus, 1998), 70–71; translation of the verses by Michael Cooperson in an unpublished paper.

21. With respect to Saracen women in the *Chansons de Geste,* see de Weever, *Sheba's Daughters,* 29. Laura Fishman has explained that the idealization of Native American women served as a vehicle to reprimand their European counterparts; Fishman, "French Views of Native American Women in the Early Modern Era: The Tupinamba of Brazil," in *Women and the Colonial Gaze,* ed. Tamara L. Hunt and Micheline R. Lessard (New York, 2002), 65–78.

22. Ashley Manjarrez Walker and Michael A. Sells, "The Wiles of Women and Performative Intertextuality: 'A'isha, the Hadith of the Slander and the Sura of Yusuf," *Journal of Arabic Literature* 30 (1999): 55–77.

23. For an analysis of the concept of *fitna,* see Fedwa Malti-Douglas, *Woman's Body, Woman's Word: Gender and Discourse in Arabo-Islamic Writing* (Princeton, NJ, 1991), 106, and Fatima Mernissi, *Beyond the Veil: Male-Female Dynamics in Modern Muslim Society* (Bloomington, IN, 1987). According to Walid Saleh, women as *fitna* are not only a source of social disorder; they are also implicated in the apocalyptic horror; Saleh, "The Woman as a Locus of Apocalyptic

Anxiety in Medieval Sunni Islam," in *Myths, Historical Archetypes, and Symbolic Figures in Arabic Literature: Towards a New Hermeneutic Approach,* ed. Angelika Neuwirth et al. (Beirut, 1999), 123–145.

24. Ibn al-Nadim, *Al-Fihrist* (Cairo, n.d.), 351. In medieval French epic, Muslim women are also depicted as playing a role of disloyalty and treason whereby the Frankish heroes are captured and the emir imprisons them in his dungeon, but his daughter, in love with one of the Franks, commands the jailer to release them and hides them in her room, finally enabling them to escape from the palace. See de Weever, *Sheba's Daughters,* 112.

25. Al-Isfahani, *Kitab al-aghani,* 8:73.

26. Al-Jahiz, *Kitab al-hayawan,* 7 vols., ed. 'Abd al-Salam Harun (Cairo, 1938–1948), 7:28; in this connection, see Jonathan P. Berkey, "Circumcision Circumscribed: Female Excision and Cultural Accommodation in the Medieval Near East," *International Journal of Middle Eastern Studies* 28 (1996): 19–38. See also 'Abd al-Jabbar, *Tathbit,* 1:157, 167.

27. Angeliki Laiou, "Women in the History of Byzantium," in *Byzantine Women and Their World,* ed. Ioli Kalavrezou (New Haven, CT, 2003), 23–32; Stavroula Constantinou, *Female Corporeal Performances: Reading the Body in Byzantine Passions and Lives of Holy Women* (Stockholm, 2005), 164; Alice-Mary Talbot, "Women," in *The Byzantines,* ed. Guglielmo Cavello (Chicago, 1997). Alexander P. Kazhdan points out that there was no special term to designate women's quarters and that there is no evidence confirming the existence of a Byzantine gynaeceum. See Kazhdan, "Women at Home," *Dumbarton Oaks Papers* 52 (1998): 1–17. See also Lynda Garland, "The Life and Ideology of Byzantine Women: A Further Note on Conventions of Behavior and Social Reality as Reflected in Eleventh and Twelfth Century Historical Sources," *Byzantion* 58 (1988): 361–393. Averil Cameron talks about a constant dialectic in Byzantium between the language of denial and the language of desire; Cameron, "Desire in Byzantium—the Ought and the Is," in *Desire and Denial in Byzantium,* ed. Liz James (Aldershot, 1999), 205–213.

28. 'Abd al-Jabbar, *Tathbit,* 1:167–168, 170–171. Laws separating the sexes in monastic life were enunciated in the early conciliar legislation and reiterated in the middle Byzantine period. Dorothy Abrahamse, "Women's Monasticism in the Middle Byzantine Period: Problems and Prospects," *Byzantinische Forschungen* 9 (1985): 35–58.

29. Monasteries were also places for excursions for the lesser folk to eat, drink, and listen to music. Patricia Crone and Shmuel Moreh, *The Book of Strangers: Medieval Arabic Graffiti on the Theme of Nostalgia* (Princeton, NJ, 2000), 13.

30. Abu al-Faraj al-Isfahani, *Kitab adab al-ghuraba',* ed. Salah al-Din al-Munajjid (Beirut, 1972), 34–35; translation from Crone and Moreh, *Book of Strangers,* 32–33.

31. Al-Isfahani, *Kitab adab al-ghuraba',* 26–27.

32. Ibid., 66–68; translation from Crone and Moreh, *Book of Strangers,* 60–62.

33. Abu al-Hasan al-Shabushti, *Kitab al-diyarat,* ed. G. 'Awwad (Baghdad, 1966), 93.

34. André Miquel, *La geographie humaine du monde musulman jusqu'au milieu du XIème siècle,* 3 vols. (Paris, 1967–1980), 1:150.

35. Sizgorich, *Violence and Belief,* 270.

36. Michael Uebel, *Ecstatic Transformation: On the Uses of Alterity in the Middle Ages* (New York, 2005), 5.

37. Al-Jahiz, "Kitab al-radd 'ala l-nasara," in *Rasa'il al-Jahiz,* 4 vols., ed. 'Abd al-Salam Harun (Cairo, 1979), 3:303–351, at 221–222. See also James Bellamy, "Sex and Society in Islamic Popular Literature," in *Society and the Sexes in Medieval Islam,* ed. Afaf Lutfi al-Sayyid-Marsot (Malibu, 1979), 22–42.

38. Al-Jahiz, *Kitab al-hayawan,* 1:124; al-Mas'udi, *Muruj,* 8:148; al-Jahiz, "Kitab al-radd 'ala l-nasara," 22–23. See A. Cheikh Moussa, "Gahiz et les eunuques ou la confusion du même et de l'autre," *Arabica* 29 (1982): 184–214.

39. 'Abd al-Jabbar, *Tathbit,* 1:168. On the large participation of eunuchs in the annual religious procession that took the Byzantine emperor from the Imperial Palace to the Great Church, see Ibn Rusteh, *Kitab al-a'laq al-nafisa,* ed. M. J. de Goeje (Leiden, 1892), 123–125.

40. Al-Jahiz, *Kitab al-hayawan,* 1:24–25. Eunuchs in the Abbasid state were all imported, castration being forbidden in Islamic law. Cristina de la Puente, "Sin linaje, sin alcurnia, sin hogar: Eunucos en el Andalus en época Omeya," in *Identidades Marginales,* ed. Cristina de la Puente (Madrid: Consejo Superior de Investigaciones Científicas, 2003), 147–193.

41. Al-Jahiz, *Al-Radd,* 221–222; Abu 'Ubayd al-Bakri, *Jughrafiyat al-andalus wa uruba min kitab al-masalik wa al-mamalik,* ed. A. al-Hajj (Beirut, 1978), 98; Nizar Hermes, *The European Other in Medieval Arabic Literature and Culture, Ninth–Twelfth Century AD* (New York, 2012), 60.

42. Ibn Abu Usaybi'a, *'Uyun al-anba' fi tabaqat al-atibba',* ed. Nizar Rida (Beirut, 1965), 184–185.

43. 'Abd al-Jabbar, *Tathbit,* 1:221–222.

44. Text and translation in James E. Montgomery, "Ibn Fadlan and the Rusiyyah," *Journal of Arabic and Islamic Studies* 3 (2000): 9, 21.

45. Miquel, *La geographie humaine,* 2:347.

46. Ibn Munqidh, *An Arab-Syrian Gentleman and Warrior in the Period of the Crusades: Memoirs of Usama ibn Munqidh,* trans. Philip Hitti (London, 1987), 164–165; see also André Miquel, "Les croisades vues par un musulman: L'autobiographie d'Usama ibn Munqidh," *Revue des sciences morales et politiques* 14 (1986): 559–570; Paul Cobb, *Usama ibn Munqidh: Warrior-Poet of the Age of Crusades* (Oxford, 2005), 82.

47. Abu Shama described, in flowery rhyming prose, the arrival of "three hundred beautiful Frankish women." He accused them of sexual profligacy, stating that they had come to offer relief to the Franks who wanted their services, the priests themselves having condoned this conduct. Hillenbrand, *The Crusades,* 273–274.

48. Aziz al-Azmeh, "Mortal Enemies, Invisible Neighbours: Northerners in Andalusi Eyes," in *The Legacy of Muslim Spain,* ed. Salma Khadra Jayyusi (Leiden, 1994), 259–272.

49. Salah al-Din al-Munajjid, *Qasidat Imbratur al-Rum* (Beirut, 1982), 46; Nizar Hermes, "The Byzantines in Medieval Arabic Poetry: Abu Firas' Al-Rumiyyat and the Poetic Responses of al-Qaffal and Ibn Hazm to Nicephorus Phocas' Al-Qasida al-Arminiyya al-Mal'una (The Armenian Cursed Ode)," *Byzantina Symmeikta* 19 (2009): 35–61.

50. Suzanne Stetkevych, *The Poetics of Islamic Legitimacy: Myth, Gender, and Ceremony in the Classical Arabic Ode* (Bloomington, IN, 2002), 145–146, 152, 165.

51. Ibid., 176.

52. Ibid., 175. For an analysis that takes into account modern novels, see Heiko Wimmen, "Ammuriyyah as a Female Archetype: Deconstruction of a Mythical Subtext from Abu Tammam to Jabra Ibrahim Jabra/Abdulrahman Munif," in Neuwirth et al., *Myths, Historical Archetypes, and Symbolic Figures,* 573–582.

53. Cobb, *Usama ibn Munqidh,* 80; Hadia Dajani-Shakeel, "Some Aspects of Muslim-Frankish Christian Relations in the Sham Region in the Twelfth Century," in *Christian-Muslim Encounters,* ed. Yvonne Yazbeck Haddad and Wadi'Zaidan Haddad (Gainesville, FL, 1995), 193–209.

54. Irvin C. Schick, *The Erotic Margin: Sexuality and Spatiality in Alteritist Discourse* (London, 1999), 66.

55. For a classification pertaining to the "authentic" Ottoman woman vis-à-vis the West, see Reina Lewis, *Rethinking Orientalism: Women, Travel, and the Ottoman Harem* (New York, 2004), 144–167.

56. Al-Muhassin b. 'Ali al-Tanukhi, *Kitab al-faraj ba'da al-shidda,* 5 vols., ed. 'Abbud al-Shalji (Beirut, 1978), 4:5–6.

57. Al-Tanukhi, *Nishwar al-muhadara wa akhbar al-mudhakara,* 2:117. A *mahram* is a man within a degree of consanguinity precluding marriage.

58. Syafiq Mughni, "Hanbali Movements in Baghdad from Abu Muhammad al-Barbahari," 249–250; Bouhdiba, *La sexualité,* 231; and A. Mazaheri, *La vie quotidiènne des musulmans au moyen âge, Xème au XIIIème siècle* (Paris, 1951), 64. The *muhtasib* was the person entrusted with the supervision of markets and of moral behavior in a town.

59. Maria Rosa Menocal, *The Arabic Role in Medieval Literary History: A Forgotten Heritage* (Philadelphia, 2004), 44.

60. Schick, *Erotic Margin,* 13.

61. Valerie Traub, "The Past Is a Foreign Country? The Time and Spaces of Islamicate Sexuality Studies," in Babayan and Najmabadi, *Islamicate Sexualities,* 1–40.

62. Schick, *Erotic Margin,* 57–58.

63. Ali Behdad, "The Eroticized Orient: Images of the Harem in Montesquieu and His Precursors," *Stanford French Review* 13 (1989): 109–126; Inge E. Bower, "Despotism from under the Veil: Masculine and Feminine Readings of the Despot and the Harem," *Cultural Critique* 32 (1995–1996): 43–73; Emily Apter, "Female Trouble in the Colonial Harem," *Differences* 4 (1992): 205–224.

64. This is also the case with the Ottoman harem. See Reina Lewis, *Gendering Orientalism: Race, Femininity, and Representation* (London, 1996), 164. The stereotypes linked to Byzantine sexual practices are also similar to the images of the Muslims that developed in France in the Middle Ages and the Renaissance.

See Guy Poirier, "Masculinities and Homosexualities in French Renaissance Accounts of Travel to the Middle East and North Africa," in *Desire and Discipline: Sex and Sexuality in the Premodern West,* ed. Jacqueline Murray and Konrad Eisenbichler (Toronto, 1996), 155–167.

65. Stephen Greenblatt, *Marvelous Possessions: The Wonder of the New World* (Chicago, 1991), 12–13; Nancy Bisaha, *Creating East and West: Renaissance Humanists and the Ottoman Turks* (Philadelphia, 2004), 7.

66. The Christian authors of Spain were similarly reluctant to render the Moor as sodomite, "a defensive measure made necessary by the very conventionality of those familiarizing discourses that blurred the lines of cultural difference between Christian and Muslim"; Gregory S. Hutcheson, "The Sodomitic Moor: Queerness in the Narrative of the Reconquista," in *Queering the Middle Ages,* ed. Glenn Burger and Steven F. Kruger (Minneapolis, 2001), 99–122.

67. The term belongs to Anne McClintock, *Imperial Leather: Race, Gender, and Sexuality in the Colonial Contest* (New York, 1995), 22.

5. Fashioning a New Identity

1. Sizgorich, *Violence and Belief,* 31–33.

2. Ibid., 204.

3. 'Imad al-Hilali, *Mu'jam a'lam al-nisa' fi al-qur'an al-karim* (Beirut, 2010). Amina Wadud suggests that women's roles in the Qur'an fall into one of three categories: "a role which represents the social, cultural, and historical context in which that individual woman lived . . . a role which fulfills a universally accepted female function . . . a role which fulfills a non-gender specific function"; Wadud, *Qur'an and Woman: Rereading the Sacred Text from a Woman's Perspective* (New York, 1999), 29.

4. Asma Afsaruddin, "Early Women Exemplars and the Construction of Gendered Space: (Re)defining Feminine Moral Excellence," in *Harem Histories: Envisioning Places and Living Spaces,* ed. Marilyn Booth (Durham, NC, 2010), 23–48; Barbara Freyer Stowasser, "The Status of Women in Early Islam," in *Muslim Women,* ed. Freda Hussain (London, 1984), 11–43.

5. Ibn Sa'd, *Tabaqat,* 8:277.

6. Ibn Hisham, *Al-Sira,* 1–2:657; Ruth Roded, *Women in Islamic Biographical Collections: From Ibn Sad to "Who's Who"* (Boulder, 1994), 37–38.

7. Ibn Sa'd, *Tabaqat,* 8:230.

8. Ibid.

9. Ibid., 8:413; Asma Afsaruddin, "Literature, Scholarship, and Piety: Negotiating Gender and Authority in the Medieval Muslim World," *Religion and Literature* 42 (2010): 111–131.

10. Al-Waqidi, *Kitab al-maghazi,* 269; translation from Faizer, *Life of Muhammad: Al-Waqidi's "Kitab al-maghazi,"* 131–132. Ibn Hisham, *Al-Sira,* 3–4:81–82. Asma Afsaruddin summarizes the account in *First Muslims: History and Memory* (Oxford, 2008), 70–71.

11. Al-Waqidi, *Kitab al-maghazi,* 271; translation from Faizer, *Life of Muhammad: Al-Waqidi's "Kitab al-maghazi,"* 132. Ibn Hisham, *Al-Sira,* 3–4:67. Alfons Teipen has noted that Ibn Ishaq's presentation emphasizes the participation of

Jahilite women and suppresses evidence of Muslim women's presence on the battlefield. It is al-Waqidi who provides a wealth of information on the participation of Muslim women at the battle of Uhud. Teipen, "Jahilite and Muslim Women."

12. Ibn Hisham, *Al-Sira*, 3–4:78–79; translation from Guillaume, *Life of Muhammad*, 379–380. On Hind, see Ibn Hisham, *Al-Sira*, 3–4:69.

13. Ibn Hisham, *Al-Sira*, 3–4:167–168.

14. Ibid.; translation from Guillaume, *Life of Muhammad*, 425–426.

15. Ibn Sa'd, *Tabaqat*, 8:14.

16. Al-Baladhuri, *Ansab al-ashraf*, vol. 1, pt. 1, p. 241; Ibn Hisham, *Al-Sira*, 1–2:188–189, 238.

17. Al-Baladhuri, *Ansab al-ashraf*, vol. 1, pt. 1, p. 259; Uri Rubin, *The Eye of the Beholder: The Life of Muhammad as Viewed by the Early Muslims: A Textual Analysis* (Princeton, NJ, 1995), 51, 103–104.

18. Ibn Hisham, *Al-Sira*, 1–2:187.

19. Ibid.; al-Baladhuri, *Ansab al-ashraf*, vol. 1, pt. 1, p. 274.

20. Al-Bukhari, *Sahih*, #3,816 and #3,817.

21. Al-Bukhari, *Sahih*, #3,818; al-Baladhuri, *Ansab al-ashraf*, vol. 1, pt. 2, p. 1032.

22. Translation from Abbott, *Aishah*, 48. See also Spellberg, *Politics, Gender, and the Islamic Past*, 154–155.

23. M. J. Kister, "The Sons of Khadija," in *The Life of Muhammad*, ed. Uri Rubin (Aldershot, 1998), 59–93. For the Shi'a, her importance stems also from being the mother of Fatima and the grandmother of the Shi'a imams. Rawand Osman, *Female Personalities in the Qur'an and Sunna: Examining the Major Sources of Imami Shi'i Islam* (New York, 2015), 107.

24. Ibn Hisham, *Al-Sira*, 1–2:240; translation from Guillaume, *Life of Muhammad*, 111. See also G. H. Stern, "The First Women Converts in Islam," *Islamic Culture* 13 (1939): 290–305; Nabia Abbott, "Women and the State in Early Islam," 106–126.

25. Al-Bukhari, *Sahih*, #3,432; Muslim, *Sahih*, #2,340; al-Baladhuri, *Ansab al-ashraf*, vol. 1, pt. 2, p. 1020.

26. Ibn Hisham, *Al-Sira*, 3–4:301; translation from Guillaume, *Life of Muhammad*, 496.

27. Al-Bukhari, *Sahih*, #4,750. Schoeler has shown that the version of al-Bukhari concerning the slander against 'A'isha is the closest to the basic form of the story, the tradition being barely modified from the story that appeared at an early date. Gregor Schoeler, *The Biography of Muhammad*, trans. Uwe Vagelpohl, ed. James E. Montgomery (New York, 2011), 80–98.

28. Ibn Hisham, *Al-Sira*, 3–4:301; translation from Guillaume, *Life of Muhammad*, 496.

29. Al-Bukhari, *Sahih*, #4,750; Ibn Hisham, *Al-Sira*, 3–4:302; translation from Guillaume, *Life of Muhammad*, 496. Ibn Hanbal, *Al-Musnad*, 18: # 25, 499. For this episode, see Spellberg, *Politics, Gender, and the Islamic Past*, 61–74.

30. Walker and Sells, "The Wiles of Women." See also Gayane Karen Merguerian and Afsaneh Najmabadi, "Zulaykha and Yusuf: Whose 'Best Story'?," *International Journal of Middle East Studies* 29 (1997): 485–508.

31. Pseudo-Jahiz, *Al-Mahasin wa al-addad,* 322; Ibn ʿAbd Rabbih, *Al-ʿIqd,* 6:87.

32. The entire episode is found in Ibn Hisham, *Al-Sira,* 3–4:297–303.

33. Ibn Saʿd, *Tabaqat,* 8:65. Detailed discussion is found in chapter 4 of Spellberg, *Politics, Gender, and the Islamic Past.*

34. Ibn Shahrashub, *Manaqib Al Abi Talib,* 3 vols. (al-Najaf, 1956), 2:335; Spellberg, *Politics, Gender, and the Islamic Past,* 129–130. Having analyzed the chapter on women included in the *Book of Government* by Nizam al-Mulk (d. 485/1092), Spellberg concluded that in arguing that female influence in government results in nothing but disaster, Nizam al-Mulk selected ʿAʾisha as his single Islamic female example. Denise Spellberg, "Political Action and Public Example: ʿAʾisha and the Battle of the Camel," in Keddie and Baron, *Women in Middle Eastern History,* 45–57.

35. Al-Masʿudi, *Muruj,* 3:115; Spellberg, *Politics, Gender, and the Islamic Past,* 136.

36. El-Hibri, *Parable and Politics,* 210.

37. Ibn ʿAbd Rabbih, *Al-ʿIqd,* 4:317; Spellberg, *Politics, Gender, and the Islamic Past,* 133–134. Mohja Kahf has suggested the idea of *mujadila* (the interlocutor) as a way to conceptualize women's compositions in the textual materials of early Islam; Kahf, "Braiding the Stories: Women's Eloquence in the Early Islamic Era," in *Windows of Faith: Muslim Women Scholar-Activists in North America,* ed. Gisela Webb (Syracuse, 2000), 147–171. For a recent discussion of the *mujadila,* see Jardim, *Recovering the Female Voice,* 184–216.

38. Ibn ʿAbd Rabbih, *Al-ʿIqd,* 4:314.

39. According to Sulayman al-Naddawi, she transmitted a total of 2,210 hadith and consequently ranks fourth in terms of the number of transmitted hadith, after Abu Hurayra, ʿAbdallah b. ʿUmar, and Anas b. Malik; al-Naddawi, *Sirat al-sayyida ʿAʾisha umm al-muʾminin,* trans. from Urdu by Muhammad Hafiz al-Naddawi (Damascus, 2010), 244. Asma Sayeed, *Women and the Transmission of Religious Knowledge in Islam* (Cambridge, 2013), 34; Roded, *Women in Islamic Biographical Collections,* 28.

40. Aisha Geissinger, "The Exegetical Traditions of ʿAʾisha: Notes on Their Impact and Significance," *Journal of Qurʾanic Studies* 6 (2004): 1–20.

41. Al-Bukhari, *Sahih,* #3,433, #3,769, and #3,770; Muslim, *Sahih,* #2,431.

42. Denise Spellberg, "The Politics of Praise: Descriptions of Khadija, Fatima and ʿAʾisha," *Literature East and West* 26 (1990): 130–148.

43. Ibn Saʿd, *Tabaqat,* 8:74–76; Barbara F. Stowasser, *Women in the Qurʾan: Traditions and Interpretations* (New York, 1994), 116; Afsaruddin, *First Muslims,* 160.

44. Ibn Abi Tahir Tayfur, *Kitab balaghat al-nisaʾ,* 25–26.

45. Ibn Saʿd, *Tabaqat,* 8:74.

46. Michel Dousse, *Maryam al-muslima,* trans. from French by ʿAbdu Kasuha (Damascus, 2008), 190; see also ʿAli al-Tahtawi, *Al-Fath al-anʿam fi baraʾat ʿAʾisha wa Maryam* (Beirut, 2005).

47. Abu Muhammad b. Jarir al-Tabari, *Jamiʾ al-bayan fi taʾwil al-qurʾan,* 12 vols. (Beirut, 1992), 8:325–326.

48. Fakhr al-Din al-Razi, *Al-Tafsir al-kabir,* 34 vols. (Cairo, 1938), 21–22:203.

49. Spellberg, "ʿAʾisha bint Abi Bakr," *Encyclopedia of the Qurʾan.*

50. Matthew Pierce, "Remembering Fatimah: New Means of Legitimizing Female Authority in Contemporary Shi'i Discourse," in *Women, Leadership, and Mosques: Changes in Contemporary Islamic Authority*, ed. Massoda Bano and Hilary Kalmbach (Leiden, 2012), 345–362.

51. Al-Waqidi, *Kitab al-maghazi*, 249, translation from Faizer, *Life of Muhammad: Al-Waqidi's "Kitab al-maghazi,"* 122.

52. Al-Bukhari, *Sahih*, #3,767.

53. Ibn 'Abd Rabbih, *Al-'Iqd*, 3:231. Slightly different versions of this report are included in Muslim, *Sahih*, #2,450; Ibn Sa'd, *Tabaqat*, 8:26–27; al-Baladhuri, *Ansab al-ashraf*, vol. 1, pt. 2, p. 1321.

54. Verena Klemm, "Image Formation of an Islamic Legend: Fatima, the Daughter of the Prophet Muhammad," in *Ideas, Images, and Methods of Portrayal: Insights into Classical Arabic Literature and Islam*, ed. Sebastian Günther (Leiden, 2005), 181–208.

55. Denise L. Soufi, "The Image of Fatima in Classical Islamic Thought" (PhD diss., Princeton University, 1997), 204–206.

56. "David Pinault, "Zaynab bint 'Ali and the Place of the Women of the Households of the First Imams in Shi'ite Devotional Literature," in *Women in the Medieval Islamic World: Power, Patronage, and Piety*, ed. Gavin R. G. Hambly (New York, 1998), 69–98; Firoozeh Kashani-Sabet, "Who Is Fatima? Gender, Culture and Representation in Islam," *Journal of Middle East Women's Studies* 1 (2005): 1–24; Syed Akbar Hyder, *Reliving Karbala: Martyrdom in South Asian Memory* (Oxford, 2006), 80; Klemm, "Image Formation of an Islamic Legend."

57. Al-Baladhuri, *Ansab al-ashraf*, vol. 1, pt. 1, pp. 1018, 1032. See Christopher Clohessy, "Weeping Mothers: Tears and Power in Fatima and Mary," *Islamochristiana* 36 (2010): 101–115; Jane Dammen McAuliffe, "Chosen of All Women: Mary and Fatima in Qur'anic Exegesis," *Islamochristiana* 7 (1981): 19–28; Jane Damen McAuliffe, "Fatima," *Encyclopedia of the Qur'an*; Barbara Freyer Stowasser, "Mary," *Encyclopedia of the Qur'an*.

58. Jane I. Smith and Yvonne Y. Haddad, "The Virgin Mary in Islamic Tradition and Commentary," *The Muslim World* 79 (1989): 161–187.

59. Stowasser, *Women in the Qur'an*, 73, 118.

60. Dousse, *Maryam al-muslima*, 197–198; Smith and Haddad, "The Virgin Mary"; Husn Abboud, *Al-Sayyida Maryam fi al-Qur'an al-karim: Qira'a adabiyya* (Beirut, 2010), 115.

61. Aziz Al-Azmeh, *Islams and Modernities* (London, 1993), 27, 100.

62. Qudsia Mirza, "Islamic Feminism and the Exemplary Past," in *Feminist Perspectives on Law and Theory*, ed. Janice Richardson and Ralph Sandland (London, 2000), 187–208.

63. Jacob Lassner, *Demonizing the Queen of Sheba: Boundaries of Gender and Culture in Postbiblical Judaism and Medieval Islam* (Chicago, 1993), 4.

64. Al-Bukhari, *Sahih*, #7,101. This nonprophetic statement is preserved in the *Sahih* as a reflection of the high endorsement it enjoyed among the traditionalists.

65. Saleh, "The Woman as a Locus of Apocalyptic Anxiety," 123–145.

66. Stowasser, *Women in the Qur'an*, 8.

67. Ibn Shahrashub, *Manaqib Al Abi Talib,* 3:102–103.
68. Stowasser, *Women in the Qur'an,* 105–107, 115; Sayeed, *Women and the Transmission of Religious Knowledge,* 22.
69. Margaret R. Somers, "Narrative Constitution of Identity: A Relationship and Network Approach," *Theory and Society* 16 (1992): 605–660; see also Sizgorich, *Violence and Belief,* 48.
70. Qur'an 3:103. Anecdote in Muhammad al-Washsha', *Kitab al-fadil fi sifat al-adab al-kamil,* ed. Yahya al-Jabburi (Beirut, 1991), 210. On Fatima's inheritance, see al-Baladhuri, *Ansab,* vol. 1, pt. 2, p. 1256; and al-Bukhari, *Sahih,* #3,711 and #3,712.
71. Burt, "Al-Khansa' "; Bint al-Shati', *Al-Khansa'* (Beirut, n.d), 40–43. It is bewildering that not one verse has survived in which al-Khansa' is lamenting her children.
72. In his introduction to Munir Ghadban, *Hind bint 'Utba* (al-Riyad, 1982), 5–14.

Conclusion

1. Aziz al-Azmeh, "Barbarians in Arab Eyes," *Past and Present* 134 (1992): 3–18; Thomas Sizgorich, "Do Prophets Come with Swords? Conquest, Empire, and Historical Narrative in the Early Islamic World," *American Historical Review* 112 (2007): 993–1015.
2. William E. Shepard, "Sayyid Qutb's Doctrine of Jahiliyya," *International Journal of Middle Eastern Studies* 35 (2003): 521–545. See also Emmanuel Sivan, *Radical Islam: Medieval Theology and Modern Politics* (New Haven, CT, 1985), 22–23; Ian Buruma and Avishai Margalit, *Occidentalism: The West in the Eyes of Its Enemies* (New York, 2004), 120. Joseph Massad has pointed out that Qutb and other Islamists have accused Western civilization of having failed the test when compared with Islamic civilization, especially mentioning the degeneration of European societies as a result of the permissiveness *(ibahiyya)* among their youth. See Joseph A. Massad, *Desiring Arabs* (Chicago, 2007), 126.
3. Dipesh Chakrabarti wrote about the nineteenth-century Santal in a somewhat comparable way in *Provincializing Europe: Postcolonial Thought and Historical Difference* (Princeton, NJ, 2000), 109–110.
4. Hilma Granqvist, *Muslim Death Burial: Arab Customs and Traditions Studied in a Village in Jordan* (Helsinki, 1965), 45.
5. Lila Abu Lughod, *Veiled Sentiments* (Berkeley, 1988), 69, 198.
6. Simon J. Williams, *Emotion and Social Theory: Corporeal Reflections on the Irrational* (London, 2001), 2.
7. Chakrabarti, *Provincializing Europe,* 98; Levinson, "Bodies and Bo(a)rders"; Daniel Boyarin, *Carnal Israel: Reading Sex in Talmudic Culture* (Berkeley, 1993), 229.
8. Gyanendra Pandey, "The Prose of Otherness," *Subaltern Studies* 8, ed. David Arnold and David Hardiman (Delhi, 1994): 188–221.
9. Nancy Bisaha, *Creating East and West: Renaissance Humanists and the Ottoman Turks* (Philadelphia, 2004), 7.

10. Tahar Labib, "The Other in Arab Culture," in *Imagining the Arab Other: How Arabs and Non-Arabs View Each Other,* ed. Tahar Labib (London, 2008), 47–90. On al-Tahtawi's experience, full of anxiety and ambivalence, see Tareq El-Ariss, *Trials of Arab Modernity: Literary Affect and the New Political* (New York, 2013), 19–52.
11. As Fatima Mernissi remarks, those making any pronouncements regarding the status of women have to justify their actions by citing precedents in religious history and tradition; Mernissi, "Women in Muslim History: Traditional Perspectives and New Strategies," in *Women and Islam: Critical Concepts in Sociology,* ed. Haideh Moghissi, 3 vols. (London, 2005), 1:37–50.
12. A. D. DeConick, *Recovering the Original Gospel of Thomas: A History of the Gospel and Its Growth* (London, 2005), 69; Gyanendra Pandey, *Remembering Partition: Violence, Nationalism, and History* (Cambridge, 2001), 204–205.

Acknowledgments

This book has benefited from the input and help of numerous people. My colleague Bilal Orfali extended his thorough knowledge of the Islamic field at every stage of composition, doing so with a dedication and generosity that only a profound love for scholarship and a genuine friendship can explain. My friend of more than twenty-five years, Sarah Chayes, has unfailingly supported me in all my writing ventures. Michael Cooperson allowed me to use his beautiful (yet unpublished) translation of an Arab poem that describes the beauty of Byzantine female captives. I wish to thank Deborah Callaghan, Tayeb El-Hibri, Susan Karani, Samer Traboulsi, Maya Yazigi, Tara Zend, Yasmin Shafei, Brittany Frye, and the anonymous readers for their invaluable input in improving the manuscript in a variety of ways. Conversations with Kristen Brustad, Paul Cobb, Tarek El-Ariss, Susan Kahn, Letizia Osti, Maurice Pomerantz, Walid Saleh, and Maaike van Berkel were challenging and rewarding. I also thank my editor at Harvard University Press, Sharmila Sen, for believing in this project and providing balanced criticism at every turn. None of them is responsible for any errors of fact or interpretation this book may contain.

I also would like to acknowledge my friends and colleagues who, over the years, helped me hone themes and ideas that relate to the substance of this book: Margaret Hunt, Manuela Marin, and Hugh Kennedy. Panagiotis Agapitos, Kathryn Babayan, Cristina de la Puente, and Maria Mavroudi gave me opportunities to discuss my work in public forums. The time I spent as a visiting scholar at the Center for the Study of Women at UCLA, at Harvard University, and at the Center for the Study of Gender and Sexuality at New York University provided much-needed stimulation and education. In this connection my gratitude goes to Sondra Hale, Roy Mottahedeh, William Granara, Rabab Abdulhadi, and Carolyn Dinshaw.

I also wish to acknowledge the financial assistance of my institution, the American University of Beirut, which allowed me to present my work in progress in a number of venues, notably at meetings of the School of Abbasid Studies where I benefited from the feedback of colleagues who are at once knowledgeable and supportive. I would also like to thank the staff of Jafet Library—Carla Chalhoub, in particular—for their professionalism and courtesy. A semester spent as a visiting professor at the Department of Near Eastern Studies and Civilizations at Harvard University gave me the opportunity to consult the collection at Widener Library once again.

On a more personal level, I would like to thank my colleagues at the Department of History and Archaeology at the American University of Beirut for their support and stimulation; I am especially indebted to Helen Sader, who took on some of my burdens with outmost grace. I am thankful to the Happy Hour Group for the happiness they give me; to my dearest friends, whose support and affection keep me going; and to my family for their love: my mother, my brother, Libby, Chaf, tio George, the Hajj, my cousins in the four corners of the world, Fouad, and Aida.

Some of the ideas in this book have been developed in Nadia Maria El Cheikh, "Mourning and the Role of Na'iha," *Identidades Marginales*, ed. Cristina de la Puente (Madrid: Consejo Superior de Investigaciones Científicas, 2003), 395–412, and "The Gendering of 'Death' in *Kitab al-'Iqd al-Farid*," *al-Qantara* 31 (2010): 411–436. Portions of Chapter 4 appeared in somewhat different form in *Byzantium Viewed by the Arabs* (Cambridge, MA: Harvard Middle Eastern Monographs, 2004).

Index